# Business Leadership and Culture

*To*
*Camilla*

# Business Leadership and Culture

National Management Styles in the Global Economy

Björn Bjerke

*Professor of Entrepreneurship and Small Business,
Stockholm University, Sweden*

**Edward Elgar**
Cheltenham, UK • Northampton, MA, USA

Published by
Edward Elgar Publishing Limited
Glensanda House
Montpellier Parade
Cheltenham
Glos GL50 1UA
UK

Edward Elgar Publishing, Inc.
136 West Street
Suite 202
Northampton
Massachusetts 01060
USA

Paperback edition 2001

A catalogue record for this book
is available from the British Library

**Library of Congress Cataloguing in Publication Data**
Bjerke, Björn, 1941–
    Business leadership and culture : national management styles in
the global economy / Björn Bjerke.
    Includes bibliographical references.
    1. Leadership.    2. Executive ability.    I. Title.
HD57.7.B536    2000
658.4'092—dc21                                                                99–28282
                                                                                    CIP

ISBN 1 84064 171 1 (cased)
       1 84064 627 6 (paperback)

Typeset by Manton Typesetters, Louth, Lincolnshire, UK.
Printed and bound in Great Britain by Bookcraft (Bath) Ltd.

# Contents

# Figures

# Tables

# Foreword

It is fantastic to travel. You meet different people, you get new ideas and you look at your old ideas in a new perspective. It is exciting and it is a challenge. It is even more of a challenge trying to learn to understand other cultures when you actually live and work with their people. You learn a lot in the process. Probably the most important thing you learn is about yourself, simply by getting a new perspective on yourself.

But you never stop learning. During the course of writing this book, I have presented parts of it in seminars and used sections in teaching and consulting assignments. I have also asked different people to read and comment on specific chapters. I have received many valuable comments and suggestions from people too numerous to mention. However, I would like specifically to thank the following people for their contributions:

Todd Hochstatter, an American and a good friend as well as a colleague for several years in an Arab country;

Talib Ameen, an Arab and a former colleague at the National University of Singapore;

Richard Pennell, presently at the University of Melbourne, a specialist in Arab history;

Ronald Rogers, a former colleague at National University of Singapore and an authority on several East Asian business cultures, including the Japanese;

Mitsuhide Shiraki, professor at Waseda University. He knows much more about Japanese business than I can ever hope to learn;

Hans Jansson, an expert on Chinese culture and business, presently professor at the University of Gothenburg;

Sing Keow Hoon-Halbauer, a presenter of a praised doctoral thesis at the University of Lund on how to do business with the Chinese in the People's Republic of China (PRC);

Claes Hultman, research director at the Swedish Foundation for Small Business Research, and an authority on Swedish business.

One person, however, has given me more than anybody else in matters of culture. Lena has been my life partner for more than 35 years. She has travelled with me around the world and she shares my interest in cultural issues. She is in many ways more of a cultural expert than I am. We have had many long discussions on the subject. She has enriched me with her insights, which emanate from a sincere interest in people and in a unique talent to 'read' them. She has also made me sharpen my arguments. This book has gained from those discussions.

The final result, that is, the book which the reader is holding, is my own complete responsibility, of course.

I hope this book will not discourage me from maintaining my interest in continuing to learn and appreciate one of the finest things there is in life, that is, variety.

Björn Bjerke

# 1. To understand culture

## A MATTER OF INTEREST

Business concepts come and go. One concept, which seems to have come to stay, is *culture*. It looks like one of those grand concepts. It burst on to the intellectual landscape of business in the early 1980s, and it has captured the interests of academics, journalists and businesspeople alike (Pascale and Athos, 1982; Hofstede, 1984; Peters and Waterman, 1984; Schein, 1985; Harris and Moran, 1987; Deal and Kennedy, 1988; Rohwer, 1995; Trompenaars, 1995). In fact, the concept has a rich ancestry in business. It can be traced back at least as far as the writings of Mayo and Barnard in the United States in the 1930s.

People can have many theories about why the culture concept was able to catch their interest so thoroughly at this time; perhaps the time was ripe. Maybe the reason was people's growing international interest or maybe it was an increase in the interest of human beings. One thing is clear, however: the cultural idea has led people to 'reevaluate the attributes of organizational success which are not part and parcel of the "orthodox" rationalist paradigm' (Green, 1988, p. 121).

Culture can be used for many different types of analysis. It can provide the foundation or the background for many different kinds of understanding. This study is an attempt to understand business leadership in five different national and regional contexts and to do this through the culture governing these contexts. The contexts are the American, the Arabic, the Chinese, the Japanese and the Scandinavian.

One way to formulate the basic question of this study could be: How do business leaders think as a result of their national culture, and what are the consequences for how business leadership is exercised? Also, how do business followers think as a result of their national culture, and what are the consequences of how business leadership *can* or *should* be exercised?

## THE IMPORTANCE OF HUMAN VALUES

There are many opinions about the content of a culture and these will be discussed more thoroughly later in this chapter. One common understanding, however, seems to be that it is related to human values one way or the other and, like culture, interest in human values dates back many years (Lewin, 1935; Allport, 1937; Bruner and Goodman, 1947; Kluckhohn and Strodtbeck, 1961).

The term 'value' is used in all social science subjects (for example, anthropology, psychology, sociology, business management, political science and economics). Each of them provides it with a different though not completely unrelated meaning. 'Value' is very much an interdisciplinary term, like 'system' or 'leadership'.

Maybe as a forerunner to the interest in culture, management researchers have, during the past 30 years or so, begun to recognize the importance of personal values in understanding business behaviour. According to Davis and Rasool (1988, p. 11), the impetus to this area of inquiry was given by Guth and Tagiuri (1965), who illustrated ways in which personal values influence the choice of corporate strategy.

The literature has since been replete with a preponderance of evidence suggesting a strong relationship between a manager's personal values and his or her decision-making (Haire *et al.*, 1966; Senger, 1970; Sikula, 1971; Pezeshkpur, 1975; Hughes *et al.*, 1976; Bennis and Nanus, 1985; Peters and Austin, 1985; Deal and Kennedy, 1988). So, the inquiry in this study into the relation between values (culture) and management behaviour (leadership) rests on a solid background.

## THE INTERSECTION OF ORGANIZATION AND CULTURE THEORY

The intersection of organization and culture theory is manifest in several 'thematic' or 'content areas' which are of interest to organization and management scholars, as shown in Table 1.1.

Arvonen (1989, pp. 88–89) classified definitions of culture based on different views of an organization.

a.  The organization is part of a larger culture system:
    master values, national culture, cross-cultural communication; corporate philosophy.
b.  The organization is a culture and should be studied as such:
    cognitive orientation;
    symbolism;
    psychodynamic orientation.
c.  Culture is an impressionable subsystem of the organization:
    a leadership variable;

*Table 1.1  'Organization' and 'culture'*

| Concepts of 'culture' from anthropology | Themes in organization and management research | Concepts of 'organization' from organization theory |
|---|---|---|
| Culture is an instrument serving human biological and psychological needs, for example, Malinowski's functionalism | Cross-cultural or comparative management | Organizations are social instruments for task accomplishment, for example, classical management theory |
| Culture functions as an adaptive–regulatory mechanism. It unites individuals into social structures, for example, Radcliffe-Brown's structural-functionalism | Corporate culture | Organizations are adaptive organisms existing by process of exchange with the environment, for example, contingency theory |
| Culture is a system of shared cognitions. The human mind generates culture by means of a finite number of rules, for example, Goodenough's ethnoscience | Organizational cognition | Organizations are systems of knowledge. 'Organization' rests in the network of subjective meanings shared to varying degrees, and appear to function in a rule-like manner, for example, cognitive organization theory |
| Culture is a system of shared symbols and meanings. Symbolic action needs to be interpreted, read and deciphered in order to be understood, for example, Geertz's symbolic anthropology | Organizational symbolism | Organizations are patterns of symbolic discourse. 'Organization' is maintained through symbolic modes such as language that facilitate shared meanings and shared realities, for example, symbolic organization theory |
| Culture is a projection of the mind's universal unconscious infrastructure, for example, Lévi-Strauss's structuralism | Unconscious processes and organization | Organizational forms and practices are the manifestations of unconscious processes, for example, transformational organization theory |

*Source*:  Smircich (1983, p. 342).

a product;

psychological climate.

Different conceptions of organization and culture underlie research in these content areas and variations in the way the concept of culture is used can be traced to researchers' different ways of conceiving 'organization' and 'culture'.

## THIS IS SERIOUS

Everyday understanding of the word 'culture' has connotations of proper behaviour, education and even snobbery; in short, people would be more 'cultural' if they knew how to behave, had a broader view of things that matter, and were more in line with what was expected from them:

> In everyday usage, the term *culture* refers to the finer things in life, such as the fine arts, literature, and philosophy. Under this very narrow definition of the term, the 'cultural person' is one who prefers Händel to hard rock; can distinguish between the artistic styles of Monet and Manet; prefers pheasant under glass to grits and red-eye gravy, and 12-year old Chivas Regal to Budweiser; and spends his or her leisure time reading Kierkegaard rather than watching wrestling on television (Ferraro, 1994, p. 16).

Furthermore, cultural differences are often the subject of anecdotes, and cultural blunders may provide a good laugh.

In contrast, social scientists place a much broader meaning on the term 'culture' that goes far beyond mere personal refinements. In scientific theory, culture is seen as a fundamental aspect of life. All people have culture. The only requirement for being cultured is to be human (Ferraro, 1994, p. 16).

Also, in practice, culture incompetence in business can easily jeopardize millions of dollars (or its equivalent) of resources in wasted negotiations or lead to fewer contracts, less sales and impaired customer relations. Also, the internal efficiency of a multinational corporation may be weakened if managers and workers are not 'on the same wavelength' (Czinkota *et al.*, 1994, pp. 263–264).

A deeper understanding of culture can be gained by first going to where 'it all started' academically, that is, to the anthropologists' understanding of the concept.

## ANTHROPOLOGISTS AND CULTURE

Anthropologists Kluckhohn and Kelly (1945, p. 97) have defined culture as 'all the historically created designs for living, explicit and implicit, rational, irrational, and nonrational, which exist at any given time as potential guides for the behavior of men'.

Culture is 'the man-made part of the environment', states anthropologist Herskovits (1955, p. 305).

In one book about anthropology, Lewis (1969) states:

> Every culture ... has three fundamental aspects: the technological, the sociological, and the ideological. ... The technological is concerned with tools, materials, techniques and machines. The sociological aspect involves the relationships into which men enter. The ideological aspect comprises beliefs, rituals, art, ethics, religious practices, and myths (p. 42).

Keesing (1974), another anthropologist, claims that culture is 'an individual's theory of what his fellows know, believe, and mean, his theory of the code being followed, the game being played, in the society into which he was born' (p. 89).

So, in general, anthropologists have given a very wide definition to culture, covering all sorts of values, acts and artefacts that a particular society has developed to manage life. This fits the purpose of that branch of science, of course. An anthropologist studying culture normally aims at investigating every aspect of it in order to get a complete picture of the society to which the culture belongs. In order to meet this purpose, anthropologists have set up 'cultural schemes' which embody all the cultural components. Such a cultural scheme may look as follows (Cateora, 1991, p. 73):

1.  material culture, technology, economics;
2.  social institutions, social organization, education, political structures;
3.  humans and the universe, belief systems;
4.  aesthetics, graphic and plastic arts, folklore, music, drama, and dance;
5.  language.

Studying the human way of life in different settings, anthropologists may find such schemes useful because these schemes stress the variety of culture and a total approach to trying to understand it.

The encyclopaedian presentation of culture has this 'complete' orientation. Two examples are as follows:

> Culture: the integrated pattern of human knowledge, belief, and behavior. Culture ... consists of language, ideas, beliefs, customs, taboos, codes, institutions, tools,

techniques, work of art, rituals, ceremonies, and other related components (*Ency-clopedia Britannica*, Fifteenth Edition, 1991).

Culture: the way of life of a particular society or group of people, including patterns of thought, beliefs, behaviour, customs, traditions, rituals, dress, and language, as well as art, music, and literature (*The Hutchinson Encyclopedia*, Ninth Edition, 1990).

## CULTURE IN BUSINESS

Occasionally cultural anthropologists have conducted research in industrial and corporate settings, in the beginning focusing on corporate culture in the United States (Ferraro, 1994, pp. 6–7). The human relations school of organizational research of the 1930s and 1940s produced a number of results showing the importance of informal cultural patterns in organizations (Mayo, 1933; Roethlisberger and Dickson, 1939; Gardner, 1945; Richardson and Walker, 1948). Another example of anthropologists' research on business is an attempt to show how specific configurations of values contribute to success or failure in meeting corporate goals (Davis, 1984; Frost *et al.*, 1991; Kotter, 1992).

Studies like these draw attention to the way in which organizations can be seen as miniature societies with a distinctive social structure, reflected in various patterns of action, language, discourse, laws, roles, rituals, customs, ceremonies, norms, folklore, stories, beliefs, myths and so on (Morgan *et al.*, 1983, p. 18). In short, business organizations can be viewed as mini-cultures which operate within the wider national cultural context, as well as cultures in their own right.

When organizations are studied as cultures, attention is drawn to a set of features which may elude the attention of those researchers who view organizations as formal structures designed to achieve rational ends. The culture metaphor emphasizes that organisations are full of social life, and encourages the researcher to study them from this point of view (ibid., p. 19).

It is no exaggeration to say that business scholars have adopted the cultural metaphor wholeheartedly. Over the last 10 to 15 years or so, 'culture' seems to be used in theory as well as in practice of business in an increasing number of applications.

## CULTURE AS MENTAL PROGRAMMING

Even in this modern computer age, the frustration of trying to get a personal computer to communicate with one with a different programming system may still be experienced. The problem is that, although the kind of information contained in one computer is understood by the other, the structure of the program – made up of systems of categories, of filing systems – is different.

Across cultures, the same type of interface problems may occur. People carry around 'mental programs' (Hofstede, 1980, p. 14). These are developed in the family in early childhood and they are reinforced in schools and organizations later on. Every person's mental programming is partly unique and partly shared with others. In fact, *three levels* can be distinguished in this respect, as shown in Figure 1.1.

Universal
(objective)

Cultural
(intersubjective)

Individual
(subjective)

*Figure 1.1    Levels of 'mental programming'*

The most basic (but also least unique) level of programming is the *universal* one. This is shared by all, or almost all, human beings. This includes the biological system of the human body, but also various expressive behaviours such as laughing and weeping and also associative and expressive behaviours which are found in higher animals (ibid., p. 15). Others see universals as generalizations (cultural products) that manifest themselves in all cultures. This is the same as the cultural schemes that have already been discussed.

The *individual* level of human programming is the truly unique part of ourselves (ibid., p. 16). No two people are programmed exactly alike, even if they are identical twins raised together. This is the level of individual personality. At least part of the individual subjective level of human programming must be inherited, otherwise it is difficult to explain why children of the same parents raised in very different environments may develop similar capabilities and temperaments.

It is at the *intersubjective,* cultural level that most (if not all) of mental programming is learnt. This level is shared with people who went through the same learning process and with those who identify themselves as its members, and who do not even have the same genes. With a multitude of genetic roots, societies, organizations and groups have ways of transferring these collective programmes from generation to generation with an obstinacy which many people tend to underestimate (ibid., pp. 16–17).

It is difficult to draw strict borderlines between the three levels of human programming. It is a matter of opinion among researchers of culture how to separate individual personality from intersubjective culture, how to distinguish exceptional individuals from their cultural system, and how to draw the line between culture-specific phenomena and universal ones.

Even if the enculturation process transfers knowledge from generation to generation, and even if this process goes on during individuals' entire lives, it tends to be learnt when we are very young, that is, when the mind is still relatively empty, as most of it deals with fundamental facts of life. And, furthermore, to a large extent, it goes on in a very nonconscious way. For instance, language and the many forms of nonverbal communication transmit cultural elements so subtly that individuals usually are not consciously aware of the constant reinforcement of their culture. Reactions to space and time (at what distance to others do people feel most comfortable when talking and to what extent do people want to be 'on time') are only two examples of the consequences of an almost endless number of 'rules' that determine our behaviour (Wortzel and Wortzel, 1985, p. 407).

In summary:

> Of the more than 160 definitions of culture analyzed by Krober and Kluckhohn, some conceive of culture as separating humans from nonhumans, some define it as communicable knowledge, and some as the sum of historical achievements produced by man's social life. All of the definitions have common elements: culture is learned, shared and transmitted from one generation to the next. Culture is primarily passed on from parents to their children but also by social organizations, special interest groups, the government, the schools, and the church. Common ways of thinking and behaving that are developed are then reinforced through social pressure. ... Culture is also multidimensional, consisting of a number of common elements that are interdependent. Changes occurring in one of the dimensions will affect the others as well (Czinkota *et al.*, 1994, p. 264).

Some problems can be seen with using the mechanical metaphor of a computer and programming when trying to gain insights into what culture is and how it expresses itself. One problem has to do with different programming among individuals. Even if, no doubt, the cultural influence on our development as individuals is vital (we would be helpless without it) and even if it may be said that 'our primary mode of biological adaptation is culture, not anatomy' (Harris, 1974, p. 84), how can the mechanical metaphor be used to explain the great minds throughout the history of mankind, creative free thinkers who give people ideas about what is really happening, and who decide what people are going to do and what their fate will be (Samovar *et al.*, 1981, p. 25)?

The second problem using the computer metaphor is also at the individual level, but more epistemological and also decisive in order to understand this study properly, that is, in order to work, culture must provide meaning. Hofstede's structuralist cause–effect definition of culture is not, in my opinion, enough to gain real insight into the intricate mechanisms of culture. This second problem will be discussed again later in this chapter.


## CULTURE IS THE RESULT OF INTERACTION

At this stage it is understood that culture is something *learnt* and it is *human-made*. It is also something which is *shared* in a group of people. It is common to people in a certain group or category, but different (at least partly) to people belonging to other groups or categories.

Culture is built up in all individuals in interaction with other individuals. There is thus no such thing as the culture of a hermit. If a solitary individual thinks in a certain way, that thought is idiosyncratic, not cultural (Ferraro, 1994, p. 17).

But what is shared? At the minimum, culture consists of 'a system of shared values (what is important) and beliefs (how things work) ... to produce behavioral norms (the way we do things around here)' ('The corporate culture ...', 17 October, 1983, p. 66) or to phrase it differently:

> Organizational culture is the pattern of basic assumptions that a given group has invented, discovered, or developed in learning to cope with its problems of external adaptation in internal integration, and that have worked well enough to be considered valid, and, therefore, to be taught to new members as the correct way to perceive, think, and feel in relation to those problems (Schein, 1984, p. 3).

The 'group' referred to in the above quotation has to be together long enough for its shared learning to take place. The 'group' could be, say, a sports team, a business firm, or even a nation. In addition 'teaching' should not be interpreted as any formal arrangement but rather as a result of interaction in everyday life.

This needs two qualifications. First, there is a degree to which people share a culture. Sharing a culture does not mean that every individual who belongs to it has all the same knowledge, beliefs and assumptions as every other individual (Dredge, 1985, p. 413). There are subcultures within every culture (Figure 1.2).

At a national level, for instance, factors like social class, occupational speciality, political position, religious background, age, sex and other

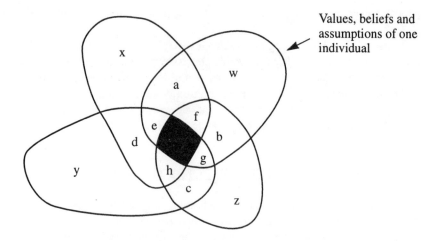

Values, beliefs and
assumptions of one
individual

*Notes*:
■ = values, beliefs and assumptions shared by all in one culture (central culture).
a–h = values, beliefs and assumptions not shared by all in one culture (subcultures).
w–z = individually unique values, beliefs and assumptions in one culture (idiosyncracies) (these
      values, beliefs and assumptions may come from other cultures).

*Figure 1.2   Culture and subcultures*

differences in social identity always mean that many aspects of a national
culture are not shared by all members (members of a nation associate with
other members in smaller groups within the whole). As one consequence of
this, every human being owns many cultures, for example, from the nation,
working life and family. Within every such culture (or subculture) members
must have interacted long enough for its members to think, feel and react in
patterned ways to give them a 'collective personality'. I prefer to express it
such that a human being has *one* 'subjective' culture (which is constantly
modified in new human interaction) which is a synthesis of influences from
many different 'public' cultures, that is, from a nation (a national culture),
from his or her working place (a corporate culture) and so on. Those values,
beliefs and assumptions people have developed as members of a nation can
be called their *national culture*; those which some of these people have
developed as members of the same working place can be called their *corporate culture* and so on. Also, national culture and corporate cultures are
related.

However, again, there is also a second, in a sense deeper, qualification.
Even if several people share the same element of a culture, this element can
mean different things to these people. I would like even to go one step

further. There is no distinction between 'this element' and 'the meaning of this element'. Culture is nothing but the meaning itself. Culture *is* meaning, or rather, 'a shared system of meanings. It dictates what we pay attention to, how we act and what we value' (Trompenaars, 1995, p. 13).

Culture, in this approach, is seen as a true social construction of meaning in the sense of Berger and Luckmann (1966). This approach is sometimes called 'phenomenological', which leads to the important difference between 'explaining' and 'understanding'.


## EXPLAINING OR UNDERSTANDING CULTURE

To claim a difference between 'explaining' and 'understanding' may seem irrelevant to some people. However, it has become customary among social scientists, though by no means among everybody, to distinguish between research activities aiming at providing objective, absolute and causal pictures of reality, and research activities aiming at providing subjective and dialectical interpretations of what is going on. It is also suggested that the term 'understanding', in contrast to 'explaining', ought to be reserved for the latter (Bauman, 1978; Bottomore and Nisbet, 1979; Cuff and Payne, 1979; Sica, 1981; Ng, 1984). Those researchers who see no basic difference between explaining and understanding (and they are adopting an explanatory approach) have traditionally been called 'positivists'. This, however, is an outdated term; I, therefore, prefer to call them 'explanaticists' (Arbnor and Bjerke, 1997, p. 45). Those researchers, on the other hand, who argue that such a difference exists (and adopt an understanding, or interpreting, approach) are called 'hermeneuticists'.

In the context of culture, an explanaticist asserts that man (including culture) can be explained by objective, external 'forces'. A hermeneuticist looks at man in a 'web', which is constructed, maintained and constantly developed by him- or herself and fellow human beings in interaction with each other. This web consists of meanings associated with all events and objects.

What was previously discussed as 'culture as mental programming' is an explanatory approach. Louis (1983), on the other hand, sees the three levels of human programming as levels of interpretation, that is, more or less generalized meaning and understanding which human beings produce for themselves. To use the example of a dog: universally speaking it is understood that dogs cannot be flown; intersubjectively speaking some people mean that dogs can be eaten; subjectively speaking some individuals claim that they are afraid of dogs.

The concept of 'meaning' can be interpreted in at least three different ways. These three ways are interrelated (Arbnor and Bjerke, 1997, p. 33):

1.  meaning = *significance* (importance) (something has a meaning = something is significant/important);
2.  meaning = *purpose* (orientation) (something has a meaning = something has a reason for being);
3.  meaning = *understanding* (content) (something has a meaning = something is not empty; it can be given an interpretation; it can be understood).

Culture is a very human matter, and it is only among humans that meaning can be talked about. Human beings can identify themselves with other human beings; they cannot identify themselves with a tree – they have nothing in common with a tree. The human world is *meaning-full*.

To illustrate this further:

> We cannot understand why individuals and organizations act as they do without considering the **meanings** they attribute to their environment. 'A complex market' is not an objective description so much as a cultural perception. Complex to whom? To an Ethiopian or to an American? Feedback sessions where people explore their mistakes can be 'useful feedback' according to American management culture and 'enforced admissions of failure' in a German management culture. One culture may be inspired by the very thing that depresses another. The organization and its structure [and culture] are thus more than objective reality; they comprise fulfilments or frustrations of the mental models held by real people (Trompenaars, 1995, pp. 19–20).

One important difference between an explanaticist and a hermeneuticist is the degree of complexity they attach to our social world, including its culture (Bjerke, 1996, p. 6). An explanaticist assumes that this world is objectively constructed and so complex that explanatics as a science must devote itself to simplifying and to reducing complexity. Such objective, simplified pictures or recreations of a reality (past, existing, imaginary or future) are called 'models'. Hermeneutics, on the other hand, assumes that this world is subjectively constructed between people in interaction and already so simplified by its actors, using all sorts of schemes, labels, concepts, norms and so on, that hermeneutics as a science must devote itself to problematizing and complicating simplicity and looking at things more holistically.

A hermeneuticist is always trying to find out what is behind or below what seems to happen. This leads to the concept of *symbols*.

## THE SYMBOLISM OF EVERYDAY LIFE

In the pursuit of our everyday tasks and objectives, it is all too easy to forget the less rational and instrumental, the more symbolic social tissue around people that gives a meaning to everyday life. In order for people to function within any given setting, they must have a continuing sense of what that reality is all about in order to be acted upon. As previously mentioned culture could be characterized as a system of intersubjectively accepted meanings operating for a given group at a given time. This system of terms, forms, categories and images interprets people's own situation to themselves. In fact, what is supposed to be distinctive about human beings compared with other creatures is his or her capacity to invent and communicate determinants of his or her own behaviour (White, 1949; Cassirer, 1953).

Symbols may consist of objects which point at something beyond themselves. So, for instance, a red light means that a person should stop his or her car, and it is possible to make people risk their lives under the banner of their national flag.

However, symbols are more than that. In fact, every system, every seating arrangement, every visit can be seen as symbolic behaviour. Each day can be looked at as a new scenario; each meeting a new setting for dramatic action. No events and no players are then too trivial to ignore in the great symbolic drama of a successful corporation (Deal and Kennedy, 1988, pp. 141–142).

> We are all emotional creatures. We feel pride, we feel slights. Our life is a drama to each of us. The winners are institutions and leaders that own up to that reality and live with us as humans – not as automatons (Peters and Austin, 1985, p. 277).

While shared meanings cannot be arbitrarily controlled, they can be communicated and possibly changed – if appealing to symbolic values.

## HOW MUCH IS CULTURE?

Considering the extensive use of 'culture' in business literature and research, it is no surprise that there is a variety in the way it is used. One 'controversy' (which is not always clearly spelt out) is whether culture is behaviour, or whether it consists of the rules governing this behaviour, or both. Four examples are set out below:

> Organizational culture is the pattern of beliefs and expectations shared by the organization's members which powerfully shape the behaviour of individuals and groups within the organization (Byars, 1987, p. 48).

> As knowledge and belief, culture exists only as thought and is nonmaterial and nonbehavioural (therefore, behaviour is guided by and reflects culture but is not the thing itself) (Dredge, 1985, p. 412).

An organization's culture can ... be described by its management in terms of the way their tasks are typically handled in the context of ... key relationships (Schwartz and Davis, 1981, p. 36).

[Culture is] the way we do things around here (Deal and Kennedy, 1988, p. 4).

This distinction will be discussed again later in this chapter.

## HOW DEEP-SEATED IS CULTURE?

People have come to understand that culture is shared, no matter how it is defined. A key issue in discussing culture is then how deep-seated it is. The degree to which a culture is conscious and open rather than nonconscious and covered has implications for how easily a culture can be studied and, in a business management context, be managed (Kilmann *et al.*, 1986, p. 89).

If culture is looked at as some kind of shared understanding, it can be placed in a consciousness–nonconsciousness continuum at three levels (Figure 1.3) (adapted from Kilmann *et al.*, 1986, pp. 89–90).

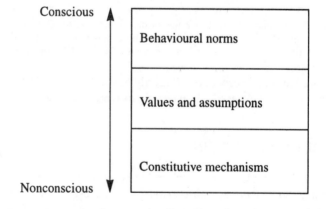

*Figure 1.3    Culture in a consciousness–nonconsciousness continuum*

*Behavioural norms* are the most overt parts of culture; they are just below the surface of experience; they are the unwritten rules of behaviour. Norms, by definition, are not written but transmitted from senior to junior, from old to young, from one generation to the next. Examples of norms are: 'don't argue with your boss', 'don't rock the boat' and 'look busy even when you're not'. When asked, most individuals can list, at least after having thought for a while, the norms that exist in their work groups.

At a somewhat deeper level lie the hidden *values and assumptions* – the fundamental drives and beliefs behind all decisions and actions. In a business context, this understanding pertains, say, to the importance of listening to peers, what stakeholders to prioritize, the nature of the environment and what learning and progress is all about.

At its deepest level, shared understanding consists of the collection of *constitutive mechanisms*, that is, those phenomenologically rooted processes of subjectification, objectification, and so on, which people operate existentially to create the social reality of any group and without which the other two levels of norms, values and assumptions cannot function (Berger and Luckmann, 1966).

Trompenaars (1995, p. 23) provides a similar model of culture as layers (Figure 1.4).

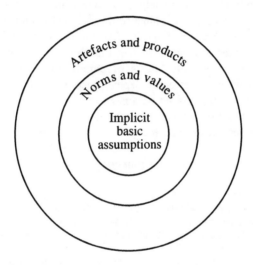

*Source*: Trompenaars (1995, p. 23).

*Figure 1.4   Culture as layers of explicity–implicity*

The reason why some values and assumptions 'disappear' into semi-awareness and why some beliefs become taken for granted and unexamined is because of *routine*. A problem that is regularly solved sooner or later becomes an underlying premise, sunk down from consciousness. This is human nature.

This means, in turn, that the effect of culture on our lives is largely unrealized (Samovar *et al.*, 1981, p. 25). People are commonly unaware of their cultural blinkers.

This can be illustrated by an experiment reported by Harris and Moran (1987, p. 103). A group of Mexican and American children were shown a series of stereograms. These were constructed such that one eye was exposed to a bullfight and the other eye to a baseball game. It was found that the children predominantly reported the scene appropriate to their culture, that is, the Mexican children tended to see the bullfight and the American children tended to see the baseball game even though they were simultaneously exposed to both scenes.

The way in which culture, at least partly, becomes the deeper level of fundamental assumptions and beliefs that are shared by members of a group, that operate nonconsciously and that define in a basic 'taken-for-granted' fashion a group's view of itself and its environment, brings to mind the concept of paradigm.

The term 'paradigm' is intimately associated with the American historian of science, Thomas Kuhn, who launched this originally linguistic term in his classic book *The Structure of Scientific Revolutions*, first published in 1962. He points out that major changes in scientific theories take place only occasionally, with what he calls 'shifts of paradigms', where the existing assumptions on which researchers depend become so unsuitable that they collapse and have to be replaced by a new set of assumptions. According to Kuhn, such a new set of assumptions cannot simply be reduced to a reinterpretation of a given set of data. It is rather (to use a psychological term) 'a change of Gestalt'.

Kuhn means that a paradigm has four components (1970, Postscript):

1. *'Symbolic generalisations'*, i.e., typical expressions used within the scientific group – what might be called jargon – which are not questioned.
2. *'Metaphysical aspects'*, i.e., typical models (they may vary along the whole spectrum from being heuristic to being ontological). These models have several functions. Among other things, they offer suitable or acceptable analogies and metaphors. They also assist in determining what will be accepted as an explanation or a solution, which also means that they determine what is to be regarded as unsolved problems.
3. *'Values'* for judging the quality of research results (e.g., that they should be formulated quantitatively) or theories (e.g., that they should be simple, consistent and probable) or scientific topics (e.g., that they should be socially useful).
4. *'Ideal examples'*, i.e., specific solutions to a problem, that the researchers confront in the beginning of their career and that can be found in 'recognised' scientific journals.

The similarities to a culture are obvious.

# CULTURE AS A MODEL – OR AS AN INTERPRETATION

It is clear that no matter what definition is given to 'culture', it is an abstraction and a model (if you are an explanaticist) or a concretization and an interpretation (if a hermeneuticist).

So, any definition/description of culture is also a theory of culture (Dredge, 1985, p. 411). The usefulness of such a definition/description should be judged when applied. If international business is studied, some aspects of human experience may be interesting; if family life is studied, other aspects may be interesting. An anthropologist may favour some kind of definition of culture, a business researcher another kind. A manager in practice may have still another understanding of culture.

My interest is to study how national culture exerts an influence on business leadership and that will flavour my choice of definition of culture, of course.

# MY CULTURAL POINT OF VIEW

To conclude, two dimensions seem important to classify various ways of defining culture:

1.  Does culture include behavioural aspects or not?
2.  Is culture conscious or not?

Based on these dimensions the following matrix can be constructed (Bjerke and Al-Meer, 1994, p. 177).

Looked at in this way, culture (in a business context) could be seen as parts or all of the cells in Figure 1.5.

1.  *Conscious behaviour*   A company may, for instance, have a formal budget process which might even start at a fixed date every year, something everyone knows.
2.  *Nonconscious behaviour*   Within a company, for instance, it may be taken for granted that at a meeting the boss sits at the head of a table and those who are nearest to his or her formal position in the organization sit as close as possible to the boss at the table as well.
3.  *Conscious nonbehaviour*   (that is, refers to values only, which in turn may influence the behaviour of those people accepting those values). In a company, an official statement about the value of avoiding accidents may be made.
4.  *Nonconscious nonbehaviour*   There are employees who find it 'natural' to always plan before action is taken, even to believe that more planning

| Culture as: | Something conscious | Something nonconscious |
|---|---|---|
| Behavioural | Example:              (1)<br><br>The budget process | Example:              (2)<br><br>Sitting down at a meeting |
| Non-behavioural (values only) | Example:              (3)<br><br>The fewer accidents, the better | Example:              (4)<br><br>Planning is good |

*Note*:   □ culture in this study.

*Source*:   Bjerke and Al-Meer (1994, p. 176).

*Figure 1.5    Culture along a behavioural–consciousness continuum*

is better than less planning. Yet this might have become a taken-for-granted value which is not questioned or debated.

My understanding of culture includes only cell (4). A definition of culture could be *basic behavioural norms, values and assumptions* (assumptions are sometimes called *beliefs), which in an interaction have been interpreted and given a meaning and which have behavioural effects without being behavioural themselves.* I want to refer to cells (1)–(3) as *cultural manifestations*, but not culture itself. So, culture (which for any individual is partly acquired as a member of a nation and partly as a member of various organizations to which he or she belongs or has belonged) will determine how members of a corporation, for example, may perceive, think, feel and act. These are learnt responses that originated as espoused norms, values and assumptions.

There are three reasons for this 'restricted' use of culture:

1. The anthropological ambition is often to present a complete design for living among civilizations which could be marginal in a larger society or even not alive today. The business researcher's ambition is almost the opposite. He or she attempts, most of all, to understand the core and logic of culture (of, for example, a firm) which is manifest everywhere and every day in abundance in any business setting.
2. Norms, values and assumptions are at the heart and soul of an individual looked at from an interpretive and understanding (not explaining)

point of view. This gives a focus to my interest. I do not, however, include (explicitly) in my understanding of culture those 'constitutive mechanisms' which were mentioned in our previously discussed consciousness–unconsciousness continuum. These 'mechanisms' are produced and operate on a micro-level (face to face) and are no doubt inevitable and decisive for any individual in any group in real life, but they are difficult to include (explicitly) in the general picture of national cultures and their consequences. Furthermore, these 'mechanisms' operate very much as *behavioural* processes (which are excluded from my definition), even if in a phenomenological sense (that is, to build up an everyday reality).

3. Culture has sometimes come to mean everything. *If* a concept excludes nothing, it becomes meaningless or, at least, loses its analytical edge.

The above definition in no way denies those intimate relations which exist between culture and cultural manifestations.

## CULTURE AND PERSONALITY

There are similarities between culture and personality as well as differences. Culture and personality are occasionally hard to separate. They interact and cultural traits can sometimes be measured by personality tests (Hofstede, 1980, p. 26). Furthermore, personality can be discussed at the level of an organization. At this level, the personality of an organization can be spoken of as an interactive aggregate of common characteristics, an intangible yet ever-present theme that provides meaning, direction, and the basis for the organization's response to its environment. Some authors (Pearce and Robinson, 1985, pp. 341–342; Byars, 1987, p. 49) claim that organizations can be talked about as warm, aggressive, friendly, open, innovative, or conservative, as well as about individuals. This comes very close to what has been previously referred to as culture.

However there are important distinctions between personality and culture. At the level of an individual, personality is a more integrated part of a person than is his or her culture (Daun, 1989, p. 45). The former is more difficult to divert from, as it is a more intimate part of his or her identity. Somebody, for instance, who is calm and thoughtful may have problems in behaving in a lively and excitable way. It is, on the other hand, relatively easier for him or her to break a cultural rule. Whether this can be done easily or not is partly a matter of what characterizes a specific personality and a specific culture, of course. However, more importantly, it does not mean that culture is something that can be shaken off whenever you want to, particularly if culture is considered to be mainly nonconscious. Nor is personality easy to change in practice. Suppose a person throughout his or her life has believed that humankind is basically good. Such a person cannot simply change his or her opinion for a more cynical one claiming that good or evil depend on circumstances (ibid., p. 46).

However, above all, cultures are not individuals: they are integrated wholes, and their logic cannot be understood in terms used for the dynamics of individual personalities. Intersubjective logic differs from subjective logic. A sociological context can, for instance, be separated from a psychological context in organizations (Table 1.2) (Louis, 1983, p. 45).

However, in a sense, it can be said that people within a particular culture think, feel and react in patterned ways that give them a collective personality.

*Table 1.2   Contexts of culture in organizations*

| Sociological context | Psychological context |
| --- | --- |
| Shared ideals; symbolic devices | Interpretive scheme |
| Cultural system of relevances | Personal system of relevances |
| Through the functions of culture, social systems achieve:<br><br>*continuity* – transtemporal stability;<br>*control* – contemporaneous stability;<br>*integration* of individual members;<br>*identity* of social group. | Within a culture:<br><br>meaning is emergent and intersubjective;<br>individuals negotiate meaning.<br>Negotiation as:<br><br>*navigation*<br>*bargaining*;<br><br>*then in situ interpretive process*:<br><br>process $\rightarrow$ negotiation $\rightarrow$ meaning $\rightarrow$ definition of situation $\rightarrow$ behaviour |

*Source*:   Louis (1983, p. 45).

# CULTURE AND CLIMATE

In the section above, warm, aggressive, friendly, open and so on, firms were discussed. Some authors even say that an organization's culture *is* 'the totality of experience, climate, personality, and atmosphere possessed by the firm' (Smith *et al.*, 1985, p. 161). Others claim they are not the same:

> Climate is a measure of whether people's expectations about what it should be like to work in an organization are being met. Measurements of climate can be very helpful in pinpointing the causes of poor employee motivation, such as lack of clarity of organizational goals, dissatisfaction with compensation, inadequate advancement opportunities, or biased promotion practices. Action to address these sources of dissatisfaction tends to improve motivation. Improved motivation ought to result in improved performance, and by and large the evidence suggests that it does.
>
> Culture, on the other hand, is a pattern of beliefs and expectations shared by the members of an organization. These beliefs and expectations produce rules for behaviour – norms – that powerfully shape the behaviour of individuals and groups in the organization. So while climate measures whether expectations are being met, culture is concerned with the nature of these expectations themselves (Schwartz and Davis, 1981, p. 33).

Schwartz and Davis continue by claiming that climate measures the fit between the prevailing culture and the employees' individual values. If those values work, the climate is 'good', otherwise 'poor', and climate is supposed to be transitory, tactical and can be changed over the relatively short term; culture is usually long term and strategic. It is, therefore, very difficult to change the latter (ibid., p. 33).

I would like to give 'climate' a deeper meaning, more intimately related to culture. A few years ago, I made a simple test in two different companies, which were unaware of each other's participation in this test (the test is described in more detail in Bjerke, 1989, pp. 354 ff). Based on the idea that a culture is reflected in its language (an idea which will be further explored in the next section), I asked most managers in both (individually and independently of each other) to tell me those 'five major words mostly spoken around here'. From these answers, I compiled two 'Top Ten Spoken Words'. The top word in one of these companies was 'return on investment'; in the other company it was 'service'. A person would not have to spend more than a few hours in each company to *feel* the difference.

That is climate to me – in the cultural mirror of language!

## LANGUAGE – A MIRROR OF CULTURE

Language is closely related to culture. It may even be referred to as a 'mirror of culture'. Language consists of arbitrary symbols with meanings that, like other cultural manifestations, must be learned and that, when following certain rules, can convey complex messages (Ferraro, 1994, p. 45). Language does not only mean words that can be spoken; there are also nonverbal aspects of language. Messages are conveyed by words used, by how the words are spoken (for example, tone of voice), and through nonverbal means such as gestures, body position and eye contact. In fact, it has been suggested that only about 30 per cent of communication between people in the same speech community is verbal in nature (ibid., p. 63). Nonverbal aspects of language also display a certain arbitrariness. It is, therefore, not surprising that the same nonverbal cue may carry with it very different meanings in different cultures and that different nonverbal cues may carry the same meaning in different cultures (ibid., p. 64).

The importance of communication is easy to understand from the following remarks (Harris and Moran, 1987, pp. 19–20):

● No matter how hard people try, they cannot avoid communicating. All behaviour in human interaction has a message value and is communicating something to the persons present. While silent with words, body language is communicating. People communicate by activity or inactivity, by the colour of skin as well as the colour of clothes and by the gift given or not given. All behaviour is communication because all behaviour contains a message, whether intended or not.

● Communicating does not necessarily mean understanding. Even when people agree that they are communicating or talking to each other it does not mean that they have understood each other. Only when meaning is attached to a behaviour – any behaviour – it is a message. This has several implications (Ferraro, 1994, pp. 11–12). Not only can any verbal or nonverbal behaviour function as a message, but behaviour may occur either consciously or nonconsciously (for example, nervous behaviour like fingernail biting or staring) and frequently unintentionally (like blushing).

● Communication is irreversible. Communication cannot be taken back. It can be explained, clarified and restated, but it cannot be wiped out even if people may sometimes wish it could. Once communication takes place, it is part of an experience and it influences present and future meanings.

● Communication takes place in a context. The context of communication cannot be ignored that occurs at a certain time, in some place,

using certain media. Such factors have message value and give meaning to the communicators.
- Communication is a dynamic process. Communication is not static and passive, but is rather a continuous and active process without beginning or end. A communicator is not simply a sender or a receiver of messages but can be both at the same time.

A fundamental tenet of anthropology is that there is a close relationship between language and culture. It is generally held that it is impossible to understand a culture and its manifestations fully without taking into account its language (which is also a cultural manifestation); and it is equally impossible to understand a language well outside its cultural context (Ferraro, 1994, p. 47). Culture influences language and language influences culture in a number of ways:

> Culture and communication are inseparable because culture not only dictates who talks with whom, about what, and how the communication proceeds, it also helps to determine how people encode messages, the meanings they have for messages, and the conditions and circumstances under which various messages may or may not be sent, noticed, or interpreted. In fact, our entire repertory of communicative behaviours is dependent largely on the culture in which we have been raised. Culture, consequently, is the foundation of communication. And, when cultures vary, communication practices also vary (Samovar *et al.*, 1981, p. 24).

And communication is important (Harris and Moran, 1987, p. 31):

> Communication is at the heart of all organizational operations and international relations. It is the most important tool we have for getting things done. It is the basis for understanding, cooperation, and action. In fact, the very vitality and creativity of an organization or a nation depends upon the content and character of its communications. Yet, communication is both hero and villain – it transfers information, meets people's needs, and gets things done, but far too often it also distorts messages, develops frustration, and renders people and organizations ineffective.

Language is a patterned unity greater than any of the individuals who participate in it. At the same time, language is one of the most intimate and significant constitutive features of human beings. People not only speak in that language, but think in it as well. Its categories are what each individual has available for conceptualizing and understanding the world; its framework is the basis for all but the most basic and inarticulate of people's thoughts. What can be said and thought is very largely determined by the language available. If there is no language to describe matters and events, they may not even be noticed in the first place.

People become the particular persons they are as they grow up because of the language community in which they grow up. The same is, of course, true of most cultural patterns: people become a certain person, with certain language, table manners, carriage, style of humour, taste in food and so on infinitely, all by being shaped by one culture and its manifestations rather than another. The culture, like the language that carries it, is first imposed on the individual from the outside, but eventually it becomes a part of his or her very self. The categories of a language are not formally experienced as a constraint on an individual's ability to think or to express themself; on the contrary, they are the very means that enable an individual to think articulately and to express themself.

One insight that this model or interpretation of language membership suggests, then, is that customary distinctions between individual and society, between the self and some larger whole to which it belongs, are not fixed, mutually exclusive dichotomies. Rather, they concern different aspects of, different perspectives on, a single reality. Society is not just 'outside' the individual, confronting him or her, but inside him or her as well, part of who he or she is (Bjerke, 1989, p. 279). All individuals in their relationships, including relationships with the past, constitute society. Who an individual is both distinguishes him or her from all others and relates him or her to them. And language both exemplifies that duality and is its instrument.

So, language is not a neutral vehicle (Hofstede, 1980, p. 34). People's thinking is affected by the categories and words available in their native language. During the twentieth century this has become known as the 'Sapir–Whorf hypothesis' (Sapir, 1949; Whorf, 1956). This is the idea that a speaker's own native language establishes a series of categories which functions as a kind of grid through which the speaker experiences the world and which restricts the way in which he or she categorizes and perceives various phenomena:

> [Some] linguists have posited that language may actually influence certain aspects of culture. Language, they suggest, establishes the categories on which our perceptions of the world are organized. According to this theory, language is more than a system of communication that enables people to send and receive messages with relative ease. Language also establishes categories in our minds that force us to distinguish those things we consider similar from those things we consider different. And since every language is unique, the linguistic categories of one language will never be identical to the categories of any other. Consequently, speakers of any two languages will not perceive reality in exactly the same way (Ferraro, 1994, p. 49).

People's symbolic language system can be seen as an intermediary between themselves and what is external to them; a medium to relate to the external world (Figure 1.6):

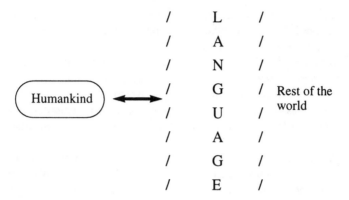

*Figure 1.6   Language between humankind and the rest of the world*

Concepts are normally seen as labels. They are supposed to designate an object or an idea: 'boy', 'house', 'manager', 'centralization of power' and so on. The concepts make it possible for people to organize and connect their perceptions of the reality, whether they are researchers or 'just ordinary' human beings. However, the concepts do more than that. People's opinion of the world 'outside' themselves is largely determined by the concepts through which it is perceived.

Human beings not only speak, they can also speak *about* language. This capacity to operate on a meta-level – to communicate about communication – seems to be unique to human beings, and absent among animals.

## CULTURE POWERFULLY INFLUENCES EVERYTHING

There seem to be several contradictions built into human nature (Peters and Waterman, 1984, pp. 55–56):

- We are all more or less self-centred, looking for a bit of praise, and generally like to think of ourselves as winners. But the truth is that our talents are spread out, and very few of us are as good as we would like to think and to face that reality daily would not do us much good.
- Our imaginative, symbolic right side of the brain is at least as important as our rational, deductive left side. We reason by pictures and stories as much as with raw data.
- On the one hand, we can hold little explicitly in mind, maybe half a dozen or so facts at one time. On the other hand, our unconscious mind is powerful, accumulating and generating a vast number of patterns, if

we let it. And there are many occasions in our professional lives where the need for complex data operations is great at the same time as we need to keep things simple.

- We are in the hands of our environment, very sensitive and responsive to external rewards and punishments, at the same time as we are strongly driven from within, self-motivated.

- We act as if expressing beliefs is important, yet action speaks louder than words. And we are watched by our environment whether we behave consistently or not.

- We desperately need meaning in our lives and will sacrifice a great deal to institutions that will provide meaning for us. We simultaneously need independence, to feel as though we are in charge of our destinies, and to have the ability to stick out.

These contradictions can be taken care of in a culture. Because of people's basic need for order and consistency, assumptions (in an interaction with other people) become patterned into cultural wholes, which tie together the basic assumptions about humankind, nature and our activities. A culture is a set of interrelated assumptions that form a coherent pattern (Schein, 1984, p. 4) and it may even contain assumptions which are mutually incompatible or inconsistent. For example, a group may believe that all good ideas ultimately come from individuals, but at the same time assume that groups can be held responsible for the results obtained, or that individuals should prioritize group loyalty.

Culture gives an individual an anchoring point, an identity, a world view, but also codes of conduct. The manner in which people consume, the priority of needs and the wants they attempt to satisfy, and the manner in which they satisfy them are functions of their culture which temper, mould and dictate their style of living. Culture powerfully influences everything from the materialistic to the spiritual. Even such a basic biological need as food has been cast into culturally defined recipes and menus and has acquired definite psychological dimensions that differ across countries. However, similar manifest cultural contrasts exist in all basic aspects of life, such as clothing, furniture and games. What people consider important or unimportant becomes dictated by culture.

> Culture is an intriguing concept. Although we can easily read a definition of it, when we begin to consider that definition and what it implies, culture becomes a prodigious and commanding notion. ... Culture manifests itself in patterns of language and in forms of activity and behavior that act as models for both the common adaptive acts and the styles of communication that enable us to live in a society within a given geographic environment at a given state of technical development at a particular moment in time. It also specifies and is defined by the

nature of material things that play an essential role in common life. Such things as houses, instruments and machines used in industry and agriculture, forms of transportation, and instruments of war provide a material foundation for social life. ... Culture also helps dictate the form and structure of our physical realm, and it encompasses and specifies the social environment permeating our lives (Samovar *et al.*, 1981, pp. 24–25).

A corporation's culture is reflected in the attitudes and values, the management style, and the problem-solving behaviour of its people (Schwartz and Davis, 1981, p. 32). It gives employees a sense of how to behave, what they should do and where to place priorities in getting the job done – how to fill in the gaps between what is formally decreed and what actually takes place (Pearce and Robinson, 1985, p. 342). In addition it embodies what it takes to succeed in the broader social and business environment in which the company operates (Deal and Kennedy, 1988, p. 107).

Culture may even influence scientific theories (Hofstede, 1980, pp. 32–33). However, in spite of the pervasiveness of culture, there are other determinants of behaviour and reality as well. Culture does not compete with or repeal the laws of, for example, technology and economics. It simply supplies the social context in which these other forces operate (Trompenaars, 1995, p. 17).


## CULTURE PROVIDES A NORMATIVE GLUE

One of the most interesting aspects of culture (maybe the most interesting one for those who research and practise business) is that it cannot be avoided, and that it paramountly determines our behaviour – normatively.

At a national level, there must be a mechanism in societies which will produce the stability of culture patterns across generations. Such a mechanism operates as shown in Figure 1.7.

In the centre, systems of societal norms, values and assumptions (here at the level of a nation) can be found, shared by major groups of the population. These originate from various ecological factors. In turn, these societal norms lead to the development and pattern maintenance of various societal institutions. Those institutions will have a strong normative bearing by reinforcing the existing systems of norms, values and assumptions, and vice versa. Systems of norms, values and assumptions of major groups of population have a strong normative bearing on how the societal institutions will operate. Change comes mainly from outside. However, nothing will happen unless interpretation and creation of meaning takes place by some members of the nation in interaction with each other.

Note that the arrow of outside influences is directed at the origins, not at the societal norms themselves. Norms, values and assumptions rarely change

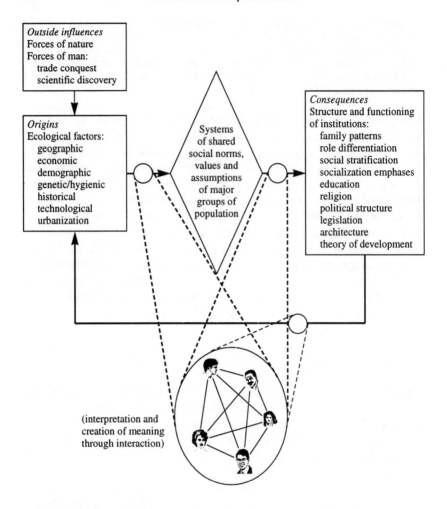

*Source*:   Adopted from Hofstede (1984, p. 22).

*Figure 1.7   The stabilizing of culture patterns*

by directly adopting them from outside, but rather through a shift in ecological conditions – they may be technological, economical, hygienic, or a combination (Hofstede, 1984, p. 22).

At the organizational (business) level, the dominant model or interpretation of culture is also to see behavioural patterns being underpinned by strong social sanctions (norms, rules and values in some kind of constitutive mechanisms) which provide the normative glue of corporate culture (Green, 1988,

p. 122). To gain an understanding of this in full, three related issues need to be approached:

- *Social morphology*   What is culture and how can it be classified?
- *Social physiology*   How does an organization's culture align itself with the environment and, hence, its performance?
- *Social engineering*   How can corporate culture be changed to improve alignment and performance?

This normative glue and its function in business organizations will be discussed further in the next chapter, but a few points could be made here. The discussion starts by following Johnson and Scholes (1988), whose main interest is strategic management.

There is a growing understanding that the strategy of an enterprise, its structure, the sorts of people who hold power, its control systems and the way it operates, tend to reflect the culture of that organization. This combines into a 'recipe' (partly unique for each enterprise) in what could be referred to as a 'cultural web' (Figure 1.8), well glued together.

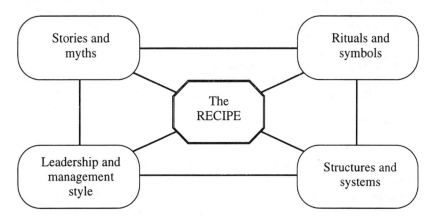

*Source*:   Adapted from Johnson and Scholes (1988, pp. 41, 119).

*Figure 1.8   The strategic recipe in a cultural web*

Critical questions that an analytical manager may ask about various aspects of the cultural web may include (ibid., p. 119):

a.   Stories and myths
    i.    What core beliefs do the stories reflect?
    ii.   How strongly held are these beliefs with power-holders?

    iii.   How pervasive are the beliefs (through the levels)?

    iv.   How do beliefs relate to strengths and weaknesses?

b.   Rituals and symbols

    i.   What language is used to describe the organization and its activities?

    ii.   What is the dominant attitude towards each stakeholder group?

c.   Leadership and management style

    i.   What are the core beliefs of the leadership?

    ii.   Which aspects are stressed in public (for example, annual reports)?

    iii.   What attributes are sought in new recruits?

d.   Structures and systems

    i.   Do structures/systems encourage collaboration or competition?

    ii.   What kind of training is given?

However, all relations in the cultural web could be seen as mutual, therefore, the normative glue becomes even stronger:

> In describing and defining the various forms and functions of symbols, language, ideologies, beliefs, rituals, and myths, it should be recognized that these concepts are to varying degrees interdependent and that there is some convergence in the way they relate to functional problems of integration, control, and commitment. These concepts direct attention toward the mobilization of consciousness and purpose, the codification of meaning, the emergence of normative patterns, the rise and fall of systems of leadership and strategies of legitimization. It is through such mechanisms and processes that culture evolves, and indeed the ever fluctuating state which we describe as an organizational culture then acts as a determinant or constraint on the way further attempts to handle issues of purpose, integration, and commitment are handled. Man creates culture and culture creates man (Pettigrew, 1979, pp. 576–577).

One thing should be clear in all this, however. In spite of what has been said about 'glue' and 'web', internal inconsistencies exist and are, in fact, quite common within cultures. Also, cultures are not fossilized artefacts but, rather, dynamic systems undergoing constant change (Dredge, 1985, p. 414).

    With few exceptions, and those exceptions are increasing in number, researchers in the business sciences have proceeded as if study of universal aspects were sufficient to understand their field. The majority of textbooks in areas such as management, organization theory and business policy take very lightly the influence and importance of culture. It is increasingly clear, however, that much of what matters in business life takes place at the cultural level (Louis, 1983, p. 43). In a way this has already been recognized in the Hawthorne studies of 'informal organization' in the 1930s, but, by and large, cultural phenomena have seemed to elude, or been overlooked by, and until recently remained on the fringe of, mainstream business sciences. This is probably partly due to the problems with coming to grips with such 'loose' concepts as values, rituals and language.

At any rate, now that the concept of 'culture' is popular, most attempts to define organizational culture have left managers in practice, who have tried it, at a loss. The usual outcome of such attempts is a list of eight to ten phrases describing the informal rules that govern the interaction of members on a management team. This may appear useful until an attempt is made to live the message of the pervasiveness of culture in everyday business life.

However, as has probably been understood in this chapter so far, the specific nature of culture is understood differently among theorists as well. They have one thing in common, though. They may call themselves cognitive, symbolic, structuralist, or psychodynamic theorists, but by using culture as a metaphor, they all consider organizations as a particular form of human expression. This is different from the views derived from the machine and organism metaphors often being used in management, which encourage theorists to see organizations as purposeful instruments and adaptive mechanisms (Smircich, 1983, p. 353).

## A SUMMARY

Culture consists of basic human norms, values and assumptions. These norms, values and assumptions have been developed (and are developing) intersubjectively. Even if they must provide meaning for carriers to be of any significance, they are still mainly nonconscious. They have an impact on behaviour, organizational (or equivalent) climate, and other cultural manifestations, but they are nonmaterial and nonbehavioural in themselves.

I see language as a mirror and a reflection of culture. I want to use my understanding of 'culture' to discuss business leadership in five different cultures, that is, the American, the Arab, the Chinese, the Japanese and the Scandinavian. I believe that no corporation can separate itself from the culture of the nation in which it operates, particularly if it is a domestic corporation.

Studies have already shown that business strategy is partly a cultural matter (Faucheux, 1977), so why not leadership?

The context in which business leadership is to be understood and exerted more operatively, that is, a corporate culture, is discussed in more detail in the next chapter.

## NATIONAL CULTURES AND CORPORATE CULTURES

Many commentators (Alvesson and Berg, 1988; Hofstede, 1993) assert that national cultures and corporate cultures operate differently and at different levels of awareness, and that it could be confusing to use a common term for both. It is true that national cultures are acquired in early childhood and that corporate cultures are acquired by socialization of new employees as they join a corporation. It is also true that national cultures only change very slowly if at all; corporate cultures may be consciously changed, even if this is not necessarily easy. However, comparing national and corporate cultures, I think it is fair to say:

- the heart of soul of national as well as corporate culture is 'norms, values and assumptions' and defined only as such, national and corporate culture could be defined in the same way, even though their manifestations may differ widely;
- the corporate culture of a firm (again culture understood as values only) from a specific nation overlaps with the culture of the same nation and these cultures, probably, do not contradict each other;
- in the end, cultures operate through individuals, where each and everybody's culture is a complex mix of cultures from his or her nation, his or her work as well as from other organizations of which he or she has been, and may still be, a member. Another story is that, as observers and researchers, nations and corporations may be discussed as units, and values may be classified as national, corporate and so on.

To conclude, national cultures can be discussed on their own but they are also part of corporate cultures; the former are introduced into the latter by people, being members of both. It is still a valid question to discuss (which is my interest) how national cultures influence business leadership.

# 2. Corporate culture

## A REMINDER

Culture is the intersubjective aspect of life. It is learnt, much of it at a very young age, and it is reinforced through social pressure. The result is that culture belongs to a whole group, not to its individuals, and we cannot avoid it. It paramountly determines our behaviour, at the same time as it gives us an anchoring point, an identity, a social place and a world view.

Because of the human need for order and consistency, our basic assumptions about humankind, nature and social activities become patterned into what may be called cultural 'paradigms' (Schein, 1984, p. 4); these assumptions form a coherent pattern. This pattern or framework is used to structure experience – to give meaning to thoughts and actions (Dredge, 1985, p. 412). It is transmitted in many ways, including long-standing and often unwritten rules, shared standards and even prejudices.

Within this general understanding of what culture means, it can be defined as being slightly different from one situation to another. Every such definition becomes, at least partly, a theory, a model or an interpretation (depending on your basic attitude to what research is for), and it suits a purpose. My purpose is to discuss business leadership in the light of national cultures. In order to gain an analytical focus and edge, I have chosen to separate culture (as norms, values, assumptions, beliefs and so on) from the way it expresses itself (as behaviour, language, organizations, institutions, artefacts and so on). This is also consistent with a common understanding that, whether culture is broadly or narrowly defined, it *includes* basic norms, values and assumptions of a human group, organization or nation. My choice of delimiting the content of culture means, among other things, that I understand language to be a mirror of culture, not part of culture itself.

Another dimension of culture is to clarify how deep-seated its shared qualities are (Kilmann *et al.*, 1986, p. 89). Values, for instance, can appear or be hidden at various levels of depth. At the conscious level, or close to it, they may appear as *behavioural norms*. Such norms are written or unwritten rules of the game. Examples of such norms could be:

- be on time at meetings;

- only wear dark business suits to work;
- do not share information with other groups.

At a somewhat deeper level lie the *hidden assumptions* – the fundamental beliefs behind all decisions and actions – that might be nonconscious cornerstones of culture. For example, some assumptions that may be shared among the members of a group or organization are:

- the future must be planned as much as possible;
- quantification of the outcome of an act makes it more certain;
- there must be superiors and subordinates in this world;
- cooperation improves motivation among participants.

As mentioned, my interest is national cultures. The hypothesis is that norms, values and assumptions in those cultures are among the most deep-seated components of the cultural package that human beings carry around with them. They are ingrained since childhood and reinforced through various social sanctions from then onwards. They have got a taken-for-granted character, and people are mainly unaware of these cultural blinkers. My definition of culture, therefore, is:

> Culture consists of basic behavioural norms, values and assumptions (beliefs). These norms, values and assumptions have been developed (and are developing) intersubjectively. Even if they must provide meanings for those, who carry them around to be of any significance, they are still mainly nonconscious. They have an impact on behaviour, organizational (or equivalent) climate, language and other cultural manifestations, but they are nonmaterial and nonbehavioural in themselves.

With the above definition I do not pretend to draw a clear-cut line between conscious and nonconscious aspects of culture (I do not even think it is possible in any general sense to do so). Also, I do not deny that what is nonconscious can be made conscious, or vice versa. Finally, I see no reason (nor find it of any interest in my case) to discuss whether value-free assumptions exist or not. I lump norms, values and assumptions together in one group without trying to separate them. For the sake of convenience, I sometimes refer to the three components of culture as simply 'values' or 'cultural values'. After all, *behavioural norms and assumptions are also a kind of values*.

## CORPORATE VALUES

*Value definitions* may sometimes differ in minor aspects, but they are generally consistent in their global meanings (Davis and Rasool, 1988, p. 12):

- Athos and Coffey (1968, p. 100) state that 'By "values" we mean ideas about what is desirable'.
- Guth and Tagiuri (1965, p. 125) suggest that values are desirable end-states.
- Kluckhohn *et al.* (1962, p. 396) define values as a conception of the desirable: 'A value is a conception, explicit or implicit, of the desirable which influences the selection from available modes, means, and ends of action'.
- Conner and Becker (1975, p. 551) assert that 'values may be thought of as global beliefs about desirable end-states underlying attitudinal and behavioural processes'.

People's values are mutually related and form value systems or hierarchies, but these systems or hierarchies need not be in a state of harmony. Most people simultaneously hold several conflicting values, such as 'freedom' and 'equality' (Hofstede, 1980, p. 19). Nearly all our 'mental programmes' (such as attitudes and beliefs) carry a value component. Humankind is an evaluating creature.

Values are the basic concepts and beliefs of an organization; as such they form the heart of the corporate culture and its manifestations. And values can be explicit or they can be hidden (Figure 2.1).

A company's *philosophy*, often called a 'company creed', commonly contains the company's beliefs, values, aspirations and priorities. Implicit, hidden

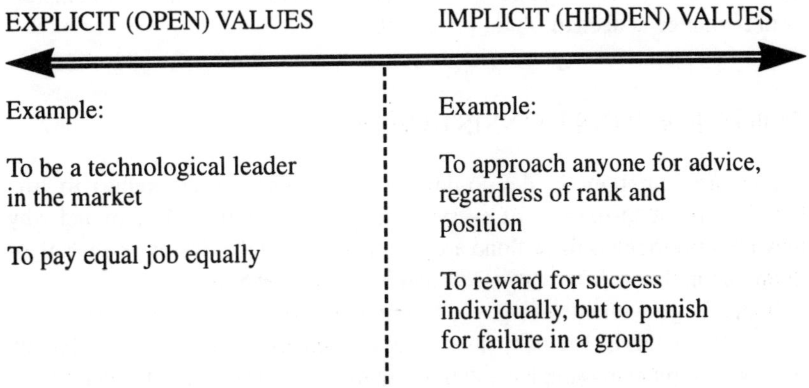

EXPLICIT (OPEN) VALUES          IMPLICIT (HIDDEN) VALUES

$$\longleftarrow \hspace{3cm} \longrightarrow$$

| Example: | Example: |
|---|---|
| To be a technological leader in the market | To approach anyone for advice, regardless of rank and position |
| To pay equal job equally | To reward for success individually, but to punish for failure in a group |

*Figure 2.1   The explicit–implicit continuum of values*

values cannot, of course, appear on a company's stated philosophy. This does not prevent this philosophy from reflecting those values, of course. Values come from experience, from testing what does and does not work in the economic environment. This experience may once have been openly expressed, but forgotten (become nonconscious) over time and still play a role.

Explicit or implicit, values are very important to a company:

> Values are the bedrock of any corporate culture. As the essence of a company's philosophy for achieving success, they provide a sense of common direction for all employees and guidelines for their day-to-day behaviour.
>
> For those who hold them, shared values define the fundamental character of their organization, the attitude that distinguishes it from all others. In this way, they create a sense of identity for those in the organization, making employees feel special. Moreover, values are reality in the minds of most people throughout the company, not just the senior executives. It is in this sense of pulling together that makes shared values so effective (Deal and Kennedy, 1988, pp. 21, 23).

It may even be said that, often, companies succeed because their employees are able to act on the values of the organization, and that cultivated corporations have a rich and complex set of values to pass on – not just products and services.

Shared values act as a kind of informal control system that tells people what is expected of them (Deal and Kennedy, 1988, p. 33). In doing so, values can be more or less pervasive in the sense of being shared by many or a few, and strong in the sense of being felt more or less intensively (characterizing corporate cultures will be discussed again later in this chapter). Pervasive and strong values may affect performance positively by increasing dedication and pointing at what should be given extraordinary attention. However, pervasive and strong values can also have a negative effect: they may be inconsistent, may become obsolescent and/or may lead to a massive resistance to change, even if change is needed (ibid., pp. 34–36).

## CORPORATIONS CONSIST OF PEOPLE

Values are important in day-to-day business. What brings values to life, however, is the *awareness* of everyone in the organization of them and why they are important. Values alone are not enough, it is the extensive sharing of them that makes a difference (Deal and Kennedy, 1988, p. 36).

It should go without saying, but corporations consist of people. The reason why I still say this is that too many standard textbooks consider people explicitly in a rational planning–implementation–control sequence only at the end of this sequence, that is, when it is time to discuss implementation of plans, when activities which have been decided upon are to be organized, when control systems are to be designed and the like. However, people are often not objectively rational and, even if they should fit such a model, they should be in there from the start. Competition is a challenge to any participating firm. This challenge cannot be taken on by new technology and economic resources alone. Technological innovation and resource allocation (as all organizational activities) are results of *human* processes (Pascale and Athos, 1982, p. 21).

Businesses are human institutions, not fancy offices, bottom lines, budgets or strategic analyses. People make businesses work, and the real existence of corporations lies in the hearts and minds of its employees (Deal and Kennedy, 1988, p. 4).

Believing that people are a company's greatest resource and acting accordingly means, among other things, to keep in mind the implicit, but powerful, force of values shared by the members of the organization of a company (which in turn shape the behaviour of its individuals and groups) and to realize that managing people is not through (or at least not directly through) memos from budget meetings or computer reports, but through the subtle cues of a culture. All too often, the tools of management are seen and acted upon in technical rather than symbolic terms. Great firms tend to do an artful job of blending explicit procedures and formal controls with implicit social controls (Pascale, 1985, p. 34).

Managing corporate cultures is possible, especially as we continue to improve our understanding of this important concept. This will be discussed again later in this chapter. Right now it is enough to point out that managing culture cannot be done by treating it as a 'thing' or an 'object', which has been successfully established by a group of senior managers solely to meet their needs for internal order and external responsiveness (Davis and Rasool, 1988, pp. 17–18). At a minimum, organizations should be conceived as socially sustained cognitive enterprises, where their members (all of them) are thinking as well as acting (Smircich, 1983, p. 350).

## CULTURE IN A WEB OF SHARED MEANINGS

There is not one, single, straightforward approach to explaining or understanding culture and its manifestations. There are at least two. They have been referred to as explanatics and hermeneutics in Chapter 1. They may also be called the *rationalist* and the *interpretist* approaches (Figure 2.2).

The rationalist view assumes that a trigger will have a direct effect through a set of cultural values. This culture set will normally not be modified or changed by this trigger. One example of this view is Hofstede's (1980; 1984) discussion of culture as 'mental programming'.

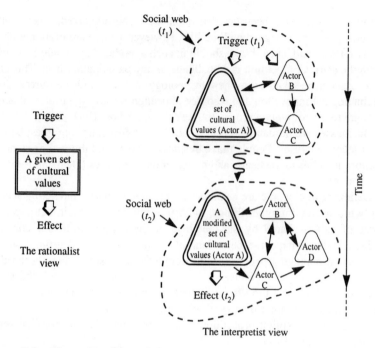

*Figure 2.2    The rationalist and the interpretist view*

The interpretist view is not just more complicated but fundamentally different. It is a more dynamic view, where trigger as well as effect and involved actors (carriers of cultural values) are placed in a social web, and where the *inevitable* interpretive process may alter the social web, the trigger and/or the effect, as well as (even if less likely) the cultural values themselves. Interpreters can be outsiders (for example, a researcher) as well as insiders (members of the web in question).

The basic presumption of the interpretist approach to understanding culture (an approach which is colouring this book) is that the *full* meaning of things (and acts) is not given *a priori* in the things (and acts) themselves. Instead, meaning results from interpretation (Louis, 1983, p. 41). There is a social web, which includes shared meanings, in every organization, and changing meanings is a communication process. The participants of this process seek to convey their message in a variety of mutually reinforcing ways. Some are continually more sensitive to the constructions that are placed on words and actions than others. They are also more convincing in their language play. They may be called 'change agents' (this will be discussed further in Chapter 10).

Instead of viewing culture in terms of social control (values and norms predicating behaviour), or as static behaviours constraining change, interpretive theory redirects attention to the way people collectively make sense of the world in which they live and their own position within it. It recognizes that we tend to be blind to our own assumptions when we are locked inside them. Yet it recognizes that these assumptions do change in response to novel situations and to social interaction. Through working with, talking to, and socializing with other people across organizational boundaries, individuals make sense of, that is they attach meaning to, events, actions, words and things (Green, 1988, p. 124).

If nothing else, the interpretist view is more realistic than the rationalist view. However, remember what has been said so far: *every* definition, explanation or understanding of culture is a theory and is there to suit a specific purpose. I believe in the interpretist view. I have found it very useful when (for instance working as a consultant) studying individual organizations in depth over extended periods of time. All discussions in this study are based on this view, even if it is not always *explicitly* stated. Other researchers, consultants or practitioners may adopt the 'simpler', rationalist view. This could be because of other beliefs or other purposes or both.

## THE SYMBOLIC LIFE OF CORPORATIONS

Closely related to the interpretist view is to study organizations from a symbolic point of view (Arvonen, 1989, p. 153):

- A *symbol* can be an object, a relation, a routine; symbols are acts, words or physical objects which are of informational value to us.
- Symbols have *associative values*. They contain information over and above what is manifest. Symbols are associated with other symbols, consciously as well as unconsciously.
- *Interpretation* is a psychological process of retrieving information from our environment, moulding and integrating it with our own beliefs.

An interpretation means to see things, events and acts as something (beyond themselves). Symbols are the same. They are seen as something, pointing beyond themselves. So, for instance, a dove is a common symbol of peace, and stretching the index finger and the middle finger slightly separated in a V-shape in the air, may point at 'victory'.

Organizations can be seen as full of symbols. In fact, structure and strategy may be more symbolic than substantive (Deal and Kennedy, 1988, p. 6). A budget can be seen as a commitment, a seating arrangement in a meeting as an implemented version of the organization chart (the general manager has the head seat and his or her deputies are sitting close by), a reserved parking space as a sign of a high position in the company.

Almost all activities going on in an organization can be studied from a symbolic point of view. Three aspects are commonly studied as such, that is, *rituals*, *language* and *myths*.

Much of the work of a company is carried out in the form of prescribed work rituals. Managers are engaged in rituals in their day-to-day life as well (ibid., p. 68), including writing memos, or holding meetings and so on. When involved in such rituals, managers may also see them as, for instance, processes of coordination, integration and motivation.

An amazing amount of decision-making in an organization is done symbolically – for the sake of the very process of decision-making – not its outcome (the decision) (Broms and Gahmberg, 1983, pp. 488–489). Studies by Lindblom (1959), March and Olsen (1976) and Westerlund and Sjöstrand (1979) show that many organization plans are never implemented or are implemented in another form than decided. However it does not mean that most planning is futile. It may give a sense of purpose to participants. Furthermore, many tools involved in decision-making (like portfolio analysis, cost curves, capital budgeting calculations and extrapolations) can be seen as rituals that give individual managers a comfortable feeling that they employ the best available managerial technology when carrying out their key responsibilities of decision-making, even though these tools may not have any significant influence on the decisions themselves (Deal and Kennedy, 1988, p. 69).

One example of symbolic thinking can be illustrated by a job I once had as a consultant, where the first day was spent by the general manager of the client taking me around, showing me the factory and the premises of the main site, where he was working. He spoke in the meantime about how modern his company was in its thinking and of how much they tried to apply new management techniques. When, at the end of the day, we came to his office, he pointed at a huge flow chart on the wall and explained with pride that the chart showed how a major extension was going on at the moment in his company. As I knew that such diagrams may have their major use in controlling and adjusting a project, I asked him where they were in the chart (the position of the extension) at that moment. His answer was, 'I don't know – but it is nice, isn't it!'

The most important management ritual is possibly the *formal meeting*. All companies have them, but their form varies widely in terms of (ibid., p. 70):

- the number held;
- the setting;
- the table's shape;

- who sits where;
- number and composition of attendees;
- the conduct.

The idea of symbols is not adopted by everyone:

> One difficulty we find in dealing with this subject [of symbolic behaviour] stems from baggage that comes along with the word 'symbolic' for the hard-nosed, rational manager. Somehow, given the macho jargon of Western management theorizing, describing an executive's behavior as 'symbolic' suggests something other than the 'tough-minded stuff of decisive strategic decision-making'. But symbolic it is (Peters and Austin, 1985, p. 271).

In the use of language another symbolically significant activity can be found. Like culture, its use may be conscious or nonconscious, and can exercise an influence in a variety of ways:

> It is the language which shapes organizational reality. The shop floor worker who attends a financial meeting for the first time may quite understandably find the language of the accountants a very foreign one. And even after learning that language, he or she may well still find that the concepts and jargon used, define a 'reality' which is contrary to that which is sought for. The language of profit and loss, return on investment, etc., may not facilitate a decision consistent with the reality which the people on the shop floor wish to enact.
>
> The use of language is rich in symbolic significance. It carries patterns of meaning which do much to evoke and define the realities of organizational life, and is a topic central to the analysis of organizational symbolism (Morgan *et al.*, 1983, pp. 10–11).

It is possible to distinguish three social functions of language (Table 2.1) (which may act in combinations), that is, the *cognitive*, the *political* and the *motivational* (Normann, 1970, pp. 24–26).

*Table 2.1   The social functions of language*

| | |
|---|---|
| A. | *Cognitive* = it defines reality |
| B. | *Political* = it may promote change |
| C. | *Motivational* = it directs attention |

A.  Language is working like a cognitive filter, which permits us to see what is already in the language (and consequently what is already reality for us).

B.  Bringing a new concept into an established conceptual frame of reference can have normative consequences, even if it is not directly perceived as a political act.

C.   In order for people to be motivated, it is necessary for them to have knowledge and a directed attention. Language may give them such knowledge and attention.

Some researchers and writers claim that what they refer to as myths are embedded deep in the subconscious. Myths are then regarded as values *clothed as a picture* (Broms and Gahmberg, 1983, p. 482). Myths are images. Abstract values, such as 'good' and 'bad', have little effect as such, but if those values appear in the form of an image (for example, good = St George, or bad = the Dragon), they suddenly start to work on the imagination of great masses of people. These value-laden images are myths (ibid., p. 482). In every culture (maybe mostly at the national level) there are such images, for instance, the 'American Dream', the 'Nationalistic Germans', or simply 'We Arabs'. These images can be transmitted at the national level by, for instance, the flag, and at the corporate level by, for example, trademarks. However, there are other, more subtle, ways of transmission.

The reason why myths are so powerful is that they are not only thought, they are also felt. The entire personality may be involved. It is important to realize that the scientific concept of myth has little to do with the everyday connotation of nonsense or nontrue. Rather, analysing the mythology of organizations is a recent research method to find the value set behind every sane judgement. The method is based on the belief that there exists a deeper, but, in its own way, a fully realistic picture of reality, and this deeper reality is tied to values, which in turn are tied to subconscious images (Broms and Gahmberg, 1983, p. 483).

The symbolists claim that:

> Traditional organization and management theory has for the most part failed to grasp the full significance and importance of the symbolic side of organizational life, because of its overwhelming commitment to models based upon mechanical and organismic metaphors of organization. Such models over-simplify the nature of organizations in creating a focus upon their formal and intendedly rational aspects, rather than upon their character as complex patterns of human activity. The rationale for studying organizational symbolism stems from recognition of this all important fact: that organizations are not simple systems like machines or adaptive organisms; they are human systems manifesting complex patterns of cultural activity. Members of an organization are able to use language, can exhibit insights, produce and interpret metaphors, are able to vest meaning in events, behaviour, and objects, seek meaning in their lives – in short, can act symboli-cally. This symbolic capacity is enhanced by their association in formal organizations so that institutions develop a history, a common point of view, and a need to process such complexity through symbolic means. Organizations are by their very nature symbolic entities, and a fully adequate theory of them must per force also be symbolic in its content (Morgan *et al.*, 1983, pp. 3–4).

Symbolism is important to every culture, and a symbolic approach to understanding organizations is interesting indeed, but very little of it will be *explicitly* used in the main part of this book (Chapters 4–9), as the discussion is here kept at a very general level. However, it will be important to bring up again in the final chapter (10), where the culturally sensitive leader will be discussed, what may even be referred to as a 'symbolic manager'.

## CULTURE IN A NETWORK

Every organization has an informal network. Studies of what managers do each day indicate that 75 per cent of their time is spent communicating (Harris and Moran, 1987, p. 61). The primary means of communication within an organization is its informal network; it ties together all parts of, for instance, a corporation without respect to position or titles. This network is important because it not only transmits information but also interprets the significance of this information for employees. It does so by being carrier of the corporate values, including the cultural ones. Deal and Kennedy (1988, p. 86) even claim that 90 per cent of what goes on in an organization has nothing to do with formal events, but that the real business goes on in the network.

According to the same authors, everybody in an organization has another job (apart from the official one): to operate in a network. The authors discuss the characters in this network in their own specific imaginative terms (ibid., pp. 87–98):

- *Storytellers* Storytellers are in a very powerful position because they can change reality. Through this they may influence people's perceptions – possibly without them knowing it.

  The tales that storytellers tell explain and give meaning to the workaday world. Storytellers maintain cohesion for the corporation and provide guidelines for everyone to follow. Storytellers also preserve institutions and their values by imparting legends of the company to new employees. They will also reveal much about what it takes to get ahead in the organization.
- *Priests* Priests are the designated worriers of the corporation and the guardians of the cultural values. These people are always accessible, they always have time to listen to a confession, and they always have a solution to any dilemma, even a moral one.

  To be a priest figure requires a maturity or seriousness beyond years. These people, therefore, tend to be older than their colleagues.
- *Whisperers* Whisperers have no formal portfolios, but are still the

'powers behind the throne'. The source of their power is not their formal position, but their boss's ear.

Two skills are required of whisperers. First, they must be able to read the boss's mind accurately. Second, they have to build up a vast support system of contacts throughout the organization and work hard to keep in close contact with the network.

- *Gossips*  Gossips know all the names, dates, salaries and events that are taking place in the organization.

  Gossips are not expected to be serious people; and they are not always expected to tell the truth. They are expected to entertain. For this entertainment alone they are tolerated, even liked.

  Their role in reinforcing a culture is vital. Gossips can spread their news more quickly because they talk at the lunch table or during the coffee breaks.

- *Secretarial sources*  In the network of supporting culture, a clerk or a secretary can be more important than a high-ranking manager. They can sometimes tell more about what an organization is really like, what is really going on, who is angry with whom, and so on, than anyone else. They can do this because secretarial sources form a relatively stable network of uninvolved and therefore unbiased participants.

- *Spies*  Spies are loyal people who keep managers informed about what is going on. The best spies are those who are liked and have access to many different people; they hear all the stories, and they know who is behind them.

  Sharp spies keep their fingers on the pulse of the organization. Smart managers associate with the spies to find out what is going on and to verify various rumours and to balance the information they get elsewhere.

- *Cabals*  Cabals exist everywhere in an organization. These are people who form a group (sometimes with only two members) joining together for a common purpose. These groups can offer strength and backing to the culture but they can also be counter-productive.

The network of an organization gives not only an implicit social control. It also forms an important part in socializing new members. The network of a corporation is, therefore, a major factor in determining its culture. Other determinants of a corporate culture include its environment and its history, but they operate and come alive *through* the corporate network.

# TO CHARACTERIZE CORPORATE CULTURE

Corporations are different from each other. With an open mind and with some observational skill it is easy to get a feel for how different cultures are manifest in various organizations by spending a day in each. There are trivial patterns such as variations in dress, jargon and style, but something else is going on as well. There are characteristic ways of, for instance, making decisions, relating to bosses and choosing people to fill key jobs (Schwartz and Davis, 1981, p. 30). It should, therefore, be possible to characterize a corporate culture in more general terms, but how?

In the 1980s, numerous consulting firms paid a great deal of attention to the need for an operational assessment of a company's culture. All approaches seem to have one thing in common: rather than trying to assess culture directly, culture is 'measured' when viewed as the product of selected factors common to all organizations (Pearce and Robinson, 1985, p. 344). One well-known example of this is the suggestion by McKinsey & Co. to see culture in a set of seven interacting variables (Waterman *et al.*, 1980):

1.  staff: what kind of people a firm has;
2.  style: how managers and employees conduct themselves;
3.  skills: what a firm knows how to do;
4.  systems: what patterns of communication go on inside the firm and to the outside;
5.  structure: the firm's organizational design;
6.  shared values: superordinate goals or the corporate culture;
7.  strategy: plans.

The key idea is that when there is a 'goodness of fit' among these seven variables, corporate strategies are more easily implemented and corporate objectives are, therefore, more readily accomplished.

I do not deny such efforts as being useful in the hands of the right consultant for specific purposes, but they really do not shed much light on culture as such. Also, culture is not, as we have come to understand, just another variable beside, for instance, skills and strategy.

There are attempts to classify corporate culture into various groups. For instance, Miles and Snow (1978, p. 14) talk about organizations as, among other things, 'defenders' or 'prospectors'. The prevailing beliefs of defenders are essentially conservative, where low-risk strategies, secure markets and well-tried potential solutions are valued. In contrast, prospectors' dominant beliefs are more related to innovation and to breaking new ground. Here management tends to go for higher-risk strategies and new opportunities. The different beliefs, values and assumptions within these two different types of organization are also manifest more widely. For example, stories in defenders are typically about historical stability and consensus whereas in prospectors they are about growth and change, with tales of dissension rather than consensus. The routines in the two types of organization are also different: prospector organizations tend to have less rigid approaches to decision-making and planning, for example, with less of an emphasis on formal relationships between people and groups.

Deal and Kennedy (1988, pp. 107–108) propose four general categories or types of corporate culture, which are decided by two factors in the marketplace: the degree of risk associated with the company's operations, and the speed at which companies – and their employees – get feedback on whether decisions or strategies are successful or not. The four generic cultures are:

1.  *The tough guy, macho culture*   This is a world of individualists, who regularly take high risks but also get quick feedback on whether their actions were right or wrong.
2.  *The work hard/play hard culture*   The rule here is fun and action, and employees take few risks, all with quick feedback; in order to succeed, the culture encourages them to maintain a high level of relatively low-risk activity.
3.  *The bet-your-company culture*   These are cultures with big stakes decisions, where years may pass before employees know whether decisions have paid off; in other words, a high-risk, slow-feedback environment.
4.  *The process culture*   This is a world of little or no feedback where employees find difficulties in measuring what they do; instead they concentrate on how it is done. Another name could be given for this culture when the processes get out of control – bureaucracy!

The problem with classifications, such as those outlined above, is that they tell more about how culture manifests itself in behaviour and so on than about culture as such (as norms, values and assumptions). Also, even if they may be logically complete (covering all possible kinds of culture), the variables behind the classification seem, in most cases, to be very dependent on the country where the background research was conducted (most of them are based on studies of corporate America).

One proposal to classify corporate cultures, which seems more universal and also more to the point of culture as values, is presented by Trompenaars (1995, pp. 139–140). He distinguishes different corporate cultures along two dimensions, that is, equality – hierarchy and orientation to the person – and orientation to the task (Figure 2.3).

Corporate culture

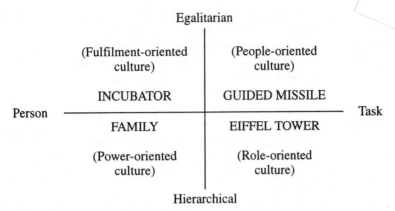

Egalitarian

| (Fulfilment-oriented culture) | (People-oriented culture) |
|---|---|
| INCUBATOR | GUIDED MISSILE |
| FAMILY | EIFFEL TOWER |
| (Power-oriented culture) | (Role-oriented culture) |

Person ————————————————————— Task

Hierarchical

*Source*:    Trompenaars (1995, p. 140).

*Figure 2.3    Corporate images*

The above four metaphors illustrate the relationship of employees to their notion of the organization. (This classification will be discussed further in Chapter 9).

There are also attempts to classify *national* cultures. The most well known or most quoted is probably the one employed by Hofstede (1984; 1980). He characterizes 40 different countries using four dimensions:

a.   *Power distance*    The extent to which inequalities are accepted and tolerated by superiors and subordinates.
b.   *Uncertainty avoidance*    The extent to which people need structure in their lives.
c.   *Individualism/collectivism*    The extent to which individuals or groups are the norm.
d.   *Masculinity/femininity*    The extent to which traditional male values like assertiveness of self or traditional female values like caring are promoted.

Having the ambition to discuss how national culture may influence business leadership, there is no point in studying culture on its own without also looking at the way in which it affects what goes on inside organizations. Three aspects of cultural impact have been proposed by Kilmann *et al.* (1986, pp. 88–89). They are *direction*, *pervasiveness* and *strength*.

The direction of impact is the course that culture is causing the organization to follow. Does culture influence behaviour so that present organizational goals are accomplished, or does culture push members to behave in ways that are counter to the existing formal mission and goals of the organization?

The pervasiveness of impact is the degree to which a culture is widespread, or shared among all members of the organization. Is the culture seen very differently by various participants within the organization or not?

The strength of impact is the level of pressure that a culture exerts on members in the organization. Do members feel compelled to follow the dictates of the culture, or do they feel that the culture only mildly suggests that they behave in certain ways?

The above aspects of a culture are commonly interrelated but they might not be. For instance, regardless of direction, culture may be strong without being pervasive (various parts of the company may hold strong but different values, not being able and/or willing to agree among themselves on which are the most important ones).

The consequences of direction, pervasiveness and strength are not to be misunderstood. There is no obvious relation between any of them and business success! The relations between business culture and business success will be discussed later in the chapter.

Finally, as previously discussed, any definition – and then also any characterization – of culture is a theory (a model or an interpretation). The test of a good classification or characterization of culture (for instance, strong or weak, pervasive or fragmented, innovative or staid, traditional or modern) is *not* whether it is 'right', but whether it is 'useful'!

## CULTURE AND LEADERSHIP

There are, of course, other relations between culture and leadership than the impact of national culture on business leadership. Managers in a firm (as well as other employees), be they leaders or not, have a culture (not only from the national level) which is more or less shared and common. This fact influences, often implicitly, how they manage themselves and other employees, and how they conduct their business, for example, decisions they make about the organization's relationship with its environment and about its strategy.

The choices managers make consequently reflect their view of reality – the beliefs and norms that have served them and their company well during their career (Schwartz and Davis, 1981, p. 35). These choices will also reaffirm the corporation's culture and reinforce the expected behaviour across the organization.

It may even be said that the job of leaders (be they managers or not) *is* culture:

> One might go so far as to say that a unique function of 'leadership' as contrasted with 'management' or 'administration', is the creation and management of culture.

At the same time, all leaders are influenced by their own prior cultural learning. Furthermore, once leaders have created a culture, they may well become constrained by that culture and find that they no longer can lead the group into new creative avenues. A complex interplay of creative and constraining forces operates both inside the leader and in the group. The resolution of such potentially conflicting forces becomes, then, one of the central tasks of leadership (Schein, 1985, p. 171)

The leadership aspect of culture is related to creating purpose and commitment. One important mechanism for doing so, of course, is the corporate language – as a manifestation of culture.

## CULTURE AND BUSINESS SUCCESS

It seems as if culture is having a major effect on the success of the business, somehow. It is common to read statements such as 'the well-run corporations of the world have distinctive cultures that are somehow responsible for their ability to create, implement, and maintain their world leadership positions' (Schwartz and Davis, 1981, p. 47) or 'companies that have cultivated their individual identities ... have an edge' (Deal and Kennedy, 1988, p. 15). However, drawing the conclusion from this that a strong and pervasive culture, directed by formal decree, means business success is *not* correct, as mentioned previously. The picture is much more complicated than that. The actual content of the culture and the degree to which it relates to the environment (present or future) seem like the critical variables here, not strength, pervasiveness or direction. It could be possible to hypothesize, for instance, that young organizations strive for culture strength and pervasiveness as a way of creating an identity for themselves, but older groups may be more effective with a weak total culture and diverse subcultures to enable them to be responsive to rapid environmental change (Schein, 1984, p. 7).

Some commentators claim that there are situations where top managers should consider the reshaping of a culture, above all its direction, for instance (Deal and Kennedy, 1988, pp. 159–161):

- when the environment is undergoing fundamental change, and the company has always been highly value-driven;
- when the industry is highly competitive and the environment changes quickly;
- when the company is mediocre, or worse;
- when the company is truly at the threshold of becoming a large corporation – a Fortune 100-scale corporate giant;
- when the company is growing very rapidly.

Even if strong and pervasive cultures do not necessarily mean that companies will lose their ability to renew themselves if necessary – companies can be fostered into living with change as many excellent companies have proven (Pascale, 1985, p. 37) – it is commonly so that a culture is a barrier to change. A culture can prevent a company from adapting, because culture is inherently conservative, resisting change and fostering continuity (Pearce and Robinson, 1985, p. 343; Deal and Kennedy, 1988, p. 159; Czinkota *et al.*, 1994, p. 264). On the other hand, corporate cultures probably change more often than national and family cultures do, as the former are more open and more dependent on the environment. The latter may even contain values *not* to change, but instead to support traditions.

However, culture is very deeply rooted, as we have previously mentioned. It is, therefore, far too complex and multifaceted to succumb to push-button control. You do not control it, at best you shape it (Green, 1988, p. 121), and shaping it cannot be done by technical tools like structure, systems and procedures – at least not alone. This process must also take place in conceptualized as well as in symbolic terms (ibid., p. 121).

There are also several dilemmas associated with shaping a culture (ibid., p. 124):

1. It requires a good appreciation of a person's own culture. Unfortunately, insight is frequently blurred. It is not easy to *really* understand oneself.
2. Contingent cultures are required. Excellent cultures are only excellent if they are contingent upon their respective environments.
3. Managers seeking to change corporate culture must have the legitimacy to do so:

> How can people who are reared within a particular value and belief system and who are judged according to their adherence to the rules, then turn around and overthrow the system that in nurturing them has also enchained them? Leaders who change direction run the risk of being regarded as heretics, turncoats, or plain incompetents. External change agents or newcomers may be ignored or won over. Consultants' views are rejected on the grounds that 'they don't really understand the problems' and new leaders succumb to the culture once an initial 'honeymoon period' is over (Green, 1988, p. 124).

However, five types of basic managerial actions which may aid the difficult process of changing organizational culture are (Pearce and Robinson, 1985, pp. 353–354):

a. *Chief Executive's role*   The CEO has to visibly lead the organization in such fundamental change, and play his or her symbolic role accordingly, that is, communicating the need for change and recognizing initial success, as well as his or her substantive role in making hard decisions. The top-management team must create the pressure for change and set unequivocally demonstrative examples. This will be discussed again in Chapter 10.

b.  *Who is hired and promoted*   One key way to begin the process of changing values and norms is to bring in new people who share the desired values. On the other hand, companies can also remove employees who strongly resist or blunt efforts to revamp the old culture, which, in extreme cases, could mean changing top management.

c.  *Change the reward structure*   To link the reward structure and the desired change is a powerful way of changing values and behaviour. Compensation is the most obvious reward, but such things as resource allocation, perks and other visible 'rewards' help positively reinforce desired change.

d.  *Clarify desired behaviour*   Unless managers are fully aware of the behaviour required to get things done in the new culture, they will not change how they approach tasks and relationships. So planning teams and other educational vehicles must clarify what the 'new rules' are and how the new behaviour will enhance development and advancement.

e.  *Foster consistency between desired change and rewards*   One element is certain in changing culture: employees cannot be fooled. So consistency between what is said to be important and what is rewarded as such is critical in cultural change. If employees find inconsistency in this respect, they will become confused, then reluctant to change and eventually intransigent.

In all this discussion about changing a culture, people should be clear about at what depth they are changing it. Do people, for instance, really change the basic direction, pervasiveness and/or strength of cultural values or are they 'only' reshaping cultural manifestations? The theme 'culture and change' will be discussed throughout this study many times.

## THE CULTURE–STRATEGY ALLOY

*Strategy* is commonly understood as general ideas about how to relate an organization to its environment, principles for various decisions taken, and rough outlines of how major objectives, resources and accomplishments of the organization are related to each other. These ideas, principles and outlines have normally a long-term orientation. They are focused on questions such as, 'What is the basic mission of the organization?', 'What are the justifications for its existence?', and 'Why should the environment be willing to pay for its products and services?'

Culture gives employees a sense of how to behave, what they should do and where to place priorities in getting the job done. Culture is, as mentioned earlier, filling the gaps for employees between what is formally decreed and what actually takes place. As such, culture is of critical importance and a powerful driving force in, for instance, implementation of strategy (Pearce and Robinson, 1985, p. 342). (This does not mean, which is commonly held, that the discussion of culture in strategic contexts can be postponed until the strategy is to be implemented; see Chapter 10).

Traditionally, strategy has been viewed as the *response* of an organization to its environment. If the environment changes, alert and responsible management rethinks and adjusts strategy as necessary. However, the organization has severe limitations on making such readjustments (Johnson and Scholes, 1988, p. 37). This is not due to traditional limitations most often discussed in the literature, that is, constraints in the environment itself that hinder change (competitive action, government legislation and so on), and internal organizational resource constraints (a lack of finance or a less adequate organizational structure, for example).

Obviously, strategic changes involve many actions, which may require months and years to accomplish. Old businesses may have to be divested, new products may have to be developed, market tests may be required, manufacturing facilities may have to be built and so on. However, in a more subtle but at the same time more decisive way, strategic change requires a basic rethinking of the beliefs and assumptions by which the company defines and carries on its businesses (Lorsch, 1986, p. 97).

So, the traditional view of strategy omits a major influence on strategy formulation which has to do with the strategy-makers themselves (Johnson and Scholes, 1988, p. 37). It is too simple to think of strategy as a causal response to the environment for it is evident that, faced with similar environments, organizations will respond differently. This response is, however, to a large extent influenced by the past experience of the managers and by the more general social and political processes in the organization (ibid., pp. 37–38). As mentioned in Chapter 1, there is, in fact, in every organization a unique set of perceptions, which could be called a 'strategic formula' or a 'recipe', that is, a group of attitudes, which can be relatively spread (at least among senior managers) and often taken for granted, and which concerns ideas about where the competencies and skills of the company are situated. It is important to understand that a strategic formula is not just a set of abstract principles, but it is very significantly impregnated with the company's culture. It is also embodied in such things as routines and control systems, myths, symbols and different kinds of formal and informal structures.

So, mundanities and routines buried deep in companies' cultures may be the most accurate reflections of why things work the way they do, and of why some firms succeed with their strategies where others fail (Schwartz and Davis, 1981, p. 31). If it is possible to get at the way in which these minutiae determine an organization's ability to create and to carry out strategy – that is, learn how to evaluate corporate culture – a great deal can also be learnt about how to manage a large organization through a period of strategic change. Strategy no longer becomes a manipulable and controllable mechanism that can be changed at the drop of a hat (Green, 1988, p. 121). Rather, strategies are usually progressing gradually, what Quinn (1980) refers to as 'incrementally'.

A carefully shaped strategy may make or break a company, and a corporate culture may make or break a strategy, therefore, an active and mutual attention must be directed towards culture as well as strategy, when discussing the company's future. Firms appear to have a better chance of achieving corporate objectives when the corporate culture and strategy are in alignment (Hickman and Silva, 1984, pp. 81–82; Smith *et al.*, 1985, p. 161).

Every change of strategy (in fact every organizational change) may involve what Schwartz and Davis (1981, pp. 36–37) refer to as a 'cultural risk'. The degree of such risk depends on the answers to two questions:

1. How *important* is each organizational approach to the success of the strategy?
2. How *compatible* is the approach with the current culture?

Figure 2.4 provides a simple but useful framework for managing the strategy–culture relationship by identifying four basic situations a company may face (Pearce and Robinson, 1985, p. 346).

| Changes in key organizational factors that are necessary to implement the new strategy | Many | Link changes to basic mission and fundamental organizational norm (1) | Reformulate strategy or prepare for long-term, difficult change (4) |
|---|---|---|---|
| | Few | Synergistic focus on reinforcing culture (2) | Manage around the culture (3) |
| | | High | Low |

Potential compatibility of changes with
existing culture

*Source*: Pearce and Robinson (1985, p. 346).

*Figure 2.4  Managing the strategy–culture relationship*

1.  *Link to mission*    A company in cell 1 faces implementing a new strategy that requires several changes in structure, systems and procedures. At the same time, most of the changes are potentially compatible with the existing organizational culture. Companies in this situation are usually successful companies that want to grow further, for instance, by either seeking to take advantage of a major opportunity or attempting to redirect major product/ market operations consistent with core, proven capabilities. Such companies are in a very promising position: they can pursue a strategy requiring major changes leaning on the power of cultural reinforcement.

Companies seeking to manage a strategy–culture relationship in this situation need to emphasize four basic considerations. First, the mission provides a broad official expression of the organizational culture, therefore, top executives should use every forum available to stress the message that the changes are linked to the company mission. Second, existing personnel carry with them the shared norms, values and assumptions of the organization, therefore, such personnel should be used as much as possible to fill positions created in implementing the strategy. Third, care must be taken if adjustments are needed in the reward system. These should be consistent with currently rewarded behaviour. Fourth, key attention should be paid to changes that are least compatible with current culture so that current norms are not disrupted.

2.  *Maximize synergy*    A company in cell 2 is in an enviable position. It needs only a few organizational changes to implement a new strategy; and those changes are potentially compatible with the current culture. A company in this situation should emphasize two broad themes. First, take advantage of this position to reinforce and solidify the company's culture. Second, use this time of relative stability to remove organizational roadblocks to the desired culture.

3.  *Manage around the culture*    A company in cell 3 must make a few major organizational changes to implement its new strategy. At the same time, these changes are potentially inconsistent with current organizational culture. It is critical for a firm in this situation to understand whether these changes can be made with a reasonable chance of success.

Several steps can facilitate managing around culture, for instance, create a separate division; use task forces, teams or programme coordinators; subcontract; bring in an outsider; or sell out. The key idea is to create an alternative method of achieving the change desired without directly confronting the incompatible cultural norms, values and assumptions. As cultural resistance diminishes, the change may be absorbed into the organization.

4. *Reformulate*  A company in cell 4 faces the most difficult challenge in managing the strategy–culture relationship. The company in this situation must make several organizational changes to implement its new strategy. However the number and nature of the changes are incompatible with current norms, values and assumptions.

When faced with such massive change and cultural resistance, a company should ask itself if it is really necessary to change many of the fundamental organizational factors, and if the changes can be made with any real expectation that they will be acceptable and successful. If the answer is 'no', the company should seriously reconsider and reformulate its strategic plan.

On the other hand, for many businesses facing this dilemma, reformulation of the strategy may not be in the long-term interests of the firm. It could be that major external changes necessitate a new strategy that requires difficult changes in the fundamental culture of the organization. In this situation, several basic managerial actions – both symbolic and substantive – should be considered as the bases for cultural change.

> For all the hype, corporate culture is real and powerful. It's also hard to change, and you won't find much support for doing so inside or outside your company. If you run up against the culture when trying to redirect strategy, attempt to dodge; if you must meddle with culture directly, tread carefully and with modest expectations ('The corporate culture ...', 17 October, 1983, p. 72).

Finally, it is all a dynamic matter. One possible way to reflect this is to relate culture and strategic choice to the life cycle of a business (Table 2.2).

*Table 2.2   Culture, lifestyle and strategic choice*

| Lifecycle stage | Key cultural factors | Implications to strategic choice |
| --- | --- | --- |
| 1. Embryonic | 1. Cohesive culture<br>2. Founders dominant<br>3. Outside help not valued | 1. Try to repeat successes<br>2. Related developments favoured |
| 2. Growth | 1. Cultural cohesion less<br><br>2. Mismatches and tensions arise | 1. Diversification often possible<br>2. Vulnerability to takeover<br>3. Structural change needed for new developments<br>4. New developments need protection |
| 3. Maturity | 1. Culture institutionalized<br><br>2. Culture breeds inertia<br><br>3. Strategic logic may be rejected | 1. Related developments favoured<br>2. Incrementalism favoured |
| 4. Decline | 1. Culture becomes a defence | 1. Readjustment necessary but difficult<br>2. Divestment may prove necessary |

*Source*:   Johnson and Scholes (1988, p. 197).

# 3. Business leadership and national culture

## MANAGERS AND LEADERS

'Management' is a word used extensively in business literature as well as in business practice today. Its use dates back to the time in the history of industrialization when owners became separated from administrators, that is, when the former had too many manufacturing sites to handle themselves; so they put 'managers' in charge to run some of these sites (Jay, 1987, p. 92).

Later, the use of the word 'manager' became ubiquitous when ownership was spread over many individuals and institutions, and when such legal business firms as 'Ltd', 'Inc.' and so on were established and individuals were appointed to 'manage' planning, supervising and controlling tasks in those firms.

Today the word 'management' stands for almost any type of administration at various business levels (strategic as well as tactic) and different ownership arrangements (private as well as public), but also administrative positions in nonbusiness organizations such as sports teams, labour unions and government institutions.

'Leadership' and 'management' are rarely today taken as synonyms. Some see leadership as a function of management: 'The managerial function of leading is defined as the process of influencing people so that they will contribute to organization and group goals' (Koontz and Weihrich, 1988, p. 392). Others see leadership as a 'higher order or capability' than management: 'A leader is an individual within an organization who is able to influence the attitudes and opinions of others within the organization; a manager is merely able to influence their actions and decisions' (Byars, 1987, p. 159). Peter Drucker has long pointed out that managers are people who do things right (efficiency); leaders are people who do the right things (effectiveness).

However, for a company to be underled and overmanaged could be as dangerous as for a company to be overled and undermanaged; therefore, the ideal is a combination of solid management and clever leadership.

## UNDERSTANDING LEADERSHIP

Nobody has a good all-purpose definition of leadership (Barnes and Kriger, 1986, p. 15). Even if, for most of us, the word conjures up an image of one leader with followers, understanding leadership can be confusing, even emotional (ibid., p. 15). Burns (1978, p. 15) cites one study with 130 definitions of the term. Another book (Bass, 1981) notes over 5000 research studies and monographs on the subject, concluding that there is no common set of factors, traits or processes that identifies the qualities of effective leadership.

Yet, according to one source, three different approaches to understanding leadership exist (Barnes and Kriger, 1986, p. 15):

1. the leader as a hero-person;
2. leadership as a set of personal attributes;
3. contingency theories of leadership.

These are briefly looked at in turn.

## THE LEADER AS A HERO-PERSON

Many books and articles have been written about the founders and developers of business empires. Many of these books have also become bestsellers. Most of them are American, though an increasing number come from other parts of the world as well.

It seems, somehow, that such books (often autobiographies) have become even more popular these days. If this is because we need business leadership heroes more in present volatile economic times or because these types of people have actually made a comeback is hard to say. At any rate, the combination of business leadership and individual success seems to fascinate many researchers, authors and readers. Whether such studies, from a social science point of view, give much more than a few hours of entertainment is arguable.

Deal and Kennedy (1988, pp. 39–41) summarize the impact of heroes in business in six dimensions:

- making success attainable and human;
- providing role models;
- symbolizing the company to the outside world;
- preserving what makes the company special;
- setting a standard of performance;
- motivating employees.

## LEADERSHIP AS A SET OF PERSONAL ATTRIBUTES

Much research has focused on identifying the traits that leaders possess, the competencies they have or (closely related) their style (considerate, structuring, autocratic, democratic, *laissez-faire* and the like). In order to illustrate this, here are two classics:

a. Blake and Mouton's *Managerial Grid*
b. Likert's *Four Systems of Management*

Building on previous research that showed the importance of a leader's having concern both for result and for people, Blake and Mouton (1964) developed a simple device to dramatize these concerns. The resulting grid, shown in Figure 3.1, or a variation of it, has often been used as a means of managerial training and of identifying various combinations of leadership styles.

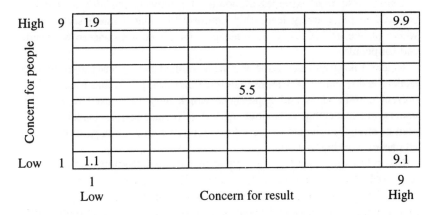

*Source*: Adapted from Blake and Mouton (1964, p. 10).

*Figure 3.1 The managerial grid*

The grid has two dimensions: concern for result and concern for people. 'Concern for result' includes the attitude of a manager/leader toward a wide variety of things, such as the quality of policy decisions, procedures and processes, creativeness of research, quality of staff services, work efficiency and volume of output. 'Concern for people' is likewise interpreted in a broad way. It includes such elements as degree of maintenance of the self-esteem of workers, placement of responsibility on the basis of trust rather than obedience, provision of good working conditions and maintenance of satisfying interpersonal relations.

Blake and Mouton recognize four extremes of style. Under the 1.1 style (referred to as 'impoverished management'), managers concern themselves very little with either people or results and have minimum involvement in their jobs. At the other extreme are the 9.9 managers, who display in their actions the highest possible dedication both to people and to results. They are the real 'team leaders' who are able to mesh the production needs of the enterprise with the needs of individuals.

Another style is 1.9 management (called 'country club management' by some), in which managers have little or no concern for results but are concerned only for people. They promote an environment where everyone is relaxed, friendly and happy but no one is concerned about putting forth a coordinated effort to accomplish enterprise goals. At another extreme are the 9.1 managers (sometimes referred to as 'autocratic task managers'), who are concerned only with developing an efficient operation, who have little or no concern for people and who are quite autocratic in their style of leadership.

Using these four extremes as points of reference, the idea is that it is possible to place every leadership approach, or management style, somewhere on the grid. Clearly, 5.5 managers have medium concern for results and for people.

Rensis Likert and his associates have studied the patterns and styles of leaders and managers for more than three decades. Likert and Likert (1976) present certain ideas and approaches which have been used in trying to understand leadership behaviour. An effective manager as leader is, then, seen as strongly oriented to subordinates, relying on communication to keep all parties working as a unit.

Likert has suggested four systems of management. System 1 management is described as 'exploitive–authoritative'; these managers are highly autocratic, have little trust in subordinates, motivate people through fear and punishment with occasional rewards, engage in downward communication and limit decision-making to the top. System 2 management is called 'benevolent–authoritative'; these managers have a patronizing confidence and trust in subordinates, motivate with rewards and some fear and punishment, permit some upward communication, solicit some ideas and opinions from subordinates and allow some delegation of decision-making but with close policy control.

System 3 management is referred to as 'consultative'; these managers have substantial but not complete confidence and trust in subordinates, usually try to make use of subordinates' ideas and opinions, use rewards for motivation with occasional punishment and some participation, engage in communication flow both down and up, make broad policy and general decisions at the top while allowing specific decisions to be made at lower levels and act consultatively in other ways.

In general, Likert found that those managers who applied the System 4 approach had greatest success as leaders. This type of management is the most participative of all and is referred to as 'participative–group'; System 4 managers have complete trust and confidence in subordinates in all matters, always get ideas and opinions from subordinates and use them constructively, give economic rewards on the basis of group participation and involvement in such areas as setting goals and appraising progress toward goals, engage in much communication both down and up and with peers, encourage decision-making throughout the organization, and otherwise operate among themselves and with their subordinates as a group.

There is no strict difference between 'managers' and 'leaders' in these kinds of classic study. Nevertheless, based on the two studies presented here (among others), Koontz and Weihrich (1988, p. 438) conclude that leadership skill seems to be a compound of at least four major ingredients:

1. the ability to use power effectively and in a responsible manner;
2. the ability to comprehend that human beings have differing motivation forces at different times and in different situations;
3. the ability to inspire;
4. the ability to act in a manner that will develop a climate conducive to responding to and arousing motivations.

In general, classic studies on leadership as a set of personal attributes have yielded many interesting results but they also have limitations. Few leaders possess all the attributes, and many nonleaders may possess many or even most of them. Also, the attribute approach gives no guidance as to how much of each characteristic a person should have. Furthermore, many of these so-called 'attributes' are really patterns of behaviour.

The most serious limitation for a project like the one presented in this study on business leadership in several different cultures is, however, that the overwhelming number of published research studies have been done in the West, most of them in the United States. It also seems as if almost every study has tried to confirm the hypothesis that the more people are allowed to participate, delegate, trust others and behave democratically, the more effective they are as leaders. In many cultures outside the American one, this does not have to be so at all, as will be seen. Other cultures may also define words like 'participation', 'delegation', 'trust' and 'democracy' differently.

One example of more modern leadership research is presented by Bennis and Nanus (1985) and Bennis (1989). They suggest that four competencies are evident to some extent in all leaders:

1. *Attention through vision*   The ability of leaders to draw others to them,

not just because they have a vision but because they communicate an extraordinary focus of commitment.

2.  *Meaning through communication*   To make dreams apparent to others and to align people with them, leaders must communicate their vision. Communication and alignment work together.
3.  *Trust through positioning*   Trust is essential to all organizations. Leaders manage trust through reliability.
4.  *Deployment of self*   Leaders know their skills and deploy them effectively. Without management of self, leaders can do more harm than good.

These results also seem more general to me in the sense that they are less 'culturally biased'. A version of the above competencies will be discussed in Chapter 10.

## CONTINGENCY THEORIES OF LEADERSHIP

Every social system requires and produces leaders, who have a function in that system (Arvonen, 1989, p. 31). Every epoch in history is asking for its own type of leadership as an expression of existing values in society. In medieval society, leadership was built into social institutions and by religion. In industrial society, leadership had a major role in planning and supervising work – technological rationalism was combined with patriarchal values. In information society, discussion is very much about people looking for charismatic leaders who can provide meaning in life and reduce modern uncertainties at the same time as social structures become more horizontal, and time as well as distance is disappearing.

This is how history is understood in the West. However, all societies, no matter where, are asking for leaders in their own terms, exerting their function in their own environment. This is very much what this study is all about.

In such a functional perspective, trying to understand business leadership can be achieved by understanding its context, a so-called *contingent approach*. Research has been done, again mostly in the United States, on variations in styles of top-level executives, especially of the chief executive officer (Steiner and Miner, 1986, p. 56). This research is often, similar to the one on leadership as attributes presented in the last section, based on studies to find out when delegation, participation and industrial democracy are adequate. One factor associated with the extent of decision-sharing at the top, for instance, appears in general to be the degree to which a company is involved in intense competition, and in product competition in particular.

It appears that where a company faces intense competition in its environment, the chief executive officer not only utilizes a more participative style in decision-making but also introduces more control to be sure the delegated decisions are carried out as intended, so:

> [There is] a strong case for matching managers in charge of businesses, and their styles, as closely as possible with the strategic demands of the business (Steiner and Miner, 1986, pp. 61–62).

One well-known contingency approach to management style, which could also be discussed in terms of leaders and followers, has been suggested by Tannenbaum and Schmidt (1973). They propose a continuum of management behaviours:

1. manager makes decision and announces it;
2. manager sells decision;
3. manager presents ideas and invites questions;
4. manager presents tentative decision subject to change;
5. manager presents problem, gets suggestions, makes decision;
6. manager defines limits; asks group to make decision;
7. manager permits subordinates to function within limits defined by superior.

Which of these management/leadership approaches is taken will be influenced by:

a. *Forces in the manager*, including his or her value system, confidence in his or her subordinates, leadership inclinations and feelings of sensitivity in an uncertain situation.
b. *Forces in the subordinates*, including their need for independence, readiness to assume responsibility, tolerance for ambiguity, interest in the problem, identification with the goals of the organization, knowledge and expectation of decision-sharing.
c. *Forces in the situation*, including the type of organization, the effectiveness of the group, the nature of the problem and the pressure of time.

For my purpose of this study, trying to understand business leadership through national cultures, I see two major drawbacks in the leadership studies presented here:

1. They seem to concentrate on formal leaders only, or at least on leaders at the very hierarchical top of the organization.
2. The results seem to be very dependent on the national culture where the studies have been conducted, that is, mainly the USA. Furthermore,

corporate culture processes (conditioned partly by the nation where the corporation is operating) are rarely taken into consideration.

## FORMAL AND INFORMAL LEADERS

In a sense, all approaches to leadership that have been seen so far are correct, but none is sufficient:

> All deal more with the single leader and multi-follower concept than with organizational leadership in a pluralistic sense. None deals well with the complexities that arise from the fact that managers are both leaders and followers, because of the very nature of organizational hierarchies. All bosses, including CEOs, are also subordinate to other people or pressures.
>
> Nor do any of these approaches deal effectively with another fact of organizational life – that informal social networks exert an immense influence which sometimes overrides the formal hierarchy. A boss in one context may be a subordinate, relative, friend, or colleague in other company settings. A person's formal job status may be clear in the hierarchy, but that is only one part of an organization's network of relationships. Less formal network ties often dominate a person's or group's role behaviour.
>
> All of this reminds us of what we often forget. Leadership goes beyond a person's formal position into realms of informal, hidden, or unauthorized influence. Moreover, we need to remember that leadership, or the lack of it, is usually better recognized by the so-called followers than by the formal leaders. To some extent, these perceptions depend upon a person's formal status, but they also depend upon the roles that a person is assigned, chooses, or is allowed to take by others (Barnes and Kriger, 1986, pp. 15–16).

Very few organizational leaders could be called hero-leaders in a hierarchy. There is a need for leadership concepts that go beyond the notion of a formal leader with many followers (Barnes and Kriger, 1986, p. 16). What is necessary is a more holistic organizational picture, where leader roles overlap, complement each other, and shift from time to time and from person to person.

This extended theory of organizational leadership involves (ibid., p. 17):

1. many potential 'leaders' in changing role relationships, who
2. move from often vague concepts of purpose and vision into
3. struggles with perceived certainty and uncertainty, and
4. reach patched-together decision actions in
5. a spiralling process involving higher and lower, newer and older producers, actors and audiences.

This concept of organizational leadership includes both formal hierarchy and informal or quasi-formal networks (Figure 3.2).

|  | Formal | Informal |
|---|---|---|
| In hierarchy | *Example:*<br><br>New CEO | *Example:*<br><br>Secretary to CEO |
| In networks | *Example:*<br><br>Shop steward | *Example:*<br><br>Mr Jones |

*Figure 3.2   Multiple leadership*

A formal leader in hierarchy can be a newly appointed chief executive officer (CEO). A formal leader in networks can be a shop steward selected by the local trade union. An informal leader in hierarchy can be somebody acting as the real brain behind a weak boss. An informal leader in networks can be anybody listened to, no matter his or her formal position.

Effective organizational leadership involves hierarchical and social network leaderships working in complementary tension patterns over time. Multiple leaderships and their tensions come from competing hierarchies and networks (Barnes and Kriger, 1986, p. 17). Hierarchies and networks are mutually exclusive, or complementary aspects of leadership. Management must constantly develop new leadership patterns in each (ibid., p. 17).

Barnes and Kriger (1986, pp. 24–25) call their pluralistic leadership approach a 'shoelacing theory'. This theory is based on the following assumptions:

1.  We need to stop talking as though executive leadership in decision-making is primarily a one-person drama played by CEOs or formal leaders only. That is an illusion, not an accurate report of how organizational leadership works.
2.  We also need to observe and use paradox as a clue for action. For example, it takes a hierarchical leader to take the step toward exaggerated trust. Only such a step can begin the complementary networking process. That means stepping outside of one's hierarchical role to create potentially competitive networks. Hierarchical leadership is needed to create and support useful networking leaderships. Though less obvious, the opposite is also true.
3.  Managers need to consider, and work on developing, complementary skills. They need to create bases of trust across formal boundaries, built

more upon what one is willing to give up than upon what one can take away. Managers must also face up to the meaning of networking leadership as complementary to hierarchies, so that people in both roles maintain some autonomy while also looking for ways to shoelace across the gaps. They might begin by looking beyond any critical tension, dichotomy, or opposite.

4. Networking leaderships offer flexibility for exploring uncertainty and ambiguity, as when hierarchical leadership wishes to search out an uncertain environment or explore new areas of opportunity which will eventually need hierarchical leaderships to run them. The two perspectives must be shoelaced actively back and forth so that neither, especially the more dominant hierarchical perspective, prevails when the other would be more useful. The skill is to keep each independent and yet complementary. That is easy to say and very difficult to do.

Culture (as norms, values and assumptions) is known to be implicit and informal, and it operates mainly through the network of an organization. To study leadership in hierarchies only is not just one-sided, but also misleading.

## THE ESSENCE OF LEADERSHIP IS FOLLOWERSHIP

It is the willingness of people to follow that makes a person a leader. Moreover, since people tend to follow those who, in their view, offer them a means of satisfying their own personal goals, the more managers are able to understand what motivates their subordinates and colleagues, and the more they reflect this understanding in carrying out their management actions, the more effective they are likely to be as leaders (Koontz and Weihrich, 1988, p. 439). In the words of Colin Marshall, a former English business leader (British Airways):

> What is the essential element any successful leader absolutely must have? I think it can be reduced to one word and a rather simple one at that: caring.
> I cannot claim that caring leadership is terribly clever or even terribly new. I can only promise that within my experience it works better than anything else (Bennis and Nanus, 1985, p. 27).

Leadership is partly a function of skilful deployment of personal qualities but probably more of the interactive processes between leaders and their followers and the more general processes through which purpose and commitment are generated and sustained within an organization (Pettigrew, 1979, p. 578). Culturally cultivated corporations have leaders whom managers and workers can emulate – not just faceless bureaucrats.

Another way to state this is to say that a successful leader is relying on legitimate power. Power often arises from position but it is derived from our cultural system of rights, obligations and duties whereby a 'position' is accepted by people as being 'legitimate' (Koontz and Weihrich, 1988, p. 208).

## TRANSACTIONAL AND TRANSFORMATIONAL LEADERS

So, leadership is many things (Peters and Waterman, 1984, p. 82):

- It is patient, usually boring coalition-building.
- It is the purposeful seeding of cabals that it is hoped will result in the appropriate ferment in the bowels of the organization.
- It is meticulously shifting the attention of the institution through the mundane language of management systems.
- It is altering agendas so that new priorities get enough attention.
- It is being visible when things are going awry, and invisible when they are working well.
- It is building a loyal team at the top that speaks more or less with one voice.
- It is listening carefully much of the time, frequently speaking with encouragement, and reinforcing words with believable action.
- It is being tough when necessary.
- It is the occasional naked use of power.

Most of these actions are what Burns (1978) calls 'transactional leadership'. They are necessary activities of the leader that make up most of his or her day (Peters and Waterman, 1984, p. 82). However, Burns has posited another form of leadership, which he refers to as 'transformational leadership' (ibid., 1984, p. 82). This kind of leadership builds on human beings' need for meaning, leadership that creates institutional purpose:

> The transforming leader is concerned with minutiae, as well. But he is concerned with a different kind of minutiae; he is concerned with the tricks of the pedagogue, the mentor, the linguist – the more successfully to become the value shaper, the exemplar, the maker of meanings. His job is much tougher than that of the transactional leader, for he is the true artist, the true pathfinder. After all, he is both calling forth and exemplifying the urge for transcendence that unites us all. At the same time, he exhibits almost boorish consistency over long periods of time in support of his one or two transcending values. No opportunity is too small, no forum too insignificant, no audience too junior (Peters and Waterman, 1984, pp. 82–83).

Tichy and Devanna (1986, pp. 271–280) profile a number of common characteristics that differentiate transformational leaders from transactional managers:

- *They identify themselves as change agents*  These leaders make a
  difference and transform the organization for which they have assumed
  responsibility.
- *They are courageous individuals*  They are able to take a stand, able
  to take risks and able to stand against the status quo in the larger
  interest of the organization.
- *They believe in people*  They are not dictators. They are powerful yet
  sensitive to other people, and ultimately work towards the empower-
  ment of others.
- *They are value-driven*  They are able to articulate a set of core values
  and exhibit behaviour that is quite congruent with their value positions.
- *They are lifelong learners*  They are able to talk about mistakes they
  have made. However, they do not view them as failures, but as learning
  experiences.
- *They have the ability to deal with complexity, ambiguity and uncertainty*  They are able to cope with and frame problems in a complex,
  changing world.
- *They are visionaries*  They are able to dream, able to translate those
  dreams and images so that other people can share them.

It may be agreed that through culture (probably transformational more than
transactional), leaders can and should influence how other employees act and
how they spend their time. How this is done varies from one national (and
often corporate) culture to another. Tichy and Devanna's list above is based
on experiences in the Western world. The same goes for Deal and Kennedy's
(1988, pp. 76–77) view of which social standards leaders can influence, that
is:

a. *Language standards*  Much of what goes on in a company is simply
   people talking with one another. Setting standards for how they do this
   has a strong influence on the culture. I believe, as does Pettigrew (1979,
   p. 578), that the capacity to use the full power of words – to make words
   talk – is one of the unexplored characteristics of successful leaders.
b. *Public decorum*  Leaders should decide what they want and then stick
   with it.
c. *Interpersonal behaviour*  Behavioural rituals determine who feels appreciated and who is downtrodden. A good leader will think this through
   and make the right kind of standard explicit.

# MY UNDERSTANDING OF LEADERSHIP

My definition and discussion of leadership has to do with culture. And culture has to do with people. I am looking for a leadership concept which at the same time as being independent of any specific culture (national or corporate) can also be used to take culture and culture's consequences into consideration in general.

I believe that all cultures have hierarchies as well as networks and that formal and informal leaders are found everywhere. I also believe it is possible to find transactional and transformational leaders of some kind in all cultures. Consequently, I think I am in a better position to understand my cultural issue by not, which seems to be common in much leadership research, neglecting networks, informality and transforming behaviour. For my purpose, therefore, formal as well as informal leaders, operating in hierarchies as well as in networks, playing a transactional and/or transformational role, are within sphere of interest.

I am interested in any kind of leaders who (influenced themselves as well as influencing others by their national norms, values and assumptions) act in a business setting. Individual people within a business organization in any position, without necessarily being heroes or formally appointed to power, can have followers, that is, have a strong influence in shaping the standards and beliefs of the organization.

So, remember, this study is *not* about leaders as outstanding individuals, or to phrase it differently, it is more about leaders than leaders' leaders ('Leadership jazz', June, 1994). This does not deny the fact that some people are more change agents than others, and more likely to be found in senior positions.

Culture as well as business leadership in general has been discussed. My ambition, as stated previously, is to analyse business leadership in various national cultures. What is left, therefore, before actually focusing on the five 'nations', is to discuss how national cultures could and should be understood. That will be the next topic.

# RELATIONS SOCIETY–CORPORATIONS

This study is based on the cultural metaphor. Developed primarily within the realm of anthropology, this metaphor draws attention to the way in which organizations can be seen as miniature societies with a distinctive social structure of, among other things, a set of more or less implicit basic norms, values and assumptions, reflected in various patterns of action.

Organizations will not often, if ever, reach the depth and richness of socially shared understanding, characteristic of the paradigmatic cultures studied by anthropologists (Wilkins and Ouchi, 1983, p. 469), but at the same time, it is known, for instance, that culture plays a major role in many aspects of overseas business success (Wortzel and Wortzel, 1985, p. 408). So, culture is important, somehow, at the level of business organizations as well.

The biggest single influence on a company's culture is the broader social and business environment in which the company operates (Deal and Kennedy, 1988, p. 13), and any company's corporate culture reflects, to a large extent, the broader national culture, of which the company is a part:

> [National] cultural elements are related one to another in an environmental system made up of a number of organizational subsystems including business enterprises. To understand a culture, it is necessary to know that the parts of the larger cultural system and smaller organizational subsystem are interrelated and interact in an ongoing process of conflict and cooperation and accommodation. For managers involved in international business, the nature and scope of the interrelationship among individuals, firms, and the [national] culture in which they are located is critically important (Wortzel and Wortzel, 1985, pp. 407–408).

National culture is manifest in a total pattern of lifestyles in a particular society. Corporate activity and national culture are closely intertwined, so that national cultural activity and understanding are essential to corporate activity, whether international or not. The culture of a nation where a company is operating will affect and have different consequences on many business variables, different from nation to nation. It is not hard to believe, for instance, that the configuration of the organization, work structuring and coordination and the career system will be typically different from nation to nation. So there is all the more reason to make comparative studies of variation in managerial and employee practices and attitudes across countries (Haire *et al.*, 1966, pp. 180–181). This study is one such attempt.

A nation's culture might influence any aspect of the management process. To give just one example: North America has a tendency to separate the person from his or her product. In other cultures, particularly in Asia and the Middle East, the totality of the person is important (Harris and Moran, 1987, p. 12). In overall terms, the national cultural impact is reflected by basic beliefs and behaviours of the people of the nation. Other examples where the culture of society can affect management approaches are:

- the extent to which power is centralized or decentralized;
- willingness among people to take risks;
- how people are rewarded and on which criteria this is done;
- to what extent people are interested in change;
- how loyal employees are to their place of work.

Variables like these, and many more, will be introduced as this study develops.

In comparative national management studies, culture is usually considered to be a background factor (almost synonymous with country), an explanatory variable (Ajiferuke and Boddewyn, 1970), or a broad framework (Cummings and Smidt, 1972) influencing the development and reinforcement of beliefs. The literature sometimes has a macro-focus, examining the relationship between culture and aspects of organization structure, sometimes a micro-focus, then investigating the similarities and differences in attitudes of managers of different cultures (Everett *et al.*, 1982). A conception of the culture–organization relationship that is portrayed schematically in Figure 3.3 (Smircich, 1983, p. 343) is common.

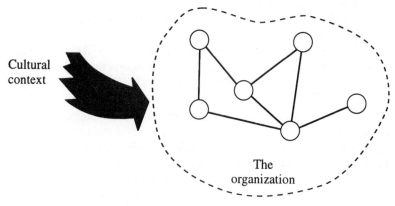

Cultural context

The organization

*Source*: Smircich (1983, p. 343).

*Figure 3.3   Culture as an independent factor*

This literature is extensive and has been subjected to several major reviews and critiques (for example, Roberts, 1970; Bhagat and McQuaid, 1982). There are also conflicting positions in the cross-cultural management literature concerning the relationship between culture and management practices (Kelley and Worthley, 1981, p. 164). Harbison and Myers (1959) have stated that as nations industrialize, beliefs concerning leadership change and increasing constraints are placed upon management's authority. In 1963, Winston Oberg proposed the converse of this 'convergence hypothesis':

> Cultural differences from any country to another are more significant than many writers now appear to recognize. A convergence claim is hardly warranted by either evidence or institution at this stage in the development of management theory (Oberg, 1963, p. 142).

In one article, Negandhi (1975) states that there is increasing evidence to support the contention that management practices, behaviour and effectiveness are as much, if not more so, functions of such contextual variables as size, technology, location and market conditions as they are of sociocultural variables. In the same year and the same journal, Bedeian stated: 'It is a well-established fact that different cultures possess different organizational norms and behaviours standards and that they recognize these as legitimate forms of influence' (Bedeian, 1975, p. 899).

Kelley and Worthley (1981, p. 165) see three basic reasons for the different positions regarding the linkage between culture and managerial attitudes, behaviour and effectiveness:

1.  The vague definitions of culture.
2.  The methodological difficulties of accurate translation and having a representative sample.
3.  Most empirical cross-cultural management studies do not isolate the impact of culture but are actually national studies that also reflect other factors such as education and economic and legal systems.

I am not totally free of these problems myself. My definition of culture is distinct and limited, representative samples are inadequate with my research orientation (this will be discussed again later in this chapter), and I do not see any reason to separate cultural factors and 'education and economic and legal systems', apart from the fact that these systems are cultural manifestations, not culture itself (as norms, values and assumptions). However one problem remains, that is, translation. This book is written in English, a language which, like all languages, contains its own assumptions and reflects its own group of cultures. To what extent that is a serious problem is up to you to decide.

## UNDERSTANDING OTHER COUNTRIES

Basic for understanding values and their development is that people tend to stick to what is well known, to an already given environment and form of life that they are used to (Daun, 1989, p. 28). The fact that people are a product of their own culture makes it difficult for everybody, researchers, ordinary human beings and leaders alike, to live in a cultural context at the same time as questioning it (Smircich, 1983, p. 355). It is difficult to engage in contextual, reflexive leadership and research, with the requirement of examination and critique of people's own assumptions and values. It is difficult; but that is what a cultural framework for leadership and research urges people to do.

As nearly all meanings attached to life are affected by values, practically all are affected by culture, and this is reflected in human behaviour. The strength and depth of cultural knowledge and beliefs, therefore, makes it difficult not only to question a person's point of view but also to adopt another's. The overwhelming majority of people everywhere approach intercultural experience from a position grounded strongly in *ethnocentrism* (Dredge, 1985, p. 416). Ethnocentrism is the practice of judging people of other cultures by the standards of one's own. It takes a prolonged stay abroad and mixing with other nationals to recognize the numerous and often subtle differences in behaviour, because that is how society has moulded people. Studies have proved that people are blind to their own culture (Phillips-Martinsson, 1992, p. 18). In order to be able to work successfully with and for persons from other cultures people must, therefore, first understand their own culture.

In the past, business managers who did not want to worry about the cultural challenge could simply decide not to do so and concentrate on domestic markets. In today's business environment, a company has no choice. It will face international competition even if it still operates only domestically. In this new environment, believing that concern about culture and its manifestations is a waste of time often proves to be disastrous (Czinkota *et al.*, 1994, p. 263). In addition, because of serious and costly errors, many managers, executives and technicians working in multicultural environments are now asking themselves questions such as (Harris and Moran, 1979, p. 21):

1.  What must I know about the social and business customs of country X?
2.  What skills do I need to be effective as a negotiator in country Y?
3.  What prejudices and stereotypes do I have about the people in country Z?
4.  How will these influence my interaction?

The study of organizational behaviour at management schools, which in the past almost exclusively reflected the American viewpoint, is now conducted from a variety of perspectives that consider the cultural norms, values and assumptions in the area being studied (Harris and Moran, 1979, p. 21). It is fair to say that managers have become more sensitive to the variety of cultural manifestations in the modern world. However, on a more basic (cultural) level than simply differences in behaviour in various countries, the nature of what culture is and how multinational firms can deal with it is less understood than it should be (Dredge, 1985, p. 411). Oversimplifications can lead to dangerous assumptions, so international leaders need cultural sensitivity in their analysis of trends in world management and commerce.

Different nations have different cultural heritage which is largely invisible. The invisible part consists of values, interpersonally held by a major part of the population (but possibly differentiated by social class and ethnic group). These values (as such, and as norms and assumptions) are what have been called culture. This culture proper is transferred from generation to generation through education and early life experience. These values have grown into societal norms. Such norms are very difficult to separate from more basic cultural values. Societal norms, values and assumptions about life lead to behaviour and determine to a large extent the political, economic and organizational solutions which are feasible within that particular national culture. As mentioned several times, such behaviour and solutions are not included themselves in culture in this study, but understood as cultural manifestations.

So, there are at least two types of knowledge related to culture which an individual manager and marketer must possess in order to cope with the problems of a different culture. One is a need for factual knowledge, that is, how culture manifests itself in social customs. Such customs are relatively easy, with a bit of effort, to anticipate, study and learn. The other type of knowledge is harder to acquire; that is a more interpretive type of knowledge, an ability to understand what is behind these social customs, that is, to get at the level of social norms, interpersonal values and existential assumptions. This study concentrates on this second, *interpretive* type of knowledge of culture and many examples of such norms, values and assumptions will be discussed in subsequent chapters. A few ways in which these may manifest themselves in various social and business contexts, that is, introduce a few examples of culture as *factual* knowledge, are described in the following section.

At the factual level of understanding, managers in, for example, multinational corporations need to know the social and business customs (manifestations of culture) of the countries in which they expect to operate. A few examples of such customs are (Moore, 1982, pp. 536–540):

*Personal acceptability*    Customs relating to personal acceptability are perhaps the most important of social customs, and they differ widely. In Europe, people shake hands when they meet someone and again when they part. In Russia, they may get kissed on both cheeks, but not in India, where people do not touch when they greet each other. An Arab likes to carry out a conversation more or less eyeball to eyeball. Latin Americans also like to stay close when talking. Americans and Europeans want more distance. In Thailand, if people sit with their legs crossed, they are rude. If people place their hands on their hips, the Chinese will think that they are angry. A friendly slap on the back by a foreigner will insult an Indonesian. In England, people who are aggressive are boors. Americans and Europeans hold their forks in different hands, and, in Arab countries, people are uncouth if they eat with their left hand.

*Time in social events*   The part that time plays in social events also differs among cultures. If a person is invited to someone's house in Sweden for a meal, he or she should arrive on time. However, in Latin America, he or she should arrive at least one hour late. In Spain, two hours late is better still. This is the case for business appointments as well as for social events. In some countries, 'tomorrow' does not necessarily mean the day after. Americans are always in a hurry. They want to get on with whatever it is. Some other countries like to spend more time with preliminary discussions. Talking, negotiating and bargaining are all parts of the game. In Latin countries, as well as in the Middle and Far East, haggling over prices is expected. The discussion should not be hurried either. Pressing to get down to business right away will intimidate a Japanese just as pressing for a deadline will offend an Arab.

*Friendship and politeness*   In most parts of the world, people do business only with people they know and like. If a new company offers them a product at a lower price, local customers may say 'no' if this company's managers are new to the community or are otherwise unacceptable. In order to carry on business, a company's manager may have to be around for a while and to develop friends. The Japanese are not likely to say 'no' directly if it offends someone. With the Japanese, too, a 'yes' at first is not to be taken as a firm 'yes'. It may be just a politeness 'yes' which keeps the door open for further negotiations which later on may become a 'no'.

*The enculturation process*, or the way in which values and rules of behaviour are passed from generation to generation, begins in infancy. The major tool for this process is language. Language, including the many forms of nonverbal communication, transmits elements so subtly that individuals usually are not consciously aware that they act in response to the values and the norms of the culture (Wortzel and Wortzel, 1985, p. 407). Very often mastery of the language is required before a person is accultured to a culture other than his or her own. Language mastery, however, must here go beyond technical competency because every language has words and phrases that can be understood only in a context. Such phrases are carriers of culture; they represent special values that have been developed to view some aspect of human existence, for instance, what it means 'to succeed' or 'to be a friend'. Language capability serves four distinct roles in international business (Ricks, 1983, p. 4):

1.   Language is important in information-gathering and evaluating efforts.
2.   Language provides access to local society.
3.   Language capability is increasingly important in company communications.

4. Language provides more than the ability to communicate. It extends beyond mechanisms to the integration of contexts.

Again, it is not to be forgotten that nonverbal behaviour can be a communication process by which meanings can be exchanged between individuals. Head nods, smiles, raised eyebrows and other facial expressions or body movements have long been recognized as communication symbols (Zikmund, 1986, p. 233).

## LEARNING FROM OTHER COUNTRIES

The fact that countries have different cultures and cultural manifestations does not mean that they cannot learn from each other. On the contrary, looking across one's own border is one of the most effective ways of getting new ideas in the area of management, organization or politics. One obvious example of cultural transfers is that languages borrow extensively from each other to avoid the need for circumlocution for useful terms for which the own language has no equivalent (Hofstede, 1980, p. 35). Words are borrowed for concrete objects (*sauna* from Finnish; *smörgåsbord* from Swedish) but also for concepts with a flavour related to the cultural context of their country of origin (*laissez-faire* and *savoir-vivre* from French; *verboten* and *Weltanschauung* from German; *jihad* and *hajj* from Arabic; *kanban* from Japanese; and *guan-xi* from Chinese).

There are occasions when nations have denounced it as a shame or a defeat to borrow customs from other nations – it has even been labelled 'cultural imperialism' to do so. On the other hand, the Japanese built up their modern country by borrowing extensively from others; and South-East Asia was booming until 1997, partly because its newly industrialized countries eagerly adopted American management and Japanese institutions. That this could be progressive proves that methods in other countries are not completely culture-bound.

In spite of the fact that, by and large, culture in this study is treated as a given, independent factor, the international business entity and its leaders can, of course, act as 'change agents' in their environment by introducing new products, ideas, practices and values. However, deep-rooted norms, values and assumptions are slow to change.

Modernization, perceived as a process whereby the old and the new ways of life mix and coexist, will invariably result in tension between the modern and the traditional. A country may, therefore, achieve economic progress and become modern in some but not all aspects of human life. It could become 'neo-traditionalist'; new and modern in form and style but not in substance or essence (Muna, 1980, p. 102). In my words: *a nation may change its cultural manifestations without changing its culture!*

## ISSUES WHEN 'MEASURING' NATIONAL CULTURE

As there is much misunderstanding when approaching a different culture in practical life, there are many potential pitfalls when trying to comprehend what is done when attempting to characterize or to measure a culture and trying to understand the consequences of such attempts. It is advisable, therefore, *to read this section carefully* to get a proper perspective on the remainder of this study.

First of all, is a nation a meaningful unit of analysis? In one way, nations merit special consideration in the study of cultures because they are the most 'complete' human groups that exist (Hofstede, 1980, p. 26). As organizations, nations are defined both according to territory and citizenry, and people are all ascribed one by birth (Ahrne, 1994, p. 62). However, the degree of cultural integration varies between one nation and another, and may be especially low for some of the newer nations.

Even then, any nation could be looked at from a multicultural point of view. Most nations are very complex and subculturally heterogeneous. Even if reasonably homogeneous, there are many potential cultural dimensions to consider, therefore, when nations are studied from a cultural point of view, this can only meaningfully be done with a limited group in mind (in my case, businesspeople). Even then, try to concentrate on one or a few phenomena (in my case, leadership).

Furthermore, when national cultures are compared, do not compare single individuals. In all nations, there is a huge variation around any kind of 'centre' or 'norm'. Many individuals do not fit this 'typical' picture. However, in every nation, experiences 'are joined together' intersubjectively, somehow, and there are feelings of belonging or nonbelonging among the inhabitants in a nation. Even with a limited group in mind (in my case businesspeople) it is fair to say that it is possible, in every nation, to find leadership behaviour which does not fit my characteristic at all – and may even gain from diverting from it! On the other hand, from an intersubjective point of view, it sounds logical that a more effective business organization should fit in with the national culture, if for no other reason than that fewer people would feel alienated.

So, how should a picture of a national culture be read? To answer this question the distinction between explaining – the rationalist view – and understanding – the interpretist view – will have to be brought up again. Those who attempt to *explain* a national culture are looking for 'typical' characteristics in the sense of 'most frequent' among the members of the culture. However, this 'most frequent' does not have to mean that it exists in absolute majority. It is enough for an explanaticist that, in a comparative perspective, a characteristic is more common in one nation compared with another to get a description of their differences. What is consequently typical for a nation in an explanatory perspective is, then, its specific *distribution* of cultural characteristics and the percentage of individuals that share a certain profile (Terhune, 1970, p. 259). What might then be a unique national characteristic is the dominating combination of cultural traits (Daun, 1989, p. 135). The explanatory orientation commonly leads to a conclusion among researchers that they are looking at the value system shared by a majority among the middle classes in a society.

Applying an *understanding* approach, such as my own, makes things different. For an interpretist, a statistical distribution of a cultural characteristic cannot exist having a physical reality of its own – because meaning cannot be quantified!

> Cultures can be distinguished from each other by the differences in shared meanings they expect and attribute to their environment. Culture is not a 'thing', a substance with a physical reality of its own. Rather, it is made by people interacting, at the same time determining further interaction (Trompenaars, 1995, p. 25).

An understanding orientation is also based on a specific view on representativity. A representative sample (in a statistical sense) consisting of some members of a national population providing a 'true', even if minimized, picture of the culture makes, therefore, no sense (does not even exist). On the other hand, as long as a person is *in* a cultural interaction, he or she is (or becomes) a *carrier*, even if unconsciously so, of the culture in question. 'The problem' with a picture of culture for the understanding researcher, then, is a matter of studying various cultural manifestations (hopefully as much as possible actually living in the culture or, at least, listening to and/or reading about statements from its members – possibly indirectly through documentations from other researchers) and from such studies arriving at an interpretation concerning norms, values and assumptions among the members of the culture. This picture is a 'typified' (or 'ideal-typified') description, that is, a picture valid only given certain specified idealized circumstances, circumstances which never exist in full at the same time in reality. It could be said that the remainder of this study provides typified descriptions, that is, descriptions of business leadership in various cultures as if leaders in those cultures were true to their type – behaving logically and naturally consistent as a consequence of their particular cultural norms, values and assumptions. Business leadership will rarely, if ever, appear in such pure forms in reality.

Cultural pictures are consequently, with an understanding and interpretive approach, by necessity a product of the researcher's interpretive efforts more than true pictures in the sense of being 'average' or 'typical'. However, this does not mean that these pictures are completely subjective and up to the researcher alone. They should, at least, be adequate in the sense of being truly accepted by other researchers with a similar orientation 'knowing' about the culture in question, 'fit' theirs and the researcher's own data (which are mainly qualitative), and be meaningful to the members of that culture (these people should feel 'at home' in these pictures). If so, the pictures are a good typified (but not typical) description (more information about differences between 'average', 'typical' and 'typified' descriptions can be found in Arbnor and Bjerke, 1997, p. 61; Bjerke, 1997; and Bjerke, 1999).

It could be said that explanaticists want to make particular generalizations, while hermeneuticists want to make general particularizations.

I have 'collected' my information by living for several years in each of the five cultures that I describe and/or working with their nationals over extensive periods of time. I am also Scandinavian-born and have a postgraduate degree in Business based on American thinking.

Finally, no culture or society is able to create unique cultural characteristics, which are only shown there and nowhere else. Cultures overlap each other and it is possible in one culture to find individuals who are more like members of other cultures than, for instance, marginal cases in their own.

So, the five cultures illustrated in Chapters 4–8 should be looked at, not as average or typical, but as typified pictures. One possible conclusion, however, could be that they provide tendencies. If one person does not 'fit' the picture of one of the cultures at all, he or she is probably not a member of it.

## MY CULTURAL PICTURES

The next five chapters provide pictures of five different 'national cultures'. They are presented in alphabetic order, that is,

- American;
- Arab;
- Chinese;
- Japanese;
- Scandinavian.

These cultures differ greatly in homogeneity, from very homogeneous in the case of the Japanese, quite homogeneous in the case of the Arab and the Scandinavian, to very heterogeneous in the case of the Chinese and the American. For instance, several studies (Hannertz, 1969) claim that Afro-Americans in the USA exist in a separate cultural world rather than in a 'branch of the American cultural tree'. Furthermore, regional differences exist in all the five cultures (as in all cultures; see Humes, 1993, p. 111), particularly in the American and the Chinese.

Furthermore, looking at only business means that I automatically exclude many Chinese (who are farmers) and most women in the Arab and the Japanese cultures (who are very little involved in business there, if at all, at least in public).

The five cultures could have been presented in a uniform framework along the same set of dimensions or variables, previously provided. There is certainly no shortage of such cultural dimensions being proposed in other studies (Table 3.1 provides examples of some possible classification variables).

I have decided not to use such a uniform framework but try, instead, to present the five cultures on their own terms. There are several reasons for this:

a. My research orientation means that I try to avoid placing too much of my own structure on others' reality but, instead, aim at understanding these others on their terms.
b. There is no consistent or systematic research done on the five cultures. There is, for instance, lots of research on the American culture, hardly any on the Arab. Nor is my experience from the five cultures uniformly patterned. It consists mainly of daily impressions, only occasionally taken down as notes. I will allow myself to be quite speculative at times.
c. I hope you will be more stimulated by reading my pictures, which are not only typified but also have been 'painted with a rather broad brush'.

Each of the five cultures will be presented along a set of 'themes' which are allocated to each and every one of them according to my understanding of their peculiar nature. This does not mean, of course, that these themes are exclusive to the culture in question, only that, in my interpretation, they are more 'dominant' there.

Chapters 4–8 will end with a summarized typified picture of the business leader in the culture being discussed.

## BEFORE WE CONTINUE

My project can be described as follows:

I want to analyse to what extent we can understand, and account for, business leadership behaviour (formal as well as informal, in hierarchies as well as in networks, transactional as well as transformational) by understanding basic norms, values and assumptions in five cultural nations or group of nations:

*Table 3.1   Possible variables to classify cultures*

| Country X | Culture dimension | Country Y |
|---|---|---|
| *Vague*<br>Few generally recognized social classes; social mobility is high; status is unrelated to class | Class structure | *Distinct*<br>Overt social classes exist; mobility among classes is restricted; status is dependent on class |
| *Short*<br>Hierarchical fluidity; rank decided by achievement; equality of superiors and subordinates | Power distance | *Long*<br>Solid hierarchy; rank decided by background; inequality of superiors and subordinates |
| *Scientific*<br>Logic and scientific methods utilized | Problem-solving | *Traditional*<br>Following precedent or adapting old procedures to new ones |
| *Pragmatic*<br>Information interpreted in context of use and action in practice | Modes of thinking | *Universalistic*<br>Information interpreted in context of general principles or ideologies |
| *Democratic*<br>Manager is expected to ask subordinates before decision; consultation accepted procedure | Decision-making style | *Autocratic*<br>Manager is expected to decide individually or using experts; informal discussions with subordinates avoided |
| *Unbalanced*<br>Object of work is wealth; stress on salaries, bonuses, fringe benefits and so on | Concepts of achievement | *Balanced*<br>Object of work is self-actualization; in addition to money, employees need recognition, belonging and so on |

*Table 3.1    continued*

| Country X | Culture dimension | Country Y |
|---|---|---|
| *Low-contextual* Most of the information is contained in the message; what is said is 'black and white' | Interpretation of communication | *High-contextual* Strangers must be 'filled in' before they can understand the message; what is said is 'grey' |
| *Individualistic* Reliance on individual initiative, self-assertion, and personal achievement and responsibility | Personal orientation | *Collectivistic* Emphasis on belonging to organizations or clans; acceptance of group decisions, values and duties |
| *Rank-dependent* Social standing and esteem linked primarily to managerial position and advancement in organizational rank, class origin nonessential | Social status of managers | *Class-dependent* Social standing and esteem derive primarily from class origin, organizational rank secondary |
| *Weak* Nuclear family structure with husband–wife relationship central; children socialized mainly outside kinship structure and become 'autonomous' on reaching adulthood; kinship influence on business slight | Kinship | *Strong* Close identification with family and kin; children socialized mainly in extended family structure; deep commitment to family honour, loyalties and responsibilities; kinship and business ties coincide |

- American;
- Arab;
- Chinese;
- Japanese;
- Scandinavian.

I do this in order to gain an understanding of business leadership as well as of culture. Then, in Chapter 9, I compare the five cultures in various respects. In Chapter 10, I end the book by discussing some consequences of my findings for business leadership of today.

Here are some important points to bear in mind:

- I do not intend to join any public debate on good or bad cultures even though, due to the nature of the subject, some of you may feel provoked by my presentations. This study is not about evaluating better or worse business leadership, even if the five cultures can easily criticize each other, based on their own point of view.
- I do not pretend that business leadership can be explained or understood by national culture alone. Also, national culture can be, and is, influenced by business leadership as well.
- I want to dispel the notion that there is 'one best way' of managing and organizing a business; and I want to provide a better understanding of culture in general and business leadership in various cultures in particular.
- An important part of my 'research tool box' is a belief that symbolic and meaningful aspects of business are important. This is not always explicit in the text.
- I have a culture as well, of course. There is no 'neutral' position from which a discussion of the five cultures presented in this study can be held. A culture-free discussion of culture is impossible.
- There are cultural (as well as business leadership) similarities as well as differences among the five cultures.

So, let us see:

- how much of a Frontier there is still in an American;
- how much of a Bedouin there is still in an Arab;
- how much of a Mandarin there is still in a Chinese;
- how much of a Samurai there is still in a Japanese;
- how much of a Viking there is still in a Scandinavian.

# 4.   American culture

## INTRODUCTION

The USA (also called 'America' in this study) is a big country in more than one sense. The size of its economy, for instance, is roughly 20–25 per cent of the world economy. Its impact on the rest of the world is, therefore, difficult to neglect for anybody, particularly in business.

Due to its size, but also due to the fact that it is built up by a mix of immigrants and their descendants, the American culture is more complex and varying than most other cultures. Any attempt to delineate an American national culture is consequently hazardous (Samovar *et al.*, 1981, p. 66). In the USA, white American middle-class cultural characteristics are considered dominant, but even then they do not encompass many significant characteristics among, for example, American Indians, Afro-Americans, Mexican Americans, and Japanese Americans.

Nevertheless, it is generally understood that a relatively clear American *business* culture (of relevance to our leadership) exists. There is also an impressive amount of research being done discussing this topic. And, even if in America, as in other countries, there is often a difference between the *corporate* culture of large corporations and smaller companies, say in strength and/or family feeling (Trompenaars, 1995, p. 161), they may both be part of the *national* culture.

In global discussions of culture, America is often placed in an Anglo-American group together with countries such as Canada, Australia, the United Kingdom and Ireland (Ronen and Shenkar, 1985, p. 449).

Some American culture themes follow in the rest of this chapter.

## PROGRESS AND GROWTH

People in America tend to be future-oriented rather than oriented to the present or the past. It is one of their fundamental assumptions that the capacity to defer gratification (doing something that is not particularly pleasant today to further future pleasure) is a positive indication (Ferraro, 1994, p. 94). It is generally thought that with this *concentration on the future –*

together with a high value placed on action and work, which will be discussed in a later section – it is not only possible, but mandatory, to improve on the present.

A future is also anticipated to be bigger and better (Samovar *et al.*, 1981, p. 72). Americans foster a cult of progress, and belief in progress involves accepting change and the idea that change can be steered in a good direction. Progress in America is often measured in materialistic possessions, and it is perhaps most frequently associated with technological control of the environment (ibid., p. 71).

This is not only because of an optimism about people's amount of initiative and ambition, even a drive for leadership, in the American type of culture (Hofstede, 1984, p. 133), but an American approach for dealing with the human element in productivity is to concentrate attention on the environment (At-Twaijri, 1989b, p. 8).

> A basic assumption of US culture is that nature and the physical environment not only can be, but should be, controlled for human convenience. If a river overflows its banks and destroys homes and crops, dam it up or change its course; if a mountain stands in the way of convenient travel between two points, slice it off the top of the mountain or tunnel through it; if gravity is a barrier to walking on the moon, simply build a sufficiently large enough engine to propel past the earth's gravitational pull (Ferraro, 1994, p. 97).

In short, Americans assume that the environment can be subjugated to the human will, given enough time, effort and money. And it should – in the service of humankind. This exploitative attitude toward nature has led to a material richness of American society no doubt, but such a culture also ranks preservation of the environment as only a tertiary value (Sitaram and Cogdell, 1976, p. 191).

This American orientation is based on an economy of abundance, stemming from the immense physical and natural resources of an entire continent (McMillan, 1985, p. 20).

In business, American managers not only value change relatively highly but also value caution less (Davis and Rasool, 1988, p. 17). This suggests an active or dynamic orientation and a willingness to make risky decisions. Uncertainty of life is accepted as normal, and economic risks are judged by potential rewards. Many scholars have certified that the American economy is very entrepreneurial, for example, Drucker (1985).

One aspect of controlling today for the future is that managers in the American type of culture are more involved in strategy, and that they categorize strategic issues as opportunities, while some other cultures (such as the Japanese) overwhelmingly view them as problems (Sallivan and Nonaka, 1988, p. 9).

*Growth* is seen as a vital need in America in its own right (Humes, 1993, p. 112), but also to grow bigger:

> Big ... has always been the American calling card. In fact, I bet you can't drive more than seventy-five miles in any direction, from anywhere in the United States, without running into a 'biggest in the world' of some sort (Peters, 1989, p. 13).

Some outsiders see American managers as obsessed with mergers, acquisitions and short-term gains (Kobayashi, 1990, p. 8).

Controlling today (for the future) means to control time. To the American, time is seen as just another part of the environment to deal with. In a culture like the American, time is perceived as passing in a straight line, compartmentalized into discrete segments in a sequence of disparate events (Trompenaars, 1995, p. 10). And in America, 'time is money'; it should be carefully used, properly budgeted and should not be wasted.

> Thus, time becomes a major concern, and in fact, plays a central role in the everyday life of the typical North American. The majority of adults in the United States have strapped to their wrist a device that divides hours into minutes and minutes into seconds, so that no matter where we are we will always know the correct time. We punch timeclocks to determine the quantity of our work. We measure how long it takes a sprinter to run 100 meters in hundredths of a second.
>
> Even the biological function of eating is done in response to the clock, for we often eat because it is lunchtime or dinnertime. Several years ago a major US watch company spent millions of dollars on an advertising campaign that claimed that their watches were guaranteed to lose less than two seconds per month. Clearly, the company would not have spent that much money to convey that particular message if it was not what the American consumer wanted to hear (Ferraro, 1994, pp. 91–92).

Cultures with a sequential view of time, such as in America (and in Britain), are usually *short term* in their business strategies. Cultures with a synchronous view of time, for instance in Japan (and in Germany), are typically long term strategically (Trompenaars, 1995, p. 174). On the other hand, *promptness* in American society is highly valued. To be kept waiting is often taken as an insult or a sign of irresponsibility and, if late for an appointment, an apology is expected to be offered (Ferraro, 1994, p. 92).

There was a time when America took the ethnocentric view that they were the greatest, and that everybody else was trying to reach their standard. One example (Humes, 1993, p. 141) is an American business management professor who said: 'The only difference between the American way of doing things and the way the rest of the world does things is that the rest of the world hasn't caught up yet.'

However, the basic assumption of convergence among cultures is beginning to be abandoned in the USA (Fallows, 1989, p. 15). The Americans, being so exposed, are naturally highly criticized (as well as praised), for instance, because of overcommercialization or because of a society breaking up, going from *Gemeinschaft* to *Gesellschaft* (a distinction introduced by the German sociologist Tönnies more than 100 years ago). Occasionally, American firms successfully use American themes abroad (Koontz and Weihrich, 1988, p. 238). However, phenomena such as McDonald's and Coke in a society may mean that it has adopted a foreign cultural manifestation without necessarily having changed its own (deeper) cultural values, a possibility which was mentioned in the last chapter and which is an important distinction for business.

## MODERNITY

One aspect closely associated with progress and growth among Americans is that they live in a society where *youthfulness* is appreciated (Ferraro, 1994, p. 109). Americans tend to emphasize what is new and young by keeping up with new trends (creating many of them themselves) and maintaining a youthful spirit. The American free enterprise system has encouraged this love affair with all things new, quickly getting rid of old things. This 'throwaway', or disposable, mentality has occasionally meant that the American culture has been characterized as inhabited by 'waste makers' (Packard, 1964).

So, as part of their future orientation, Americans prefer to conform to standards that are momentarily current and up to date rather than old-fashioned (Samovar *et al.*, 1981, p. 79). No current generation of Americans wants to be called old-fashioned.

Old-fashioned, however, is not the same as conservative. Even if there is a tendency in the American type of societies to be less conservative (Hofstede, 1984, p. 140), it may be fashionable to be conservative – particularly if an aspect of the American way of life is threatened!

On the business scene, American managers endorse 'modern' management ideas and try to be up to date (ibid., p. 174). And the American business style has truly been popular (and in many parts of the world still is):

Currently the American business style is dominant because it appears to produce the efficiency required. Commenting on this, a European executive of a United States company has emphasized five major traits in the American managerial philosophy which have produced a successful penetration into other cultures. One is the belief in growth as a vital need in its own right; another is the belief in profit as a mark of efficiency and performance, and a producer of social benefits. The third is a belief in free initiative and private enterprise as a system which, in spite of its imperfections, has hitherto performed more effectively than any other. The fourth element in this philosophy is that hard decisions must be accepted for the sake of the well being of the whole organization. Such decisions include the elimination of inefficient businesses, the dismissal of weak executives, and the down-grading of conventional status symbols. The final feature is that change must be accepted in every aspect of the working existence (Brooke and Remmers, 1978, p. 52).

## MATERIALISM

The action culture in America has made available the mass-produced goods the American market wants – better than anyone else has. Americans consider it almost a right to be materially well off and physically comfortable. They expect convenient transport, a variety of clean and healthful foods and comfortable homes equipped with labour-saving devices.

> Materialism is a major force behind the American genius for devising and employing machines to provide efficiency and convenience in daily life. Americans are famous for taking all kinds of gadgets and machines with them on their trips abroad. They exhibit a strong tendency to perceive their tasks as requiring the use of machines, tools, and equipment (Samovar *et al.*, 1981, pp. 68–69).

The high value placed on *materialism* in the American culture is sometimes reflected in an ethnocentric attitude towards other individuals, groups and societies as being 'underdeveloped' or 'poor', if they do not have the high standard of living as measured by American material orientation.

Achievement is defined in terms of recognition and wealth in the American type of societies (Hofstede, 1984, p. 200). This orientation towards money and materialistic possessions may even make people prefer additional salaries to shorter working hours (ibid., p. 201). In general, American companies appear to rely much more on monetary rewards than do, for instance, typified Japanese firms (Boulton, 1984, p. 168).

## ACTIVITY AND WORK ORIENTATION

Unlike cultures in the East, the West has developed separate institutions with separate spheres of influence for the spiritual life and for the material aspects of life of human beings. The commercial institutions have been allocated the role of the latter. This means that the spiritual and social life of humankind in Western thinking is outside work (Pascale and Athos, 1982, pp. 17–18).

In fact, one of the most important distinctions in the forms of activity in American life is the separation of work from play. Work is pursued for living. Play is relief from work (Samovar *et al.*, 1981, p. 70). However, that is not all;

the American culture is also very doing-oriented. This is reflected in phrases like: 'Getting things done' and 'Let's *do* something about it'. This, together with the American materialistic way, makes the country an almost perfect example of a culture that stresses activity and work. A foreign visitor in the USA quickly gains an impression of life lived at a fast pace and of people constantly active (ibid., p. 69).

> One element in America's lexicon of values is the emphasis placed on work, activity, and achievement. Throughout [its] history as a nation, the United States has been known for its high levels of human energy, its aversion to idleness, and its preference for the person of action over the person of ideas (Ferraro, 1994, p. 95).

These values, that is, that individuals must work hard to accomplish objectives and the positive sanctions to work, achievement and activity, were brought over by some of the immigrants and were necessary for surviving and taming the wilderness. They became known as the 'Protestant ethic'. This Puritan orientation views human nature as basically evil but perfectible. Constant control and discipline of self is required.

So, Americans believe that individuals can influence the nature by hard work ('where there is a will there is a way') (Hodgetts and Luthans, 1991, p. 41). This may called 'effort optimism', which means that no goal is too remote for the individual who has the will and the determination. The converse also holds, that is, failure means that the individual did not try hard enough, is lazy, or even worthless. Promotion and pay should be based on performance, not seniority (Schwind and Peterson, 1985, p. 71), and people should be removed, or even fired, if they cannot perform (Hodgetts and Luthans, 1991, p. 41), according to the American culture.

## INFORMALITY AND EQUALITY

Americans are *informal*. This, together with goal orientation, means that Americans tend to be on the expressive side. Perhaps this is because their country is inhabited by many immigrants. In the course of history, Americans have had to break down social barriers again and again (Trompenaars, 1995, pp. 65–66). This could be a different experience from living in a more 'settled' country. In such a case, it may be harder to avoid those you grew up with; friendship tends to start early in life and lasts many years.

Informality seems to be a theme that runs through the American value system. Americans also frequently assume that informality is a prerequisite for sincerity. They may feel uncomfortable faced with formal ceremonies and strict traditions (Ferraro, 1994, p. 101). Their informality may make them resist referring to ascribed characteristics such as age and birthplace. Informality is also shown in the English language where, unlike several European continental languages, there is no difference between an informal and a formal you.

It has been suggested that *frankness* is a primary value in the American type of culture (Sitaram and Cogdell, 1976, p. 191) and that, therefore, company information should be available to anyone who needs it within the organization (Hodgetts and Luthans, 1991, p. 41).

As a consequence of informality and openness in American organizations, conflicts are seen as natural. Deviant behaviour is also not felt like a threat; people have greater tolerance and preparedness to trust others. Americans tend to exhibit emotion, yet separate it from 'objective' and 'rational' decisions (Trompenaars, 1995, p. 66). This could be seen as a result of the clear distinction between work and pleasure in the USA, a fact which has already been mentioned.

Power distance is medium in the USA. Characteristics of such a culture include (Hofstede, 1984, p. 259):

- subordinates expect superiors to consult them but will accept autocratic behaviour as well;
- ideal superior to most is a resourceful democrat;
- laws and rules apply to all but a certain level of privileges for superiors is judged as normal;
- status symbols for superiors contribute moderately to their authority and will be accepted by subordinates.

There are no generally recognized social classes in the USA, income and achievement act as the main differentiators, and the American culture emphasizes *equality* in social relationships. The value of equality is prevalent in both primary (in the family) and secondary (among friends, at work) social relationships in American society (Samovar *et al.*, 1981, p. 78). There is also relative equality of sexes in the USA (Ferraro, 1994, p. 109). Furthermore, an emphasis on external conformity easily develops out of the American premise of basic human equality: if all are equal, then all have an equal right to judge their fellows and to criticize their conduct according to commonly accepted standards (Sitaram and Cogdell, 1976, p. 51). There are, as is widely known, many people in higher official positions in the USA who have had their moral standards scrutinized in public.

The value of basic human equality and democracy is so ingrained among Americans that many of them became shocked and even frightened when they perceived that the communist world undermined such a value in substance and officially claimed otherwise.

The power distance of a culture is reflected in the superior subordinate relations in business organizations. A short power distance is an inducement to greater volume and variety of vertical communication and participative decision style. As previously mentioned, the USA has a medium power distance. It is common for such countries to advocate participation in the manager's decisions by his or her subordinates; however, the initiative towards this is supposed to be taken by the manager (Hofstede, 1984, p. 258).

The value of equality in the American culture sometimes conflicts with the values of individualism and freedom (this will be discussed in more detail later in the chapter). Opportunities, value standards, policies and practices apply to all ('universalism') in this culture; at the same time a person who, on his or her own, is able to make it and stand out above the crowd, is much admired.

Company triangles (the organizational hierarchies) are generally very flat in the USA (Trompenaars, 1995, p. 144). A hierarchy in the American culture means inequality of roles, established for convenience (Hofstede, 1984, p. 94). Promotion is both from inside and outside and based on market value ('cosmopolitanism') (ibid., p. 174). Proposals for promotion and for an increase in salary can come from the employee's direct superior, and do not have to come from the top of the hierarchy (ibid., p. 264). The organization type is implicitly structured in the American culture; managers are more interpersonally oriented and flexible in their styles, and informal employee consultation is possible without formal participation (ibid., pp. 92, 143, 216).

Increasingly popular in the American business society (which corresponds well to the calls for the destruction of bureaucracy, to the democratic norms prevalent there and to its increasingly better educated workforce) is to use task forces, integrating managers and project structures (Hofstede, 1984, p. 295). Even such a relatively complex organizational structure as a matrix could be adequate there. This is because in the American culture, problems are resolved not by referring to hierarchy, not by establishing procedures, but by horizontal negotiations (ibid., p. 217). There are fewer written rules in this culture and organizational development techniques for stimulating interpersonal openness and feedback are natural there (ibid., p. 267). Management by objectives is also an appropriate management system in the American culture (Trompenaars, 1995, p. 159).

## LOGIC, EFFICIENCY AND PRAGMATISM

From what has been understood of the American culture so far, it is natural to expect that the typified American management is very task-oriented and rational, known for solving problems successfully, quickly and decisively.

Efficiency is a primary value in the West (Sitaram and Cogdell, 1976, p. 191).
American emphasis on efficiency has consistently impressed observers.

> *Efficient* is a word of high praise in this society that has long emphasized adapt-
> ability, technological innovation, economic expansion, mass production,
> standardization, up-to-dateness, practicality, expediency, and 'getting things done'.
> The mere listing of those words and phrases reveals how the multiple extensions
> of efficiency are used as a standard against which activity is judged. ... American
> concern for efficiency at once sets this society apart from others that place greater
> emphasis upon aesthetic, contemplative, ritualistic, mystical, or other-worldly
> concerns (Samovar *et al.*, 1981, p. 70).

It has also been seen that time orientation is intense in the American culture.
So, when an American manager complains that 'I've spent the whole damn
day on the phone', he or she is giving voice to the image that a precious
resource – time – may have been wasted (Johnson, 1988, p. 42).

It may even be said that American problem-solving is *scientific* instead of
traditional. Logic and scientific methods have been internalized as the means
of solving new problems and solutions are perceived as progress or improvements. In their need to control nature, the Americans believe science and its
related technologies are the major tools for explaining it. Science (at least as
being practised in the USA) is based on the assumption that reality is and can
be rationally ordered by humans, thereby being predictable and manoeuvra-
ble. However, the prime quality of science is, in this context, not in its
applications but in its basic method of approaching problems – a rational way
of thought and a logical set of procedures for interpreting experience. This
reflects the values of the rationalistic–individualistic tradition in America
(Samovar *et al.*, 1981, p. 68). The USA has also gained many Nobel Prizes
for its contribution to applied natural sciences.

As American corporations, abetted by American universities and especially
their business schools, have confronted the challenge of size, complexity and
diversity, they have developed a disposition for sophisticated structures and
systems (Humes, 1993, p. 114).

> American organizational structures and job descriptions have long been more
> formally and more clearly defined and developed than the European or Asian.
> America-based multinationals have also stressed quantifiable standards, prescrip-
> tive manuals and the latest management fads. American managers have tended to
> trust 'scientific management' and quantitative data in their efforts to evaluate and
> improve job performance. Americans have become preoccupied with more easily
> measured and compared short-term results as reflected in growth and profits set
> forth in yearly, quarterly and even monthly statements. This predisposition has
> been fostered by American financial markets that can analyze short-term results
> more easily than long-term potential, by business schools that can teach quantita-
> tive methodology better than qualitative judgement, and by shareholders who

prefer an immediate return on their investments. Thus American businesses have stressed goals that can be quantified, progress that can be measured and the tools for these efforts (Humes, 1993, pp. 113–114).

The Americans value explicit objectives at work, and have stronger expectations concerning deadlines, policies and procedures, job descriptions and feedback. The working tasks may be specified in details (Arvonen, 1989, p. 102) and control mechanisms may be very explicit (Bjerke, 1989, p. 41).

This is not to be misunderstood. The dissimilarities in American corporations are remarkable (Humes, 1993, p. 115). The American multinationals share the predilection for growth and profits, but they often differ in the way they attempt to achieve these results. The preferred tools of management have been to attack the organization: its structure, its policies, its rules, job descriptions and task objectives. The task comes first, people second (this will be discussed later in the chapter). Organizations in American culture can, therefore, be pluriform (Hofstede, 1984, p. 142).

Practicality or *pragmatism* is a positive value in the American culture. When persons from other cultures do not show similar concern for efficiency or practicality, Americans become very frustrated (Samovar *et al.*, 1981, p. 71). What works is important (Hodgetts and Luthans, 1991, p. 71). Actions are justified by ends. Such a culture has been characterized as 'cybernetic' (Trompenaars, 1995, p. 156) in the sense that it homes in on its target using feedback signals. It rarely, if ever, changes its mind about its target. Steering, however, could be corrective, open to new means. If rules cannot be kept, they should be changed (Hofstede, 1984, p. 140).

The important business goal is profit (and share price). In general terms, the American model of management concentrates on finance and marketing (the Japanese on quality and production; the European on 'softer' people skills) ('The elusive Euro-manager', 7 November, 1992, p. 81):

> Spurred by the need to find more and better means of managing their large and complex businesses, American corporations developed well-defined structures, sophisticated systems and precise job specifications. Increasingly, their systems and processes have stressed the 'harder' quantitative data which facilitate more rigorous comparison and calculation than does the more elusive, 'softer' qualitative information. Numbers, especially financial numbers, have not only become the common denomination of diversified businesses, they have also lent themselves to more rigorous comprehensive scrutiny. Business schools, by stressing courses focusing on systems and number crunching, have promoted these principles and practices (Humes, 1993, p. 140).

Americans are taught to act on logic (Hodgetts and Luthans, 1991, p. 37). Others may be taught to act on emotion. A study by Schwind and Peterson (1985, p. 71) shows that American MBA students prefer rational thought rather than emotional thought, and logical thinking more than intuition. This suits the American textbook norm: 'fact-based' rather than intuitive management and 'fast decisions based on clear responsibilities' rather than the use of informal, personal contacts and the concern for consensus (Hofstede, 1984, p. 261).

Operating in a low-contextual culture (see Table 3.1), American management systems develop from a purely logical and economic ground. There is also less ritual behaviour in such a culture. Verbal communication relies on facts and logical explanations; statements are direct. The company is seen as a tool, and the involvement with it becomes calculative (not moral). In a study by Trompenaars (1995, pp. 17–18), a small but, compared with many other cultures, significant majority of American respondents opted for conceiving a company as a system rather than as a social group (54 per cent). In another study (Davis and Rasool, 1988, p. 15), 57 per cent of American managers were found to have a pragmatic orientation and only 30 per cent had a moralistic orientation.

The American management system is egalitarian and task-oriented, but also impersonal. That reveals a specific attitude to people in the American culture. Americans seem to assume that people are basically rational and that they can be trusted to make decisions for themselves even though, naturally, they may make mistakes. On the other hand, Americans believe that human nature is very plastic and possible to mould (Samovar *et al.*, 1981, p. 74). People should 'take orders' from the situation and act to control the situation; it is, in this tradition, possible to control the situation as well as people. The ultimate criterion of human value in an American type of culture is how you perform and to what extent you contribute to the jointly desired outcome. Change comes quickly to such a culture. New targets appear, new groups are found and old ones dissolve. All the time, however, loyalties to profession and career are greater than loyalties to the company (Trompenaars, 1995, p. 156). Motivations tend to be *intrinsic* in this culture; people are able to feel enthusiastic about, identify with and struggle towards the final product. And they are paid by performance.

A few aspects related to opinions about managers in the American type of culture are (Hofstede, 1984, pp. 94, 140):

- Managers follow the textbook norms (many textbooks come from America anyway), centred around decisions.
- There is a belief that management skills, which in themselves could be specified, do not have to be tied to a specific industry, and a belief in common sense, even though good experts are admired.
- Managers should be selected on other criteria than seniority.
- The use of power should be legitimate; authorities are there to serve.

Some characteristics of American management development programmes of relevance here are (Lindkvist, 1988, pp. 60–62):

- They are more oriented towards formulas than understanding relations and systems.
- Their objectives are well defined in advance, not a result of participants' discussions in the programmes themselves.
- Participants are earmarked, not self-selected.
- The result, not the process, is evaluated.

It is agreed that successful decision-makers should use the best available techniques of problem-solving to reach their decisions, but they must also follow proper institutional and procedural implementation of the decision environment. America has a long history of developing business leadership models. These models, however, tend to be normative (because they assume rationality) and to concentrate on the planning and making of the decision rather than on its implementation. Simplistically put, it can be said that Americans try to find the best strategy, even if it may not be fully implemented as decided. The Japanese try to find a consensus strategy that can be implemented in full, even if it may not be the objectively best one for the 'firm' as such.

Perfect rationality exists only in theory and any implementation of a decision must consider culture in the context where implementation takes place. Even if America is the world's largest exporter of management theories ('management' is a very American thing), it should not be taken for granted that these theories apply elsewhere. Also, with the increasing international challenge during the last couple of decades, many American businesses and business schools have begun to question the general applicability of their traditional emphasis on sophisticated systems, comparable statistics, accountability to the numbers and more readily taught management dynamics. However, only a few American-based multinationals have self-consciously long promoted the concept of a culture and the development of human resources (Humes, 1993, p. 141).

## INDIVIDUALISM AND ACHIEVEMENT

If people were to choose the hallmark of American culture, this should probably be the value of *the individual* (Hofstede, 1984, p. 158; Humes, 1993, p. 113; Ferraro, 1994, p. 109), that is, reliance on individual initiative, self-assertion, and personal achievement and responsibility.

The ideal of the individual is deeply rooted in American social, political, and economic institutions. Although historians, philosophers, and social scientists don't always agree on its origins or its more recent forms, there is a general understanding that the value of the individual is supreme and it is the individual who has the capacity to shape his or her own destiny (Ferraro, 1994, p. 88).

Some fundamental characteristics of individualistic cultures are (Samovar *et al.*, 1981, pp. 75–77; Hofstede, 1984, pp. 92, 132–133, 153, 154, 166–167, 171, 173–174; Schwind and Peterson, 1985, p. 71; Arvonen, 1989, p. 102; Bjerke, 1989, p. 41; Ferraro, 1994, pp. 91, 109; Trompenaars, 1995, pp. 51–54, 142–144):

- *Nuclear families and independent children* There is a nuclear family structure with a central husband–wife relationship; parents put less value on children's obedience; everyone is supposed to take care of him- or herself and his or her immediate family.
- *Private lives and opinions appreciated* Everyone has the right to a private life and opinion; involvement of individuals with organization is, as already mentioned, primarily calculative.
- *Self-orientation and self-motivation* Identity is based on the individual; behaviour is very much determined by perception of the self; people tend to be self-motivated and their business relationships are based on self-interest.
- *Freedom and variety are important* There is more importance attached to freedom and challenge in jobs; people are supposed to choose their belongings and consumption pattern on their own and have a variety to choose from in all aspects of life; relationships with other people are developed by free choice.
- *Education promotes independence* Students put high value on education; they consider it socially acceptable to pursue their own ends without minding others.
- *Individual initiative is encouraged* Policies and practices should allow for individual initiative; employees are expected to defend their own interests; people are encouraged to make their own decisions, develop their own opinions, solve their own problems, have their own things, and, in general, learn to see the world from the point of view of the self.
- *Stronger ambition for individual advancement and leadership* Managers rate autonomy as more important; there is a stronger achievement motivation; managers aspire to leadership.
- *Individuals do the job and are rewarded as such* People believe in individual decisions rather than decisions made in a group; individuals are responsible; individuals take actions and individuals are rewarded.

- *Cosmopolitan outlook* A minimum set of relations with organization exists; people have the feeling of being an integral part of the world outside the organization; there are more 'cosmopolitans' than locals in powerful positions.
- *Strong feelings against collectivism* There are strong pressures to defend oneself from all kinds of collectivistic tendencies.

Japanese managers have, by tradition, learnt to depend on each other, to be integrated parts in a larger human unit. Not so in the West. Western (particularly American) managers have, by tradition, learnt to look for independence of others, being self-governed and self-sufficient (Pascale and Athos, 1982, p. 115). Americans assert individual differences when they seem justifiable, even if in conflict with the goals and values of the group (Harris and Moran, 1987, p. 27). Internal values are more important than external values.

America scores high on Hofstede's Masculinity Index (Hofstede, 1984, p. 189). Masculinity is here associated with independent, individual decision-making, decisiveness, being tough, but also not showing emotions.

This typified American lack of emotions is not to be misunderstood. Americans are very extrovert and can certainly show emotions – but only on single, particular issues, not to the detriment of rationality. They have also a high 'willingness to communicate' (Daun, 1989, p. 217). Americans are not supposed to show signs of shyness (even if they have the feeling). The USA has certainly a long tradition of rhetoric and students perceive a pressure and demand for high communicative skills (ibid., p. 66).

Due to Americans' deep repugnance for collectivism and social levelling, they may have problems in appreciating the concept of corporate culture. Americans, dedicated to individuality, regard 'socialization' as suspect. Stemming from this tradition, American organizations allow their members to do their own thing to a remarkable degree. Trendy campaigns like 'becoming a strong culture' might encounter resistance when members are asked to give up their idiosyncrasies:

> The crux of the dilemma is this: We are intellectually and culturally opposed to the manipulation of individuals for organizational purposes. At the same time, a certain degree of social uniformity enables organizations to work better. The less we rely on informal social controls, the more we must inevitably turn to formal financial controls and bureaucratic procedures. US firms that have perfected and systemized their processes of socialization tend to be a disproportionate majority of the great self-sustaining firms which survive from one generation to the next. Virtually none of these companies discuss 'socialization' directly. It occurs as an exercise of the left hand – something that just happens 'as the way we do things around here' (Pascale, 1985, p. 28).

An important point here is that Americans take culture less seriously in the sense of believing they are more able to manage it (such as being able to manage so many other things of business) than compared to, say, Europeans:

> The very notion that culture can be 'managed' is, in itself, culture-bound. For example, in discussing corporate culture, American managers tend to see culture as something organizations *have*; European managers are more likely to see it as something that organizations *are* and thus more dubious about being able to change it. The American assumption of being able to control one's destiny and the propensity to take action have created quite a market for how-to, self-improvement books and for books about managing across cultures (Schneider and Barsoux, 1997, p. ix).

Individual managers become much more crucial in a culture such as the American one. They accumulate individual experience, become very knowledgeable and may possess great skills. Problems may arise, however, when this knowledge and these skills are supposed to be integrated into a coherent picture in situations which are too complex for one person alone (Nonaka and Johansson, 1985, p. 185).

Another much publicized aspect of the American culture is its positive appreciation of *achievement* – being able to reach individual wealth, recognition and self-actualization. Modesty is a negligible value in the West compared to the East (Sitaram and Cogdell, 1976, p. 191).

In one study, reported by Trompenaars (1995, p. 128), 89 per cent of Americans (highest among 38 countries) believed that what happens to them is their own doing. Americans certainly like a challenge (Hofstede, 1984, p. 156) and this, together with earnings, recognition and advancement is relatively more important in this culture (ibid., p. 200). Excelling means 'trying to be the best' in America.

There is sympathy for the successful achiever in America. The strong tend to be compensated and given the rewards (Hodgetts and Luthans, 1991, p. 27). Social status of managers is dependent on rank (not class). Americans strongly disagree that respect should depend on family background (Trompenaars, 1995, p. 94). Young men (and increasingly young women) are expected to make a career for themselves; those who do not are generally seen as failures:

> The 'success story' and the respect accorded to the self-made person is distinctly American. Ascribed status (in the form of fixed, hereditary social stratification) has been minimized, and achieved status through self-motivation and hard work has been maximized (Samovar *et al.*, 1981, p. 77).

Though the American culture appreciates other kinds of achievement as well (actors, entertainers, statespeople, scientists and generals, to name but a few), promotion in business serves as the main path for moving up the ladder for most people in society. In this respect, typified American organizations apply quick evaluation and promotion, specialized career paths and short-term employment.

There is a high rate of mobility among employees in the USA. Achievement is more important then job security (Schwind and Peterson, 1985, p. 71). If employees have problems moving to another job, restructuring of their existing job, permitting individual achievement, is appreciated (Hofstede, 1984, p. 208).

Performance appraisals are greatly used in the American culture. There is also a very American way of conducting such appraisals (Table 4.1).

*Table 4.1    Performance appraisals in America*

| | |
|---|---|
| *Objective* | Fairness; employee development |
| *Who does appraisal* | Supervisor |
| *Authority of appraiser* | Presumed in supervisory role position; Supervisor takes slight lead |
| *How often* | Once/year or periodically |
| *Assumptions* | Objective appraiser is fair |
| *Manner of communication and feedback* | Criticism direct; Criticism may be in writing; Objective/authentic |
| *Rebuttals* | Will be done |
| *Praise* | Given individually |
| *Motivators* | Money and position strong motivators; Career development |

*Source*:   Harris and Moran (1987, p. 37).

## FREEDOM AND COMPETITION

As reported by Trompenaars (1995, pp. 47–48), one question that participants have been asked in his seminars is the following:

Two people were discussing ways in which individuals could improve the quality of life.

*A*    One said: 'It is obvious that if individuals have as much freedom as possible and the maximum opportunity to develop themselves, the quality of their life will improve as a result.'

*B*   The other said: 'If individuals are continuously taking care of their fellow human beings the quality of life will improve for everyone, even if it obstructs individual freedom and individual development.'

Which of the two ways of reasoning do you think is usually best, *A* or *B*?

An overwhelming majority (79 per cent) of participants from America opted for 'individual freedom' (answer *A*). Since American society is seen among its participants as an instrument for satisfying the needs of individuals, a political philosophy has developed calling for *freedom* from coercion from institutions like the church, the state and others (Ferraro, 1994, p. 88). Individuals demand independence of government policy (Lindkvist, 1988, p. 40).

Some further characteristics of this freedom are (Hofstede, 1984, p. 92):

● Authoritarian attitudes in students, if they exist, are a matter of personality, not culture.
● Employees are less afraid of disagreeing with their boss.
● Students have positive associations with 'power' and 'wealth'.

The idea of individual freedom is related to the American use of *persuasion*:

> Americans tend to dislike motives originating in others which are then applied to them. They strongly reject motivation in the form of orders, injunctions and threats emanating from authority. Probably it is this dislike which makes Americans anti-militaristic rather than a rejection of fighting or violence. ... The American concept of the self and self-motivation causes stress both in American institutions and in the general lifestyle prevalent in the United States. If coercion is disapproved and authority rejected, how do Americans manage to coordinate their lives and activities? The answer is through persuasion. The desire to act according to the wishes of others is instilled in the individual by means of examples, incentives and subtle hints of failure (Stewart, 1972, p. 71).

Closely associated with the American preference for individualism, freedom and achievement is the emphasis placed on *competition*. Most Americans want to experience the 'thrill of victory' (Ferraro, 1994, p. 103). In the study (presented earlier) by Schwind and Peterson (1985, p. 71), more American MBA students valued free competition higher than monopoly. The idea is that competition stimulates high performance.

There certainly is no dearth of evidence of the high value placed on competition, winning and getting ahead in American society. Examples provided by Ferraro (1994, pp. 104–105) range from the Anti-Trust Division in the US Department of Justice to popular games such as Monopoly (the purpose of which is to wipe everyone else off the board by getting everything for yourself).

## KNOWLEDGE AND SPECIALIZATION

The status of the individual in the West is tied to education and knowledge and, as mentioned before, in the American type of culture, experts are treated with great respect and loyalties to a profession are greater than loyalties to the company. Relationships between employees could be characterized as 'specific tasks in a cybernetic system targeted upon shared objectives' (Trompenaars, 1995, p. 159). In the previously mentioned study by Schwind and Peterson (1985, p. 71), American MBA students mainly preferred specialized training to generalized training.

In America, *specialists* are well defined (Humes, 1993, p. 112) and even part of a person's identity. In the West in general, when people from the same country meet for the first time, it appears that the initial conversation revolves around a person's occupation or profession (not family background or employer, which is common in the East) (Muna, 1980, p. 36).

American business education looks at *management as a specialist profession using rational, 'scientific' tools.* There is a generalist orientation and an elaborate educational system built into the company in Japanese management; Western management has a specialized orientation and if new skills are required, outsiders (temporary 'troubleshooters') are employed. Such outsiders can serve an integrative role at the same time as they can allow individuals to develop even more in-depth skills for future use (Negandhi *et al.*, 1985, p. 94; Nonaka and Johansson, 1985, p. 186; Lindkvist, 1988, p. 40; Trompenaars, 1995, p. 4).

> Specialist expertise has long been a hallmark of American management. Classical management itself, which has influenced business school as well as corporate thinking, has defined roles in terms of specific job descriptions and well-designated responsibilities. The increasing specificity of these roles has been concomitant with the proliferation of technical and professional specialisms and societies and specialized educational programmes. American managers have generally begun their career as specialists and their rise to management ranks has been based upon their success as specialists. Consequently, American corporations are more likely than non-American ones to hire on the basis of specialist qualifications; and they are more likely to go outside the company to find someone with specific qualifications. Thus US MBA programmes include a specialist concentration while European ones do not. US executives have long tended to be more vocationally specialized, more likely to identify their career interests with their professional specialism than with their company, and more likely to identify with a specialized faction of the company than the whole company (Humes, 1993, p. 114).

It is worth mentioning that typified American management development programmes (compared with European programmes) target managers only (not managers and other employee representatives) and the result should be definable skills, knowledge and attitudes (not learning to learn, preparedness and ability to adjust) (Lindkvist, 1988, pp. 61–62).

## A TYPIFIED INTERPRETATION OF AMERICAN BUSINESS LEADERS

The American culture has been discussed focusing on certain themes. These are summarized in Table 4.2.

*Table 4.2   The American culture themes*

---

- Progress and growth
- Modernity
- Materialism
- Activity and work orientation
- Informality and equality
- Logic, efficiency and pragmatism
- Individualism and achievement
- Freedom and competition
- Knowledge and specialization

---

Based on these themes, it is possible to give a typified interpretation of American business leaders as follows:

- They are future-oriented; want to improve on the present for growing bigger and better in the future; look at technology as one factor to control, time another.
- They accept change and think they can steer it; appreciate modernity (also in their own profession); measure progress materialistically.
- They are active, action-oriented, and dynamic; are willing to take risk; focus very much on decisions.
- They find work important, but draw a strict line between work and private life; conceive the company as a system rather than as a social group; are more involved in strategies and see them as opportunities; operate sophisticated structures and systems; are quantitative.
- They concentrate on finance and marketing – less on informal control; are very oriented to results and see profit as a measure of it.
- They are frank and sincere; are involved in straightforward, direct performance appraisals; are fact-based, not intuitively based; are less

ritualistic; think that appreciation and pay should be based on performance, not seniority.
- They are informal and on the expressive side; feel pressure for rhetoric
and communicative skills.
- They are working in flat organizations, implicitly structured; are practical and pragmatic; are flexible and interpersonally oriented; are
task-oriented, rational and efficient – even 'scientific'; are happy to
work in project structures with well-educated colleagues.
- They promote independence and individual initiatives; are expected by
subordinates to consult them; may be autocratic, but only if legitimate
and justified; support participation – on their own terms; are loyal to
profession more than to company (intrinsic motivation).
- They are individualists; may have problems in appreciating the concept of culture or, at least, take it very lightly.
- They appreciate achievement as wealth, recognition and self-actualization; admire achievers; look at business as a main source of achievement.
- They appreciate freedom and private enterprise in competition.

# 5.   Arab culture

## INTRODUCTION

Western awareness of the Arab world jumped sharply with the events in the oil business of the 1970s (some call it 'oil boom'; others call it 'oil crisis'). Before then few international businesspeople from outside the Arab world had had any direct dealings with Arab executives and little was known about Arab culture in general and Arab business behaviour in particular. At the worst extreme, some commentators depicted a caricature of Arab managerial behaviour 'as an unbounded fatalism apparently unconcerned with rational economic considerations' (Muna, 1980, Foreword).

The discovery of oil in the Middle East turned out to be a major turning point for the Arabs:

> The greatest impact on the economic, political, and social spheres of the oil-producing countries began in the 1960s. Through nationalization of the oil companies in some countries, joint-ownership plans (participation agreement) in others, and finally through the medium of the Organization of Petroleum Export-ing Countries (OPEC), the oil-rich countries are now able to reap the benefits of ownership and/or control of their oil resources. Needless to say, this development continues to have wide-ranging effects on the economies both of producing and consuming countries (Muna, 1980, p. 18).

Within a period of less than two decades, the economies of the Arab world were transformed (more in some countries than in others) from being agrarian and from trading regionally into becoming industrial with world-wide connec-tions due to revenues earned from a single commodity, that is, oil (Bjerke and Kazi, 1990, p. 1). This unprecedented economic boom encouraged the estab-lishment in oil-rich countries of welfare states able and willing to provide generous employee and public benefits. Massive government investments were designated to provide social basics like free education, free medical care and modern forms of communication and transport (At-Twaijri, 1989a, p. 48).

Due to slackening prices of crude oil and in order to secure a more sustain-able future, Arab governments have aimed at establishing a broader and more economic base, not totally dependent on oil. However, most growth of manu-facturing sectors in the Middle Eastern countries (when growth has taken place) has been based on development of the hydrocarbon industries, that is concerned with refining and production of downstream-linked petrochemical products (Bjerke and Kazi, 1990, p. 1).

The economic picture looks gloomier today for several reasons, the major one being a very low price of crude oil, but efforts are still being oriented towards industries for imports substitution in order to put less emphasis on the petrochemical industries (Bjerke and Alzamel, 1990, p. 11). Some Arab countries try to open up as tax-free ports for trade and services, or otherwise link up to the industrialized world, mainly by joint venturing (Bjerke and Kazi, 1990, p. 7).

To the West, Arabs and oil business are interlinked. However, Arabs were no strangers to business before the 1970s. Historically, they have a long tradition of trade, even with parts of the world far away from their own, a profession which has coloured the way they do business even today.

In this study, the Arab world means the Middle East west of Iran, that is, the Arab peninsula, comprising countries like Abu-Dhabi, Bahrain, United Arab Emirates, Kuwait and Saudi Arabia but also countries such as Jordan, Iraq and Syria outside this peninsula. I would also like to include Egypt (from the African continent) in my understanding of Arab culture. Even though Egypt is slightly different from other Arab countries in a social history context and called *Mustarab* ('re-Arabized') by other Arabs, it is an integrated unit in the economic development of the Middle East. Egypt, therefore, provides part of the picture of how Arab business management and leadership is functioning and where it is heading.

Ever since the emergence of the modern arrangement of the Middle Eastern states at the end of World War I, Arabs have felt themselves pushed and pulled between the demands of their own nations and the interests of the wider Arab community ('A survey of the Middle East', 28 September, 1991, pp. 4–5). In this field of various forces, Arab executives, managers and business leaders share with each other at least three closely interrelated bases of identity and commonality: 'language', 'religion' and 'history' (Muna, 1980, p. 5). These common factors have also been used to identify Arabs and membership of the Arab League.

## TRADITION AND RELIGION

One word is paramount in understanding culture throughout the Arab world. This word is *religion*. Religion relates to all aspects of life among Muslims. It also has a major impact on Arab thinking. One example is the answer given to me by a student at one Arab university when I asked him why they did not offer any courses in psychology or sociology at his university: 'We don't need it. We have the Qur'an!'

Contrary to other religious views, Islam holds that the world is totally real, or rather built up of two realities: one divine and one created (Samovar *et al.*, 1981, p. 93). Allah, the divine, created the world and everything in it for the pleasure of humankind. The created reality is available to everybody, but the divine reality is revealed only to a few.

To gain access to this divine reality there are many rules to follow for a Muslim. Religion becomes part of a Muslim's daily life, and a visitor to the Arab world who shows respect for the Islamic religion will gain a favourable reception almost everywhere. This means, among other things, refraining from drinking alcohol at social events and not exposing any kind of images, such as religious symbols, statues and so on. This also means that the visitor, whether a businessman or not, encounters a male-dominated society. Women are usually not part of the entertainment scene in the Muslim Arab world. They carry on with their own social lives, and they are not involved in business with foreigners. Ferraro (1994, p. 107) tells the story of an international bank which sent a woman to meet an important Arab sheikh, a client at the bank, when he arrived at an airport somewhere in the Western world. In keeping with the sheikh's custom, he believed that the bank was offering the company of the woman to him during his stay. The bank had a very unhappy customer to contend with when he learnt that this was not the case. Equality of women is a negligible value in Arab countries (Sitaram and Cogdell, 1976, p. 191).

Most Arab countries want to keep their societies free of undue influences from the Western world. Most of them, therefore, are very *censured*.

Generally speaking, religion can be a way of coping with an uncertain future, and religion and uncertainty avoidance appear to be meaningfully related and religion reinforces differences in uncertainty avoidance between cultures (Hofstede, 1984, p. 137).

In modern times, the dominating factor in the consciousness of most Middle Easterners has been the impact of the West (it started historically with Europe) and the transformation – some say dislocation – which it has brought. Most cultures in the Middle East are traditional and Muslim and caught in the midst of conflict and change. Some Arab political leaders feel, therefore, that:

> there is no need for the Arabs to choose between alien ideologies, such as capitalism and socialism, conservatism and liberalism, democracy and authoritarianism. Instead, they feel that these choices are unnecessary if only the tenets of the Islamic Shari'a [Islamic law] are applied as the guiding principles of economic, governmental, and community life (Muna, 1980, p. 15).

Already in 1974, the late King Faisal of Saudi Arabia declared that he wanted his country 'to achieve economic growth and modernisation without sacrificing the traditions of Islam and Arab culture' (Muna, 1980, p. 101).

The desire to maintain both the Arabic and the Islamic identity is prominent not only in political circles, but also among Arab academics and businesspeople. Arab executives find themselves in an uneasy situation of introducing change, at least as modern and scientific methods, and adapting them to their new, yet traditional work and lifestyles. It could be said that Arab executives are agents of social change in a society which itself is undergoing modernization while attempting to retain its Arab identity and character.

Many Arab managers look at Japan as a kind of reference ideal of how modernization can be achieved in a society without losing its specific cultural values.

It is a bit of an anomaly that what is possibly the richest Arab country of them all, that is, Saudi Arabia, having invested billions of riyals of oil revenue to create an infrastructure and industry in a tribal nomadic society, is perhaps more fearful of change than any of the other countries in the Arab world. At the same time, a foreigner visiting this country quickly finds out that the Saudis are very proud of what they have achieved and they do not, for instance, want to be reminded of their Bedouin background.

There is more emotional resistance to change in the Arab type of culture (Hofstede, 1984, p. 132) and problem-solving procedures follow precedent or adapt old procedures to new situations. Departure from tradition is generally presumed to be bad until proved otherwise. The Arab world is a clear example of where modernization is not the same as Westernization. American themes are not, in general, good sales arguments among Arabs – unlike among the Japanese, for instance. The value pattern in traditional societies also sets a limit to technology transfer possibilities (Kedia and Bhagat, 1988).

For the above reasons, and for others that will follow later, the usefulness of Western (American) management and leadership thinking is doubtful in Arab culture (Bjerke and Al-Meer, 1993). There may be a suspicion towards having foreigners as managers and there could also be a difference between the pattern of interaction in a group where a foreigner is present from where he is not.

Arabs are generally quite nationalistic. This is a common phenomenon among (successful) young nations. However, Arabs also see themselves as unique and do not want to be compared with others. As a consequence, it may even be difficult to find any comparative international statistics in Arab libraries!

Some Arabs, however, are critical of the slow pace of change in their countries. They claim that more change agents are needed (Muna, 1980, p. 119). Appropriate qualifications for this role would include skills of introducing change, managing resistance to change, and understanding the process of change and its consequences. They are also worried about lack of industrial mentality and extreme 'informality' and 'personalism' in the Arab world (this will be discussed in more detail later in the chapter). As it is now, new solutions sometimes present great difficulty in Arab societies. They come slowly and often after much controversy.

Arabs have little experience of working in formal organizations which, combined with belonging to a high-contextual culture, means that much of what goes on as planning, supervising and controlling is more symbolic than substantive, as will be seen. Many Arab institutions and business organizations are not very efficient, which is one reason why Arab executives prefer to use personal (family and friendship) ties instead of formal channels and apply a very personalized and informal management style (more details of this will be discussed later in this chapter). Also, in the Arab type of culture, there is less concern with fashion in management ideas (Hofstede, 1984, p. 174).

As a consequence of *traditionalism*, nationalism and a lack of trust in foreign management principles, joint venture is (as mentioned previously) a common approach for a foreigner who wants to do business in the modern Arab world. To start a business there as an outsider, you must find a local sponsor or partner (in this respect, things were not much different in the 'pre-oil' days of trading with Arabs):

> [Arab culture] has its own special breed of entrepreneurs who, with a mixture of innate desert cunning and Western sophistication, have managed to build their own business empires, both at home and in Europe and elsewhere. The ... oil boom provided dramatic examples of highly successful businessmen who moved from investing in industrial development projects to buying controlling interests in Western banks and on to financing petrochemical plants and shipping fleets [even amusement parks and computer firms, as we know]. Some [Arab] businessmen started off as importers or exporters, or both. They developed an ability to locate deficiencies in their own national economy and seeked to fill the gaps with imported skills and finished goods.
>
> Sometimes some businessmen simply position themselves midway between governments and Western firms, signing 'commission contracts', and once a reasonable capital base takes shape, these sharp investors quietly penetrate the markets in search of 'sure' investment opportunities. By moving from one market to another and from one type of investment to another, they multiply their capital base and usher themselves into the fold of millionaires (At-Twaijri, 1989a, p. 7).

The combination of education (whether at home or abroad) and the exposure to the West (through business or personal travel) has typically resulted in a bilingual Arab executive (Muna, 1980, p. 10).

# HIGH CONTEXT AND SYMBOLISM

Cultures vary in terms of how explicitly they send and receive verbal messages. Arab culture is a *high-contextual culture*. This means that communication between Arabs relies heavily on hidden, implicit, contextual cues such as nonverbal behaviour, social context and the nature of interpersonal relationships. To a foreigner, communication between Arabs may even sound very inexact, implicit and indirect.

There are many factors that may influence the climate of communication in the Middle East (Harris and Moran, 1987, p. 71):

1. the situation itself;
2. the people involved in the situation or in the communication;
3. the age of the persons communicating;
4. the level of education of the people;
5. the social status of the person involved;
6. the amount of friendliness, sincerity and honesty that are displayed by those who are communicating.

There are also differences in communicating with members of the same clan and communicating with others.

Emphasis on words without context is quite confining to Middle Easterners. Verbal accuracy is less important to Arabs and giving attention only to verbal channels of feedback in a working relationship is, to them, inappropriate.

On the other hand, Arabs generally love to talk and listen to people talking, and they have a language which is very rich and lively, as are the Arabs themselves:

> Arab cultures ... engage in overassertion, exaggeration, and repetition. The Arab language is filled with forms of verbal exaggeration. For example, certain common ending words are meant to be emphasized; frequently certain pronouns will be repeated in order to fully dramatize the message; highly graphic metaphors and similes are common; and it is not at all uncommon to hear an Arabic speaker use a long list of adjectives to modify a single noun for the sake of emphasizing the point (Ferraro, 1994, p. 54).

The Arabs have a linguistic propensity for verbal overkill. They have a tendency to overstate their case. Also, Arabs frequently engage in verbal duelling. This is known as *hija* and it dates back to old traditions when warriors would loudly ridicule their opponents with various insults while boasting of their own prowess (Ferraro, 1994, pp. 59–60). Verbal threats are commonplace in the Arabic language (a common threat is, for instance, 'I will kill you', which, of course, is not meant in a literal sense). Arabs may, therefore, sound very aggressive to a foreigner listening to (and viewing) them talking, but such threats 'function more as a psychological catharsis than as an accurate description of the speaker's real intentions. It should be kept in mind that this rhetoric feature of linguistic overassertion is just another form of verbal ambiguity or inexactness because [the language] fails to send direct, precise messages' (ibid., p. 54).

So, Arab language is a very important gate to understanding Arab culture. Verbal communication is implicative, where the subject of communication is comprehended through linkages to its environment or other events, relying on analogies, symbolisms and indirect statements. There are also conversational rules to follow for a foreigner (at least at the first meeting), for example:

a.  Avoid bringing up subjects of business before getting to know the host.
b.  Avoid any question or comment about a man's wife or any female children over the age of 12 (if close, a wife may be referred to as 'mother of children').
c.  Avoid the subjects of politics (in particular of Israel) and religion (Arabs enjoy, however, talking about political and religious matters among themselves and may be quite tense about them).
d.  Avoid private financial matters (even brothers do not discuss their pay).

This means that in a high-contextual culture such as the Arab one, nonverbal communication is very important, and there is a lot of it there. Arabs speak with their hands and use facial expressions extensively, for example:

• Arabs are taught to look a person in the eye, especially when greeting. This means that conversants must be facing each other directly, and talking while walking can cause a problem. Arabs' intensive way of looking may make a Westerner feel very uncomfortable and he may characterize it as 'gazing'.
• Arabs belong to a high-touch culture (they often, for instance, clap each other's hands after having exchanged the punch line of a joke) and stand very close when talking. A Westerner may interpret this as pushy or aggressive.
• What is *not* being said can carry more meaning than what is said. Silence may be an appropriate and expressive means of communicating. It may be more important to listen and to observe than to ask specific questions.

Details are important in such an 'intense' and 'all-penetrating' culture as the Arab one.

It can be said, generally, that asking personal, intimate questions is not for the high-contextual Middle East. Also, frankness is of secondary value to Arabs (Sitaram and Cogdell, 1976, p. 191). On the other hand, Middle Easterners are excellent interpreters of contexts and good psychologists (and skilled negotiators). Their culture trains them to be so. This has some consequences for the conduct of management training programmes among Arabs (especially if you are a foreigner) (Harris and Moran, 1987, pp. 64–66):

- The trainer's attitudes and style and his expectations of participants are important. Substance is far from enough.
- Participants are likely to expect tangible, direct and immediate feedback for their efforts. A general understanding of future benefits from learning is not an adequate reward.
- The feedback should come from the trainer. For a Middle Easterner to have his skills evaluated by, say, each of the members of his group, one after another, would seem quite unnatural, contrived, tedious and superficial.

On the other hand, sensitivity to details may lead to insensitivity to understanding the total picture. Muna (1980, p. 119) claims that Arab executives need better conceptual skills in the sense of being able to 'radar-scan' their environment and having a 'helicopter view' of the situation. This could lead to higher sensitivity to the complex processes in a fast-changing environment.

Management systems are culturally based. However, such systems are more than just rational tools; they contain elements of symbolism and rituals, and particularly so in high-contextual cultures, of course. Symbols are much developed in the Arab world, and Western managers visiting their clients and counterparts in the Middle East find themselves negotiating symbolic systems which define quite different realities from those existing in the West. This richness of symbols may seem like 'an invisible wall' to the outsider, because, like many aspects of culture and its manifestations, symbolic systems exist at an unconscious rather than a conscious level of awareness (Morgan *et al.*, 1983, p. 11).

However, these systems may be of importance at any time and at any place. Meetings, where planning activities are to take place, can be used by seniors as confirmations of their positions and relations to other seniors and as a means to avoid uncertainty. As previously mentioned, this is particularly so when formal organizations are often inefficient in such recently modernized nations as those found in the Middle East. These organizations tend, therefore, to become very ritualistic. The 'ritual Arabs' will be discussed in the next section. It is true that the Arab type of culture supports more detail in planning (Hofstede, 1984, p. 264), and that Arabic managers systematically tend to take more variables into account when making strategic decisions (Ali *et al.*, 1992, p. 212) or in purchasing decisions (Al-Mubarak, 1988, p. 23) than do, say, American managers, but this is for symbolic not substantive reasons. Western-type quantitative management systems and data-based decisions will not work as such in the Arab culture (Muna, 1980, p. 119).

In the Arab type of culture, the cultural norms make it less likely that strategic planning activities are practised in the first place, because they may put question marks to the certainties of today. If they are performed, 'particularistic' and 'pragmatic' thinking modes are emphasized (information is interpreted in the context of practical use and specific action).

Other aspects of planning and control in business in the Arab type of culture are (Broms and Gahmberg, 1983, p. 487; Hofstede, 1984, p. 264):

- Personal planning and control is supported rather than impersonal systems. This often means no formal planning at all when power distance is long (which it certainly is in Arab culture; this will be discussed later in the chapter).
- A long power distance norm also supports 'political' rather than 'strategic' thinking (Faucheux, 1977).
- There is a tendency to leave planning to specialists, and the decision will automatically be associated with the leader of the group, who will be visualized in his concrete surroundings actually making the decision (other cultures may look at the decision as such without bothering about who made it).
- Decisions are finalized before being announced.
- When planning takes place, it is a big thing (to a large extent, as previously mentioned, for symbolic reasons), but there is much less implementation and follow-up than is generally the case in the West. Merely going through the rituals of a meeting will eliminate many problems.

## SOCIAL BUT RITUALISTIC

In one sense, Arabs are very *social and informal*. For instance, titles are not a general cultural manifestation, except for royal families, ministers and high-level military officers. Arabs are generally also very generous and hospitable. On the other hand, they place great importance on manners.

Manners include such details as to be careful about hand gestures (even though Arabs 'talk' a lot with their hands, as previously mentioned). The left hand is the 'toilet' hand (never shake hands or receive something with your left hand. Believers of Islam are sometimes referred to as 'people of the right') and bodily functions, such as nose-blowing, are down-played (there are paper tissues everywhere and they are highly used). Sneezing should be followed by the expression *alhamdul'llah* ('God's blessing'). It is also considered impolite for people to expose the soles of their feet or shoes to those present (do not stretch your legs while sitting on the floor in somebody's house – a common place to sit when there are many visitors). The offer to visit an Arab's home should be accepted and the system of hospitality is based on mutuality.

Arabs are very proud: they are proud of their culture, people and achievements. They expect others to pay respect to what they are and what they have done. Nothing will motivate an Arab more than giving him pride. However, there is a caveat here. Middle Easterners, who can be very sensitive to the feelings of others, are themselves often sensitive to criticism, in particular in public (Harris and Moran, 1987, p. 65). Feedback, in the limited sense in which Westerners usually understand it, is, therefore, often felt by Arabs to be too blunt and lacking in finesse, regardless of truth.

This may have some unexpected consequences for a foreigner visiting an Arab country. It is expected, for instance, to argue about who pays the bill at a restaurant, though whoever proposed the outing is usually the host, who may feel a loss of dignity and honour, if he is not allowed to pay at the end. 'Dutch treat' is frowned upon unless among very close friends, and while visiting an Arab, you should take care not to praise or admire too vividly anything that your host owns, because the host may feel obliged to give it to you. I have very explicitly experienced such an event myself. After having been to dinner in an Arab's home, I was accompanied by my host to the street in front of his house. There, parked next to my own five-year-old small Japanese car, was his own brand new Cadillac. I could not help praising the beauty of it. I obviously used too many words. Suddenly, my host threw his car keys to me, offering to change his car for mine. It took some time for me to explain myself, in the meantime desperately trying to hide my confusion and embarrassment.

To summarize, Arabs have a strong sense of pride, dignity and honour. This is in their case associated with formalities and protocol, which are important for any foreigner to know.

Related to this is the fact that the Arab type of culture is quite ritualistic. They score high in uncertainty avoidance (Bjerke and Al-Meer, 1993, p. 32). And as much as social informal rules are not to be broken, neither are rules in a business setting (Hofstede, 1984, p. 133) (I have some reservations concerning the expression 'breaking *formal* rules' in the Arab context later in the chapter). In addition, as in all societies, rituals may play many roles in the Arab world:

Rituals, such as sacrificing to the gods, are prescribed by primitive religions to ensure the season's crop or the winning of a war. Unbelievers smile at such practices because they think they know that on the logical level the rituals do not change anything. But this is immaterial; the rituals are functional because they allow the members of that society to continue their lives as peasants or warriors together in the face of otherwise intolerable uncertainty. Of course, rituals may also be cruel and destructive, as in the case of human sacrifices.

Modern society is less different from primitive society than we sometimes think. Its basic ingredient is man, and there is no evidence that human nature has changed much in the process of modernization. In any case, we share with primitive man a need for social cohesion and a limited tolerance for uncertainty. We dispose of infinitely better technical means to defend ourselves against risks, but unfortunately these means themselves always bring new risks; and we still feel the future to be very uncertain indeed. Like the social systems of primitive man, our systems have developed their rituals to make uncertainty tolerable.

Rituals in traditional and modern society serve many other purposes besides making uncertainty tolerable. They play an important role in our establishing relationships with our fellow man and in giving meaning to our lives. Rituals in modern society are recognized in religious and state ceremonies, in the family, in youth movements and countercultures. They are less easily recognized, but equally present, in pragmatic business and public organizations.

Rituals in organizations are non-rational. They include social rituals and uncertainty avoidance rituals. They are neither silly nor superfluous; they are, however, omnipresent. There are good and bad organizational rituals. Good rituals support social cohesion and relieve stress because they concur with the values of the people involved, and they have no negative consequences for the organization or any of its members (modern society knows its human sacrifices, too) (Hofstede, 1984, p. 116).

This ritualistic orientation, combined with the extensive symbolism in the Arab world referred to earlier in this chapter, means that it is necessary to establish at least a cordial personal relationship before business there (Dredge, 1985, p. 420). An outsider rarely walks into an Arab's office and starts by discussing a business problem (Muna, 1980, p. 74).

First of all, initial contact could be very ritual and impersonal (I have had many invitation cards written in golden letters in the Arab world). Arabs (as most people in high-contextual cultures) do not give much away immediately, not even what a Westerner would call a firm handshake (it may appear quite limp). Rituals also include leave-takings.

While seeing a host in his office, interruptions may be frequent; visitors are often constantly arriving and leaving and messengers are being sent and received all the time. This partly plays the symbolic role of repeatedly confirming the incumbent's position, of course. Such confirmation is even more important in the Arab type of culture, where formal organizations are relatively fresh and not yet settled ('informally formal' Arabs will be discussed later in the chapter).

In short, the first business visit and initial business dealings should be approached as a leisurely process of 'getting to know each other' in the Arab culture. Conversation may not get around to business for several days, and it is considered rude for the visiting businessman to press the issue, to show impatience or to fail to respond to social preliminaries.

Arabs have been trained since childhood in 'reading' various social situations. However, this takes time, especially when a foreigner is involved. It is no surprise that negotiation and bargaining is an art in the Middle East (as well as in other high-contextual cultures, for example, the Japanese).

## LOYALTY AND BELONGING

Arab culture manifests a definite class structure. Some societies may define classes based on wealth, education or similarity of occupation. Sociologists commonly adopt a concept of class limits in terms of purely nonsubjective factors, such as income class (upper, middle and lower), productive and nonproductive classes, educated class, landowning class and working class. The Arab class is based on the family (tribe) and its background.

The traditional model of classes is meant to separate the society such that each class is expected to conform to its own societal model: a culturally approved pattern of behaviour. The Arab class structure, however, does not separate people as much in behaviour as in power, prestige and esteem. An Arab class signifies the cultural status of a family and, in extension, historically a tribe. An individual's status, even his or her identity, is based on this social system. Such cultural status should not be confused with legal status, even if there may be relations.

In the Arab type of culture, people are born into extended families or clans. Children are socialized in this kind of family structure and become closely identified with family and kin. Among Arabs, like the Chinese, there is a deep commitment to family honour, loyalties and responsibilities. People are motivated by security and belonging (Hofstede, 1984, p. 256). There is an intrinsic satisfaction in being loved and respected (Trompenaars, 1995, p. 160):

> It is interesting, that when Arabs meet their countrymen for the first time, they usually attempt to establish each other's family identity. In the West, on the other hand, it appears that the initial conversation revolve around a person's occupation or profession. In Japan, introductions are made with reference to one's organization or company rather than profession (Muna, 1980, p. 36).

The family concept may occasionally be extended to what is initially an outsider. It is an honour for a foreigner to be called a 'brother' by an Arab. It means that a person has been accepted as one of 'the family'.

From a wider perspective this means that the status of individual Arabs is determined primarily by their family position and social contacts, not necessarily by their own individual accomplishments (Hodgetts and Luthans, 1991, p. 37).

Arabs live in a collectivistically oriented culture. It means that individuality is a negligible value (Sitaram and Cogdell, 1976, p. 191). Care is more important than individual freedom (Trompenaars, 1995, pp. 47–48). It means also that social relations are predetermined and people think in terms of ingroup and outgroups (Hofstede, 1984, p. 167).

This tribal-based social structure is also very rigid in most Arab countries. Friendship is determined by social relationships and mainly 'locals' (not 'cosmopolitans') will be found in influential positions. However, in order for this to work, the social structure must be very stable. One consequence is common, that is, privileges are unevenly distributed; Arabs live in a collectivistic culture, but it is not egalitarian. It may even be that ordinary citizens are considered incompetent versus the authorities (Hofstede, 1984, p. 140) and that there is a pessimism about the ability to control politicians' decisions (ibid., p. 133). Also, if differences develop between people's values and the social order, this may lead to pressure toward an even stronger social order (fundamentalism), rarely towards more individualism.

It should be noted that Arab culture is not extremely collectivistic (Bjerke and Al-Meer, 1993, p. 33). There are individual differences between some of its members at least in the sense that many Arab business leaders (my focus of interest) were born and have spent their formative years in three different communities: tribal, rural and urban (Muna, 1980, p. 11). Arab culture has a 'we'-consciousness, but 'we' may refer to any of these communities (or a combination). Different classes in Arab society may, therefore, also show partly different cultural manifestations. However, most importantly for my study, as far as fundamental values are concerned (my understanding of culture), Arabs show a homogeneous pattern.

The Arab executive's managerial behaviour is heavily influenced by society's social structure and by the values, norms and expectations of its people. For instance, social standing and esteem of managers derive primarily from class origin, and organizational rank is secondary.

> The Arab executive lives in a society where family and friendship remain important and prevalent factors even in the functioning of formal institutions and groups. Consequently, ... the Arab executive relies upon family and friendship ties for getting things done within his organization and society (Muna, 1980, p. 12).

Kinship and business ties coincide. Using personal connections becomes normal – and necessary – to get the job done. 'Well-connected' people progress faster. To the Arab business mind (as well as to the Chinese business

mind), to use personal ties and connections is like a balance sheet of recipro-
cal transactions: using old 'credits' and accumulating new 'liabilities' (Muna,
1980, p. 72).

There are several consequences of this kind of cultural network on business leadership in the Arab culture (Muna, 1980, pp. 1, 12–13, 77–78, 118–119;
Hofstede, 1984, pp. 132–133, 153, 166–167, 173–174, 259; Harris and Moran,
1987, p. 66):

- Business firms are subjected to external pressures to conform with the
  societal class structure by using discriminatory recruitment and promotion policies. Personnel selection or promotion based only on
  efficiency or achievement is frequently violated in view of the importance in the Arab world of nepotism, loyalty and personal connections;
  managers are selected and promoted on the basis of seniority (which
  means much more than just professional experience in this context)
  and mostly from within.
- Impersonal Western management theories which make no allowance
  for individual differences in terms of relationships of different duration
  or levels of trust, or for persons having different positions, age or
  family ties are inadequate in many Arab settings. A Middle Easterner
  does not assume that a person is to be judged only on objective business skills and certainly does not practise it.
- Long power distance and collectivism go together in most countries as
  they do in the Arab culture. This means, for instance, that subordinates
  expect superiors to act autocratically.
- As a result of variation of policies and practices according to relationships, an Arab business executive relies heavily on highly personalized
  methods and styles in his management.
- Arab managers commonly endorse 'traditional' points of view, not
  supporting employee initiative or participating in group activity.
- The Arab businessman does business with the person, not with the
  company or the contract. This means that getting an Arab to use his
  'personal capital' built up by connections, duties and liabilities, may
  cost money (some would call it bribery).
- An Arab business leader might be able to influence his own society far
  beyond his direct business and political skills.

Some authors claim that Arab senior executives need to save time by delegating more (Muna, 1980, p. 119). By the same token, they should train, motivate
and utilize the skills of employees more; other authors notice some negative
consequences of the ruling system, for example, weaker perceived work
ethic, more frequent belief that people dislike work and that employees are

reluctant to trust each other (Hofstede, 1984, p. 92) or a general pessimism about people's amount of initiative, ambition and leadership skills (ibid., p. 133).

At any rate, more Arabs claim than not that group decisions are better than individual decisions and most Arabs believe that individual responsibility is not relevant (Trompenaars, 1995, pp. 51–54). It is important here to realize that 'group decision' does not mean a democratic decision in the Western sense of the term. If an Arab feels that a decision is taken by somebody with him in mind (possibly after having been consulted), he *feels* part of it. Arabs do not want to feel that they are left alone to get the job done (ibid., pp. 142–143). More generally, in the Middle East, the totality of the person is important (no separation between product and person) (Harris and Moran, 1987, p. 12). Arabs look at a firm as a social group rather than as a system (Trompenaars, 1995, pp. 17–18). There is an emphasis on belonging to organizations; membership is an ideal (Hofstede, 1984, p. 171). There is also an emotional dependence of an individual on organizations and institutions in the Arab type of culture. Employees become morally (not so much calculatively) involved in the company where they are employed. Subordinates and superiors also become more dependent on each other.

Organizations have great influence on their members in Middle Eastern countries. The former are expected to assume a broad responsibility for the latter, providing expertise, order, duty and security. Private life is invaded by organizations. Employees expect organizations to defend their interests. This is one reason why large companies are attractive and why labour unions are very rare in the Arab world.

Friendship and trust are prerequisites for any social or business relationship and are developed slowly. These values play a larger role in the Arab type of culture. In fact, policies and practices are based on loyalty and a sense of duty in such a culture (Hofstede, 1984, p. 173). Loyalty is seen as a virtue and considered more important than efficiency (Muna, 1980, p. 80). The latter may even be ranked as a tertiary value (Sitaram and Cogdell, 1976, p. 191).

This may have some consequences for how performance appraisal takes place in a country like Saudi Arabia (Harris and Moran, 1987, p. 37):

- its objective is placement of personnel;
- the appraiser must know the employee well;
- reputation is important;
- subjective aspects dominate objective aspects;
- criticism is given individually and not in writing.

Some special consequences of Arab values may include:

- Few Arabs disagree with the statement: 'The most important thing in life is to think and act in ways that best suit what you really are, even if you do not get things done' (Trompenaars, 1995, p. 141).
- Many Middle Easterners take great satisfaction in appearing to be helpless. Helplessness can be used as a source of power, for in this part of the world the weak are supposed to be compensated (Hodgetts and Luthans, 1991, p. 37).

As mentioned earlier, in the Arab culture employers are supposed to care for the employees in more than one respect. This may lead them to see it as important to provide not only acceptable physical conditions at work, but also to offer possibilities to use existing skills and to get further training, whenever there is a chance (Hayes and Allison, 1988, p. 75).

The low stress on efficiency among Arabs is associated with the fact that their sense of time is less strict than among Westerners. Punctuality is a tertiary value (Sitaram and Cogdell, 1976, p. 191), and it may, as mentioned already, take a long time for a visitor to see a host in his office, even if an appointment is made. A Middle Easterner does not assume or exercise control over his time. Issues and actions are triggered by whether the time is right, not on schedule or by reference to a mechanism. Patience is a virtue among Arabs (Harris and Moran, 1987, pp. 62 ff).

Some authors claim that one of the Arab business executive's gravest problems is the low value placed on time in his culture. There are, however, several pressures and reasons which inhibit a better utilization of time in the Arab world (Muna, 1980, pp. 90–91):

1. The inadequacy of the economic and organizational infrastructure. Delays and waste of time are often a result of the non-existence and/or poor utilization of such items as transportation, housing facilities, communication channels and technology.
2. A range of social pressures and constraints imposed on the executive's time, including fusion of business, social and personal life, top-man syndrome and social visits at the office.
3. The executive's role in the community and the organization. This results in heavy time commitments and obligations to the extended family, friends and employees.
4. The low level of delegation by executives. This is an obstacle to good management of time. Delegating more of the operating level decisions will relieve the overburdened executive and speed up the decision-making process.
5. The executives' person-oriented interpersonal style. This partly imposes on their time, especially with executives who use the Arab rituals and

customs while conducting business, and with those who believe in the open-door tradition.

## POWER AND FORMAL INFORMALITY

It fits well with what we have seen of Arab culture so far that organization pyramids (if they are perceivable; many organizations in the Arab world appear more like 'organized chaos'; more about this later) are very steep – steepest of all in an international comparison made by Trompenaars (1995, p. 114). They are tall and centralized (Hofstede, 1984, p. 107). What usually follows from such steep pyramids – and maybe particularly so in the Arab type of culture – is that top-down communication is dominant and that authoritarianism becomes a primary value (Sitaram and Cogdell, 1976, p. 191). The cultural manifestation of authoritative management style in the Middle East can be explained by the following (Harris and Moran, 1987, p. 67):

- Governments in the Middle East are generally authoritative. The absolute authority is vested in the hands of the ruling class.
- The social structure as previously discussed.
- The family structure – the paternalistic male Arab will be discussed later in the chapter.
- The manager in the Middle East enjoys power and to give it away could even be seen as a sign of weakness (the idea of 'power' in this context will be discussed in a later section).

To summarize, the Arab manager makes decisions autocratically and paternalistically, exerting and enjoying power in the meantime. The following quotation, referring to the 'great majority of Egyptian-owned private establishments', gives a good picture of what the structure of many Arab enterprises is all about still today:

> Here the manager is a dominant individual who extends his personal control over all phases of the business. There is no charted plan of organization, no formalized procedure for selection and development of managerial personnel, no publicized system of wage and salary classification. ... Authority is associated exclusively with an individual (Harbison and Myers, 1959, pp. 40–41).

This is what Mintzberg (1979) refers to as a 'simple structure'.

An autocratic manager may sound like a contradiction of what has been said before about Arabs not wanting to feel left alone, sometimes not even having a strong sense of individual responsibility. The point is that the combination of long power distance and collectivism found in the Arab type of culture means that social involvement develops only in horizontal relationships (I have some reservations about using concepts like 'horizontal', 'vertical' and 'chain of command', as they are normally understood in a hierarchy when applied to the Arab culture, a fact that will be discussed later in the chapter) similar to those found in various types of primary group. In vertical relationships this is not so (Hofstede, 1984, p. 153). The chain of command is rarely broken which, as mentioned earlier, may occasionally lead to loss of time and to poor communication (Muna, 1980, pp. 82–83). All seniors are expected to be consulted according to their rank. In the end, however, managers are expected to formulate decisions individually, occasionally using experts (if they are not threatening their power), and those having been consulted do not feel left alone. In Arab countries, industrial democracy (the way it is understood in the West) is basically a contradiction; it will meet with strong resistance from all (Hofstede, 1984, pp. 268–269).

> Joint decision making (or participative leadership style) is unlikely to be widely adopted by Arab managements, even for decisions which are best suited for this style. The major reasons for this are: (a) subordinates might view it as a sign of weakness on part of the executive: they expect to be consulted, but not to make the final decision; (b) Arab executives prefer and feel more at ease with the consultative decision-making style; and (c) Arab executives and subordinates tend to dislike team-work (Muna, 1980, p. 118).

So, *who* is doing something is more important than *what* is being done among Arabs. This could be called 'management by subjectives' (Trompenaars, 1995, p. 160).

Some potential and real consequences of such a situation are (Hofstede, 1984, pp. 92, 94, 107):

- other people are a potential threat to an individual's power and can rarely be trusted;
- latent conflict between the powerful and the powerless;
- the way to change the social system is by dethroning those in power;
- large wage differentials;
- low qualification of lower strata;
- large proportion of supervisory personnel;
- close supervision positively evaluated by subordinates.

The basic assumptions in a culture with a long power distance societal norm are as follows (ibid., p. 94):

- There should be an order of inequality in this world in which everyone has his or her rightful place.

- High and low are protected by this order.
- A few should be independent – most should be dependent.
- A hierarchy means existential inequality.
- Superior and subordinates consider each other as being of a different kind.
- Power is a basic fact of society which antedates good or evil. Its legitimacy is irrelevant.

Arabs score very high on *power distance* (Bjerke and Al-Meer, 1993, p. 31). They are generally very rank-conscious. This, combined with a rigid social structure (even though, for an outsider, people are dressed the same and may appear the same) means that in the Arab culture powerful people should try to surround themselves with pointers, indicating their power, that is, status symbols are very important in the Arab world. They also contribute strongly to somebody's authority.

Flaunting status symbols does not involve any conflict in a society where power-holders are expected to be entitled to privileges. It is also no surprise that in the Arab type of culture, positions where status symbols are more accessible are favoured, for example, white-collar jobs are valued more highly than blue-collar jobs (Hofstede, 1984, p. 197).

One interesting aspect of the Arab culture is that the distinction between formal and informal is not very useful. It may appear, at first, that superior–subordinate interaction is very formal and restricted and that informal discussions with subordinates are avoided. This organizational type has been characterized as 'full bureaucracy', that is, relations between people as well as work processes are rigidly prescribed (Hofstede, 1984, pp. 215–217).

However, the point is that these prescriptions are not uniform. The Arab organization does not work as a bureaucracy in the Max Weber sense! Arab executives conduct business in a leisurely way. They dislike, in fact, foreigners' 'business-is-business' impersonal notion (Muna, 1980, pp. 85–86), but that is not all. Arabs are truly more person-oriented than role- or task-oriented. Their management approach is even personal and pragmatic to the extent that procedures may differ from one occasion to the next, even if the two occasions are similar and even if in both cases rules being applied could be very strict! One estimate is that public rules and regulations are applied only about 20 per cent of the time (ibid., p. 83).

I have heard visitors saying that Arab bureaucratic organizations do not work, but they do! However, this is understandable only if you are able to untangle their complicated web of power play and get inside their high-contextual daily life. Some authors call it 'organized chaos'. Instead it could be called *'formal informality'*!

# PATERNALISM

As already discussed, the Arab executive's managerial behaviour is heavily influenced by the structure of the society outside his firm and by the values, norms and expectations of its people. One consequence of this is that the Arab manager sees himself as a father figure:

> The executive's role within his community and organization is shaped to a considerable extent by the expectations of relatives, friends and employees. The top executive, by virtue of his position in the organization, sees himself as the head of a family: employees are perceived as members of that family (Muna, 1980, p. 1).

Managers like to view themselves as *benevolent decision-makers* in the Arab type of culture (Hofstede, 1984, p. 92). However, management has many social implications in this culture. The Arab senior manager's paternal behaviour reinforces his employees' perceived role as members of a family. The ideal superior to an Arab is a paternalistic but benevolent autocrat. Employees expect organizations to look after them like a family and can become very alienated if that is not the case (ibid., p. 173).

Members of 'the extended family' in an Arab company ask their seniors for all sorts of help and assistance, including (Muna, 1980, pp. 36, 41):

- consultation on personal problems or family decisions, such as divorce or housing;
- contacts or pressure on government agencies or other institutions in matters of obtaining a passport, a visa, a driving licence or even cancelling a traffic violation;
- financial assistance and loans.

The paternalistic nature of Arab management discourages impersonality and promotes 'family' traditions. Changes may take place, of course, but only when 'father' acts.

This is closely associated with another deeply rooted tradition that has found its way into today's Arab organizations, that is, the open-door policy. This policy goes back to the sheikh's, ruler's or king's *majlis* (assembly or visiting room) where the visitor can either pay his respects, request a favour or submit a grievance. In some Arab countries it is still possible for any national to do so. Consultation is actively encouraged by the Qur'an and the *Hadith* (interpretations of the Qur'an), where it is mentioned several times.

Consultation, for some Arabs, seems to be an effective 'human relations' technique and it is used on several occasions and in various situations (ibid., p. 60): (a) to avoid potential conflicts; (b) to please, or to win over, persons who might be potential obstacles to an individual's ideas or actions; and (c) to provide the person being consulted with a boost of status.

## FATALISM

In the last chapter it was stated that Americans often believe that their future is within their own control and that it will depend on what actions they take. It is a common conception that Arabs are just the opposite, that is, being 'fatalists':

> Arab behaviour is greatly influenced by the belief that destiny depends more on the will of a supreme being than on individual behaviour. A higher power dictates the outcome of important events, so individual action is of little consequence. This thinking affects not only individuals' aspirations but also their motivation (Hodgetts and Luthans, 1991, p. 37).

This view holds that local managers in the Arab type of culture 'will not do very much creative managing. They won't plan ahead or try to do anything to mold the future' (Moore, 1982, p. 538). Furthermore, this view attributes this fatalistic indifference to the teachings of Islam (Muna, 1980, p. 93).

There are at least two objections to this view:

1.  It is too simplistic, where fatalism *does* exist, to attribute it solely to Islam without taking into account other socio-economic and political factors. Moreover, there are within Islamic teachings as many precepts exhorting initiative, rationalism and activism as there are precepts which encourage fatalism. The *Hadith* admonishes man first to think and plan ahead, then put his trust in Allah (Muna, 1980, p. 95).
2.  It is also simplistic to generalize that most Arabs (Muslims or nonMuslims) are fatalistic regardless of their socio-economic and educational background. My experience from the Arab world is that this pattern is much more complicated. The category of people of interest in this study, that is, business leaders, do not, in general, fit into this stereotypical mould.

It is perhaps the frequent use among Arabs of the phrase *Insha'Allah* ('if God is willing') which flavours the opinion among many expatriates and foreign visitors. However, instead of interpreting this phrase as a sign of resignation and inactivity, a person should (particularly in business circles) see it more as a custom and a habit than as a sign of religiousness.

*Insha'Allah* fits the Arab virtue of patience. The phrase may, of course, be a convenient excuse for inaction or be used as an easy way out, blaming an outside force if something should go wrong.

The myth of fatalism, at least among businessmen, should be laid to rest (Muna, 1980, p. 98). Past and present Arab achievements (which are in harmony with Islamic teachings) demonstrate the use of long-range planning and a desire to influence the future (ibid., pp. 95–96). There are many examples of Arabs becoming successful due to being active and hard working (At-Twaijri, 1989b, p. 22).

## EMOTIONAL AND CONFLICT-PRONE

Middle Easterners act on *emotion*; in contrast, Americans are taught to act on logic, as was discussed in the last chapter. Contrary to Oriental reservedness, emotional displays are commonplace among Arabs. There is, generally, more showing of emotions in high uncertainty avoidance countries (Hofstede, 1984, p. 140).

Arabs are also a caring kind. They score quite low in Hofstede's masculinity (Bjerke and Al-Meer, 1993, p. 33). Arab men read poetry; they are sensitive; they are often seen embracing and holding hands. Women, on the other hand, are considered to be coldly practical. It is almost like reverse sex roles compared to the West (Hofstede, 1984, p. 201). Male achievement is defined in terms of human contacts and a living environment. Money is of secondary value (Sitaram and Cogdell, 1976, p. 191).

As previously mentioned, the person with whom a Middle Easterner works is more important than the mission, the product and the job (Harris and Moran, 1987, p. 62). In short, Arabs are diffuse-affective; relational reward is love, relational punishment is hate (Trompenaars, 1995, pp. 85–87).

This has some interesting implications for Arabs communicating with each other, in particular considering their rich language. As mentioned previously, Middle Easterners love the spoken word, they tend to ramble and they do not get to the point quickly. They are also masters at flattery and appreciate compliments at the same time as they are easily outraged by even slight provocations (Harris and Moran, 1987, pp. 62–63). The communication situation is often several-to-one with countless interruptions where aggressive behaviour of self and others is accepted. Arabs are very good at holding several conversations at the same time. When a foreigner sees Arabs speaking together, he may think that they are engaged in very heated arguments.

An Arab is as quick to explode at friend as at foe. Not only is there no stigma attached to sounding off, but it is looked on as a handy safety valve – a first line of defence, or offence – that makes the ranter feel better without having done any real harm to the rantee. The other side of the instant frown, however, is the instant smile (Axtell, 1990, p. 30).

Because they act so intuitively and spontaneously, some authors say that Arabs are *conflict-prone*. Being very temperamental, Middle Easterners may try to avoid arguments at first, but once into a discussion, there is a lower readiness to compromise with opponents (Hofstede, 1984, p. 133). Peace is of negligible value in Muslim cultures (Sitaram and Cogdell, 1976, p. 191).

Arabs, however, have developed a unique mechanism for settling disputes, that is, 'the mediator'. The mediator mechanism as a manifestation in the Arab culture is described by Harris and Moran (1987, pp. 106–108) as follows:

- Mediation has for centuries been the traditional method of settling disputes on the tribal and village level, and it has been adapted to the modern world.
- Those involved in a conflict tend to feel that their honour is at stake. To give in would diminish their self-respect and dignity and be a sign of weakness. Hence, it is almost impossible for an Arab to come to an agreement in direct confrontation with an opponent.
- The task of the mediator is to separate and restrain the feuding parties. These parties are supposed to restrain themselves out of respect for the mediator. Thus the greater the prestige of the mediator, the more successful he will be.
- Reconciliation, not judgement of (legal) right and wrong, is the purpose of mediation. The mediators mediate. They do not arbitrate. They do not judge.
- A compromise through mediation does not in itself represent a compromise of personal values of the parties. Arabs also believe that mediation is rooted in a certain realism, that is, all problems do not have neat solutions; thus the need for compromise through mediation.

Nevertheless, some Arabs believe that their business executives should improve on conflict management (Muna, 1980, p. 119).

## A TYPIFIED INTERPRETATION OF ARAB BUSINESS LEADERS

The Arab culture has been discussed focusing on certain themes. These are summarized in Table 5.1.

Based on these themes it is possible to give a typified interpretation of Arab business leaders as follows:

*Table 5.1   The Arab culture themes*

- Tradition and religion
- High-context and symbolism
- Social but ritualistic
- Loyalty and belonging
- Power and formal informality
- Paternalism
- Fatalism
- Emotional and conflict-prone

- They are working in a young nation with an old culture; are often in the petrochemical industry; are often linked to the government; are relatively new on the multinational scene.
- They live in a society where religion is paramount.
- They work in a society, which is emotionally resistant to change and limiting humanware technology transfer; are generally very nationalistic; are operating a management style, heavily influenced by the traditions of Islam and Arab culture; often use problem-solving procedures which follow precedent or adapt old procedures to new situations; are occasionally critical of the slow pace of change, lack of delegation and shortage of conflict management skills; try to be agents of social change in a society which itself is undergoing modernization.
- They are influenced by expectations from their extended families; are operating in a male-dominated, collectivistic society with a definite, nonegalitarian class structure, based on families (tribes); are committed to family honour, loyalties and responsibilities, motivated by security and belonging; are merging kinship and business ties.
- They look at a firm as a social group rather than as a system for rational execution of decisions; are paternalistic (benevolent autocrats), providing all sorts of help and assistance to subordinates; consider loyalty more important than efficiency; apply a policy of a door open for consultation, but socialize only in horizontal, not vertical, directions.
- They live in a long power distance society with steep, tall and centralized organizational pyramids; are fond of power and rank-conscious, employing many status symbols, at the same time as applying a very person-oriented and personal style of management (management by subjectives).
- They apply management systems having a large symbolic load and including many ritual elements, confirming the status quo; can use

detailed planning but are less interested in following up decisions made.

- They love to talk and participate in conversations; have a tendency for verbal overkill; are sensitive to details, excellent interpreters of context, good psychologists and skilled negotiators; use a communication style which contains many implicit components and nonverbal cues.
- They have a sense of time which is less strict; look at patience as a virtue and do not consider it worth while (sometimes not even possible) to be a good time manager.
- They are not fatalistic, contrary to common belief.
- They stress manners, pride and dignity, but also generosity and hospitality.
- They are sensitive to the feelings of others but are themselves sensitive to criticism, in particular in public; are emotional, even conflict-prone (not ready to compromise face to face with opponent).

# 6. Chinese culture

## INTRODUCTION

Regardless of what the Western world thinks and says about the Chinese, it must be acknowledged that China is the world's oldest civilization among cultures existing today. Many of its old values are still preserved. Modern Greeks and Egyptians bear little cultural resemblance to their ancient fore-bears (Yang, 1991, p. 7).

> China is an ancient civilization. During the Chou Dynasty (1122 B.C. to 256 B.C.) the wheel, wire saw, diamond drill, and the crossbow were developed. In mathematics and astronomy, the Chinese were at times ahead of the Western civilization. The Pythagorean theorem of geometry was developed in China at about the same time that it developed in Greece, approximately 400 B.C. At about the same time, the Chinese mapped approximately 1500 stars, 200 years before Hipparchus mapped about one-half that number (Harris and Moran, 1979, p. 309).

China survived when other civilizations vanished. After many years of isola-tion, stagnation and internal turmoil, China is once again asserting its importance in the international community and the urge to understand the Chinese has gained a new impetus. In this effort, many Westerners claim that Chinese behaviour is confusing, unprofessional and seemingly inappropriate (Chu, 1991, p. 11). This opinion is probably more often than not a reflection of the attitudes of some Western businesspeople and politicians to measure the whole universe by Western standards (ibid., p. 11). Western management principles must certainly be challenged to do business in Asia in general and with the Chinese in particular (Lasserre and Schütte, 1995, pp. xvi–xvii).

How was Southeast Asia able to grow so fast during the past three decades or so and until recently? This subject touches upon many of the qualities that have shaped modern Asia (Rohwer, 1995, p. 22). Culture in the form of certain dominant values is a necessary condition for economic growth. How-ever, culture alone is not sufficient for such growth to occur. Two other necessary conditions are the existence of a market and a political context that allows development (Hofstede and Bond, 1988, pp. 18–19).

The first condition was there, if nothing else but in sheer numbers, for example, roughly 20 per cent of the world's population are Chinese and about two hundred million Indonesians can be added. However, the market size is not enough. Modern growth in Asia only started in some places at the end of the 1950s, when for the first time in history the conditions for a truly global market were fulfilled (Hofstede and Bond, 1988, p. 18). The other necessary condition, the political situation, hampered growth in China until 1979, when the door to the People's Republic of China was opened for trade and business in the rest of Southeast Asia, the supportive political context was present earlier, although in different ways in different countries, varying from active support to *laissez-faire* (ibid., pp. 18–19).

This study is not the place to discuss in detail the successful growth of Southeast Asia, nor its downturn since 1997. The same goes for Japan in the next chapter. It is too easy to come up with value judgements of good or bad cultural values, which I try to avoid (as mentioned in Chapter 3). However in the case of Southeast Asia, what are commonly accepted as factors behind its exceptional growth and decline are so intertwined with its cultural values (which are to be explored in the rest of this chapter) that it is worth mentioning these factors, at least briefly.

On the political side again, economic development in Asian countries has, with the exception of Hong Kong, been guided by governments. The role of governments in Southeast Asia is summarized by Lasserre and Schütte under seven headings (1995, pp. 116–123):

1.  *Development context*   Asian government involvement in economic developments aims to generate public support and an environment conducive to economic growth.
2.  *Consensus towards growth*   In Asia, as a rule, both governments and the general populace believe that everyone benefits from economic growth and that it must be shared, though not in a strictly egalitarian manner.
3.  *Business–government relationships*   Business and government cooperation is institutionalized in some Asian countries; it is informal in others and occasionally exists as a hybrid of the two.
4.  *Pro-business attitudes of the bureaucracy*   A skilled, business-oriented state bureaucracy is common.
5.  *Government in Asia: pragmatism and flexibility*   Pragmatic implementation in government policies has allowed flexibility, even in the ideological sphere.
6.  *Development orientations*   Asian countries can be divided into two distinct groups: those which have traditionally adhered to import-substitution policies and those with an outward-looking, export-led orientation. Economies that grew the fastest belong to the second group.
7.  *Direct government participation*   The majority of Asian governments have intervened directly in the economy through the ownership and

control of enterprises and through a targeted policy of public procurement.

Generally, in terms of theories of economic growth, Asia was very good at putting together some elements that make for economic growth (Rohwer, 1995, pp. 17–18) (most of these elements are still at place even in the present recession). First, Asia's workforce is growing fast and puts in long hours. Second, most of East Asia is working hard to improve the quality of its workers through education and training. Third, Asian countries have injected unusually large amounts of capital into their economies combined with high savings rates (to this was added, until recently, huge amounts of capital from outside as direct foreign investments).

A fourth element of growth – productivity, or the efficiency with which the first three elements are combined – is much harder to assess. Some have argued that this factor has not been in Southeast Asia's favour, but nobody can deny that countries in this part of the world have been good at spreading and using technology, fitting the society's cultural values with the demands of modern economic life, receptive to new ideas and foreign influence and moving up the value-added ladder as the economies have become more advanced.

The most distinctive feature of East Asia's business regime, however, is how much it has depended, and still depends, on private business. In the two decades after 1970 private investment in East Asia accounted on average for almost two-thirds of total investment (Rohwer, 1995, p. 55). In particular, most of Southeast Asia's economies cannot be understood without an examination of the Overseas Chinese – ethnic Chinese who live outside the mainland (Naisbitt, 1995, pp. 3–4). These expatriate wizards did not create the boom in Southeast Asia or in Mainland China, but they were uniquely placed to take advantage of it (Seagrave, 1996, pp. 15–16). They are the force behind modern Southeast Asia (and even present Mainland China to a great extent). They are the true *Lords of the Rim* (ibid.).

It is suggested that there have been four main patterns of Chinese migration over the years (Wang, 1992, pp. 4–9). These are:

1. the trader pattern;
2. the coolie pattern;
3. the sojourner pattern;
4. the descent or re-migrant pattern.

The trader pattern refers to merchants and artisans (including miners and other skilled workers) who went abroad, or sent their colleagues, agents or members of their extended families or clans (including those with little or no skills working as apprentices or lowly assistants) abroad to work for them, and set up bases at ports, mines or trading cities. When this proved success-ful, the business abroad could expand and required more agents or young family members to be sent out to help the new ventures.

This was the dominant pattern from early times in various parts of South-east Asia. It was clearly the dominant pattern by the eighteenth century, and the only significant pattern before 1850.

The second pattern, the 'coolie pattern', derived from the migration of large numbers of coolie labour, normally men of peasant origin, landless labourers and the urban poor. This pattern was associated with plantation economies of one era as well as the beginnings of industrialization in another. A large proportion of these contract labourers returned to China after their contract came to an end. This pattern also came to an end in Southeast Asia as a whole (by the 1920s).

The third pattern was the sojourner pattern. It is quite different in nature from the traders and coolies. Even if the term often refers to the first two patterns as well, Wang (1992) here refers to those teachers, journalists and other professionals who went out to promote greater awareness of Chinese culture and national needs.

The fourth pattern is the descent or re-migrant pattern. This is mainly a new phenomenon of Chinese movers. While they are largely foreign-born, they also include some who were born in China, Taiwan or Hong Kong who have acquired foreign citizenship and are, strictly speaking, not temporarily resident abroad.

Those patterns of interest here are the first and the second, that is, the traders and the coolies. Today, when international trade is playing a larger role than ever before in world economic development, it should be re-membered that, in the old days, Chinese entrepreneurs overseas started as traditional merchants and they had been around for a very long time (Wang, 1992, p. 181). There are many different groups of Chinese, of course. One difference of particular interest for the history of economic development in East and Southeast Asia and of relevance to understand Chinese culture in the context of business leadership, the project of this study, is the northern Chinese versus the southern Chinese in China itself. These two 'groups' (separated by the Yangtze river) have always been characterized differently (Chu, 1991, pp. 186–187; Seagrave, 1996, p. 81). The upper class, the man-darins, formed the central governments in the north. The merchants were placed at the bottom of the social structure, often had to pursue their trade unofficially and even secretly and did their best to avoid interference from others. Mandarin supervision from northern China remained a major obstacle to the rise of an indigenous capital class. The merchants and traders were forced to move south to operate autonomously and to gain momentum. When later in history southern China was also included more directly in the controlling sphere of the north, the merchants and traders started to move overseas to continue with their businesses.

Today 85 per cent of Overseas Chinese outside mainland China are from southern provinces – Guangdong, Fukien, Hainan and Guangxi (Mackie, 1992, pp. 163–164; Naisbitt, 1995, pp. 10–11).

Figure 6.1 gives an overview of the Overseas Chinese migration pattern: However, this is only part of the story. The popular myth that most Overseas

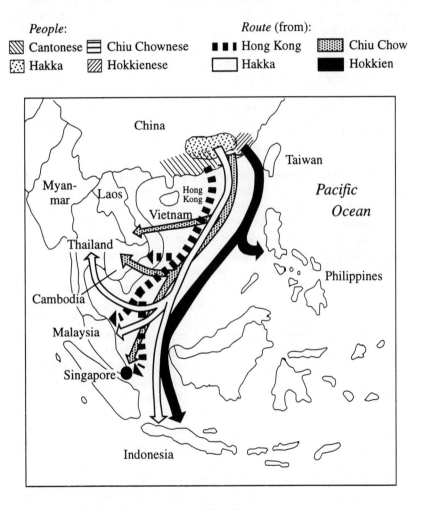

*Source*: 'The Overseas Chinese', 18 July, 1992, p. 22.

*Figure 6.1   Overseas Chinese migrant pattern*

Chinese were forced out of their home and arrived abroad as traders trained in commercial operations and funded by substantial capital is not supported by history (Limlingan, 1986, pp. 158–159). The number of Overseas Chinese grew over the centuries, as did the number of countries and areas where they came to live. Large-scale migration started only in the years between the Opium War (1830–1842) and World War II. The vast majority of these people were not trained and funded traders, but consisted of coolies and contract labour (ibid., p. 37). This coincided with the region being incorporated into the rapidly expanding world capitalist system (McVey, 1992, p. 19). Rulers thought it easier, and less disruptive of the local hierarchies, to bring in outsiders. The Chinese were easy to recruit, because their homeland was in turmoil. Adapting themselves to their new environment, the Chinese immigrants accultured to the style of the ruling groups, which in most cases were Western:

> From their allotted position as intermediaries between Western big business and the local economy, Southeast Asian Chinese business leaders gained both knowledge of modern trade and manufacturing techniques and (which Western firms rarely did) the local market (McVey, 1992, p. 21).

Table 6.1 provides a rough estimate of where Overseas Chinese live today. Being traders or recruited workers, records show that many Chinese left their homeland because their lives were impoverished and due to economic pressure (Tanaka *et al.*, 1992, pp. 3–5; Rohwer, 1995, pp. 230–231). They were also treated very differently in their new countries and often harshly (Tanaka *et al.*, 1992, p. 3). They were 'pariahs' in the sense that they could not really rely on the state to protect their interests (McVey, 1992, p. 20). As a result they developed their own support groups and, in business, financial networks and buying/selling relationships, avoiding as much as possible exposure to official control. A number of immigrant Chinese profited from their intermediary position between the rulers and the locals, using these support groups, networks and relationships to the fullest (Braadbaart, 1995, p. 180).

At the same time, the Overseas Chinese were helping their host countries. The 'boys' from Shanghai gave the first boom to Hong Kong just after World War II (Seagrave, 1996, pp. 271–272). The Chinese group known as 'Hakka' played a major role in building networks across nations and many Southeast Asian business and political leaders are Hakka (Tanaka *et al.*, 1992, pp. 13–14). Hong Kong and Singapore have served (and still serve) as key stations for the Overseas Chinese (ibid., p. 15).

As Southeast Asia grew, more than a hundred large corporate conglomerates emerged (not counting Hong Kong and Taiwan), nearly all owned or controlled by the ethnic Chinese, a number of them billionaires in any currency. They live and work across the region, but most have (as previously mentioned) their roots in South China (Seagrave, 1996, p. 14).

*Table 6.1    The Chinese living outside China*

| Continent | Thousand |
|-----------|----------|
| Africa | 100 |
| Oceania | 400 |
| Europe | 600 |
| America | 2 700 |
| Asia | 51 000 |
| of which | Million |
| Malaysia | 6 |
| Thailand | 6 |
| Indonesia | 8 |
| Singapore | 2 |
| Philippines | 1 |
| Vietnam | 1 |
| Hong Kong (*) | 6 |
| Taiwan (*) | 21 |

*Source*:    Rough figures from various sources; (*) not strictly Overseas Chinese.

Financially and organizationally, the Overseas Chinese dominate the entire Pacific Rim, the world's biggest market and cheap labour pool. They are the biggest investing group on the Mainland and, if China holds together, their influence and leverage will be immeasurably enhanced. The longer term outlook is that the Overseas Chinese will greatly increase their commercial lead over the rest of the world – and if the West does not prepare for that possibility, it is in for a major shock (Seagrave, 1996, p. 17).

Some statistics to prove our point are shown in Table 6.2 (Naisbitt, 1995, p. 3):

*Table 6.2    Overseas Chinese companies as per cent of listed companies*

| Country | (%) |
|---------|-----|
| Thailand | 81 |
| Singapore | 81 |
| Indonesia | 73 |
| Malaysia | 62 |
| Philippines | 50 |

The spread and economic power of the Overseas Chinese has no precedent in history (Drucker and Nakauchi, 1997, p. 7). They are scattered all over Southeast Asia, concentrated in family businesses and kept together by strong ties of blood, geography and business (Tanaka *et al.*, 1992, p. 3). Many industries and trades were penetrated by the sponsorship of family members in setting up and using the family wealth as a common pool (Redding, 1993, pp. 36–38). The Overseas Chinese might be called 'a prosperous multinational middle class with a small superclass on top' (Seagrave, 1996, p. 15). They run an extremely efficient opportunity-seeking machine ('Fissiparous fortunes and …', 30 November, 1996, p. 15), moving funds around in networks. They have turned the Pacific Rim into a borderless economy (Seagrave, 1996, p. 16). The key determinants behind Overseas Chinese business have been (Redding, 1993, pp. 144–145):

- paternalism;
- personalism;
- insecurity.

These determinants will be discussed in detail throughout this chapter.

The typical evolution of an Overseas Chinese business group has followed the pattern as in Figure 6.2:

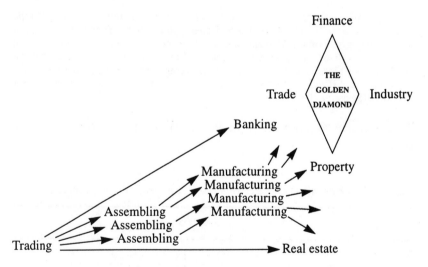

*Source*:  Lasserre and Schütte (1995, p. 107).

*Figure 6.2   Typical evolution of an Overseas Chinese business group*

The size of the Overseas Chinese economy can only be estimated. Nobody really knows. The ethnic Chinese controlled $541 billion in ten Asian stock markets in 1994 (Naisbitt, 1995, p. 3). Several sources have estimated that the Overseas Chinese control liquid assets valued between $2 and 2.5 trillion (Chen, 1995, p. 69; 'Asia's new giants', 27 November, 1995, p. 30; 'Inheriting the bamboo ...', 23 December, 1995, p. 25; 'A survey of business in Asia', 9 March, 1996b, p. 4; Seagrave, 1996, p. 15)! A safe conclusion is that the Overseas Chinese are a new economic superpower (Drucker, 1995, p. 177), probably the third largest economy in the world, outranked only by the USA and Japan. The World Bank has guessed that the gross domestic product (GDP) of Greater China (China itself plus Taiwan, Hong Kong and Singapore) in 1990 was $2.5 trillion (calculated on a purchasing power parity (PPP) basis), already ahead of Japan ($2.1 trillion) and almost half of the American figure of $5.4 trillion (Rohwer, 1995, p. 229).

The Overseas Chinese business wealth has been reduced since mid-1997 in the wake of the financial crisis in the Southeast Asia region, in some countries even drastically so, but it is still a force without which the region could not function and a force of strategic importance to thé world.

The Chinese diaspora was originally meant to be temporary. The dream was to return to the motherland one day. However, the Overseas Chinese have been more and more localized where they are, and they have been more successful outside China than they could ever have been inside. Nevertheless, the Overseas Chinese have never forgotten their roots. They have a strong desire to maintain their national identity. Their investment in China has increased rapidly since its opening in 1979 (Tanaka *et al.*, 1992, p. 5); the Overseas Chinese are today the largest investor in the People's Republic of China (Seagrave, 1996, p. 339).

> Apparently, the emigrants who left China were mainly driven by the desire to earn a living and the desire to escape domestic hardship. ... The sense of China as the Middle Kingdom remained so deep-rooted in the minds of the Chinese people that they could hardly envision leaving their homeland without intending to return at some point. The name given to those who settled in Southeast Asia was *nanyang huaqiao*, which meant that the Chinese living in the Southern Seas were thought to be temporary sojourners. In fact, many had already sojourned for decades but still held on to their dream that they would eventually return to their motherland before their death. Though it is not the same today for most Overseas Chinese, many still feel emotionally bound to China even after centuries of family settlement elsewhere. The Overseas Chinese are a major source of tourism and investment in China, even though many of them are themselves victims or the descendants of victims of the current communist regime (Chen, 1995, p. 72).

PRC attempts to attract the Overseas Chinese, of course. China is, among other things, short of financial infrastructure and knowledge of modern business management. Maybe more important, the Overseas Chinese are the only people able to supply China's greatest and most crucial need – educated people (Drucker and Nakauchi, 1997, p. 8).

> The boom on the Mainland is exhilarating to Overseas Chinese everywhere. They are proud that after centuries of humiliation China is regaining greatness at breathtaking speed – economic greatness, first, but with political leverage as a consequence. The older generation of expatriates, who have felt discriminated against in Western and Asian societies, hope a strong China will change all that. Others fear that it will (Seagrave, 1996, p. 360).

## FROM BOOM TO GLOOM

Asia's economic performance was nothing short of spectacular for several decades, with its share of the world's GDP increasing to about 25 per cent in 1997. In retrospect, however, it is clear that these very years of 'miraculous' growth contained the makings of a disaster, though few noted it at the time.

As many have since observed, systems of political, corporate and financial governance in most Asian countries failed to keep pace with the rapid growth. This failure led to several developments:

- exchange rates pegged at unrealistically high levels;
- excessive expansion of credit by loosely supervised banking systems with little regard for profitability; extensive borrowing overseas took place and cash-rich foreign lenders, looking for handsome returns on their deposits, were helping;
- a real-estate bubble which, in turn, led to a further expansion of credit, as banks continued to lend as the value of their collaterals rose.

This could not go on for ever. The economic boom turned into a financial crisis in East Asia. It started when Thailand was forced to a devaluation of its currency in July 1997. In only days, the Indonesian and Philippine currencies began to tumble as they were freed from their own long-standing anchor to the American dollar, which appreciated against all other major currencies. And the blight rumbled on, shaking every major Asian financial market. The crisis soon spread to other aspects of the East Asian economies, leading to higher unemployment, recession and even collapse of some of them.

At the same time, it should be understood that the fundamentals of most Asian economies are still in place – high savings rates, outward orientation, heavy investments in infrastructure and human resources, to name a few. However, when these economies became targets for global financial speculation, they were abruptly exposed to forces beyond their control, forces which they were ill-equipped to deal with.

The Asian collapse is widely blamed on structural problems – too much state interference in economies, 'crony capitalism' and lax financial supervision and inadequate regulatory mechanisms. However that system produced exceptional growth for several decades! The more important *direct* cause of the Asian crisis is probably the sudden exposure of these nations to the whims of unregulated speculation of international financial capital (of which some came from within the region itself) ('What sank Asia? ...' 27 July, 1998, p. 10).

It should also be understood that the Asian financial crisis has very little impact as such on the rest of this chapter, that is, the nature of Chinese business culture and its microeconomic manifestations.

Does an identifiable culture exist among so many people with such a diverse history as the Chinese? I think at my general level, talking only of business leadership, it is possible to say so. It is hard to define the business culture *in* China itself (much of it is secret and hidden from the government), but this is much clearer *outside* of it (Wang, 1992, p. 182). The business culture outside China is based on an identity (ibid., pp. 207–208). The Overseas Chinese have an ethnic identity with common values (Jansson, 1987, p. 6). The sense of Chineseness seems to have diminished little over distance or with the passage of time (Redding, 1993, p. 34). The business organizations of the Overseas Chinese are remarkably consistent in a number of key aspects (ibid., p. 115).

For Westerners, the frustrating thing about the Overseas Chinese business families has been that outsiders had little hope of understanding their real business or significantly participating in it (Rohwer, 1995, p. 235). However, that is changing, if for no other reason than because there are shifts of generation going on within many of their firms. The new generation is more open, quite often educated abroad, and its members know that the better aspects of Western management are needed as well for the next century.

## PHILOSOPHY, STRATEGY AND FUTURE

Everyone in China is at least half *philosopher* (Chu, 1991, p. 187). Also, Asian culture has no clearly defined division between religion, philosophy and business. Faith and philosophy are lived every day as a way of life. To understand the Chinese, for example in the context of business leadership, it is important to understand the principles by which they live and to what extent the teachings of their philosophers are still applicable today.

Chinese religion has no direct equivalent to Western or Middle Eastern scriptures, but there are mythologies as well as moral and ethical philosophical writings (Chu, 1991, p. 175). The oldest and most complete book of

Chinese mythology is the *Mountain Sea Scripture*. This is a combination of several works, some of which are over four thousand years old. This book maintains, among other things, that creation and development is a process of combining Yin and Yang forces, the female and male aspects of energy. This concept of a positive and a negative side of all things influences many aspects of Asian life and thought (ibid., pp. 175–176).

Philosophically, there are several major influences affecting Chinese thinking, including Confucianism, Buddhism and Taoism (Harris and Moran, 1979, p. 309; Hoon-Halbauer, 1994, p. 84). Of these, Confucianism turned out to be the most viable.

Kong Fu Ze, whom the Jesuit missionaries renamed Confucius, was born in 551 BC. Confucianism embraces two main streams of philosophy, political Confucianism and personal ethics (Naisbitt, 1995, p. 80). Political Confucianism laid down principles for a hierarchical political system culminating in the emperor. The stability of society is based on unequal relationships between people (Hofstede and Bond, 1988, p. 8). These relationships, *wu lun*, are five, each associated with its own virtue (Chen, 1995, p. 56): sincerity between father and son; righteousness between ruler and subjects; distinction or separate functions between husband and wife; order between older brother and younger brother; and faithfulness among friends.

During his own time, nobody listened to Confucius. It was not for many generations that the rulers discovered the advantage of popularizing Confucius's teachings to promote obedience and respect for authority (Chu, 1991, p. 180). Some Asian governments today are employing political Confucianism as an umbrella to legitimize their mode of governance:

> The resurgence in Confucian values, both on the part of Asian governments and the academic community, represents a campaign to ward off social decay – the weakening of work ethics, hedonistic consumption, excesses of individualism and agitation for participation in government (Naisbitt, 1995, p. 82).

Confucius's teachings on personal ethics have, on the other hand, been established among Chinese as a set of pragmatic rules for daily life (Hofstede and Bond, 1988, pp. 7–8; Lasserre and Schütte, 1995, p. 131; Naisbitt, 1995, p. 80). These rules, or values, include hard work, thriftiness, obedience, patience and perseverance. They are to be achieved through strict respect of traditional hierarchical relationships (those mentioned above) and the importance of acquiring skills and education (many of these values will be discussed throughout the remainder of this chapter).

Although Mao was fiercely opposed to Confucianism, the organizational model prescribed by him was not, in fact, very different from that of Confucius. The major difference was that Mao emphasized egalitarianism instead of a benevolent bureaucratic élite (Hoon-Halbauer, 1994, p. 90).

It may be asked to what extent Chinese business leaders are embracing Confucian values or whether it is so that the success of East Asian economies gave Confucianism a good name. 'Asian values' (a very debated concept today) are supposed to stress (Rohwer, 1995, p. 336):

- the family rather than the individual as the paramount unit of society;
- a preference for order over freedom and the common good over individual fulfilment;

hence:

- considerable deference to authority;
- frugality;
- belief in the virtues of education and hard work.

However, Confucian values did not originally support business and economic development, nor are they unique to Asia:

> Confucianism does entail respect for authority, for education, and for the family, but it was founded on a deep contempt for commercial life and an assumption that an unchanging society was the natural sort. The values that sustain Asia's societies work in some of the world's most commerce-minded countries in the midst of the fastest social and economic change in history. Nor are the values even peculiarly 'Asian'. They may not be the values by which life in America is conducted today, but they are not radically different from the values by which American life was conducted in the 1950s (Rohwer, 1995, pp. 336–337).

> Of course the Chinese do not have a monopoly of the values so glibly ascribed to Confucianism; such values would be just as familiar to a Samuel Smiles or a Victorian, and on a scientific plane it is well-nigh impossible to prove that the Chinese are more richly imbued with these virtues than the other races in Southeast Asia. But many Chinese have taken the idea of a 'Chinese spirit of capitalism' to imply ethnic and cultural superiority. There are plenty of Chinese in Singapore, for example, who believe that the place would not be the economic success that it is if it were populated, not by a majority of Chinese, but by a majority of Malays. Racial explanations of ability, while discredited scientifically, sadly still go down very well in uninformed quarters (Pan, 1991, p. 245).

Hofstede and Bond (1988, pp. 16–18) have tried to solve this 'paradox' by claiming that countries that developed favourably and strongly during the past few decades stressed those teachings of Confucius that are more oriented toward the future (especially perseverance and thrift), while some other countries not doing so well were oriented by Confucian values pointing at the past and the present. Hofstede and Bond refer to this as 'Confucian dynamism'. *Confucian dynamism* stresses the relative importance of (ibid., p. 17):

- persistence (perseverance);
- ordering relationships by status and observing this order;
- thrift;
- having a sense of shame.

One Confucian tradition, included in Confucian dynamism, is thrift, that is, savings and investment for the future (Rohwer, 1995, p. 54). The Chinese have learnt to endure hardship and to have self-discipline (Chu, 1991, p. 189). If families did not save for hard times by themselves, nobody else would take care of them when misfortune struck (Naisbitt, 1995, p. 54).

In Confucian dynamism the following values are relatively unimportant:

- personal steadiness and stability;
- protecting your face;
- respect for tradition;
- reciprocation of greetings, favours and gifts.

Of those 22 countries tested on this model by Hofstede and Bond, China, Hong Kong and Taiwan finished at the top. The model did not fit Singapore well, which ended up somewhere in the middle, but Singapore public policies owe less to Confucianism than to the rival Chinese tradition of 'legalism' (legalists are famous for laying the foundation of China through strict laws during the time of its first emperor). No true Confucian state would need to pass a law, as Singapore has done, requiring children to look after elderly parents. Singapore is probably also the most Westernized of all the Chinese countries.

It would probably be correct to label many East Asian countries 'neo-Confucian'. Three hallmarks of the Chinese are hard work, thrift and giving their children a good education (Naisbitt, 1995, pp. 13–14). There are many who assert that Chinese are hard-working, almost workaholics (Harris and Moran, 1979, p. 312; Jansson, 1987, p. 10). This is true for bosses as well as for workers (Rohwer, 1995, p. 52).

A top Asian *personal* value is self-reliance (Naisbitt, 1995, p. 73). Young men (and increasingly women) in the Chinese type of culture are expected to make a career for themselves; those who do not see themselves as failures (Hofstede, 1984, p. 207). Many Asian countries have made education for all a backbone of their development policy. There is an optimism and a passion to learn in the region, including a reverence for academic credentials (Lasserre and Schütte, 1995, p. 207); in business from the more recognized university the better (for instance, a top American university).

It is a common belief that the Chinese interest in philosophy also includes an interest in *strategy*:

Since Asians believe that the marketplace is a battlefield and that life is a series of battles, they also believe that mastering military strategy is essential for success, as well as for survival. Asian rulers have always placed great importance on studying the classical Chinese treatises on military strategy, the Bing-Fa. The common people have also studied them and continue to study them in order to apply their principles to the affairs of daily life (Chu, 1991, p. 12).

This should mean that modern business strategies applied by Asians can be seen as updated versions of old Chinese texts on military strategy.

This is a nice thought, but I believe it is a myth, at least as far as Overseas Chinese business *applications* are concerned. I have experienced these people as having many adequate business qualities. They are extremely good at exploiting opportunities and at deal-making; they are masters of financial, in particular cash, management; in short, they are a result of a long series of opportunistic tactical moves. They are persistent, enduring and may survive in business for a long time by simply accumulating slim short-term gains, but perseverance and long-term existence is not the same as strategic thinking! This subject will be discussed again later in this chapter.

## AUTOCRACY AND TRADITION

Characteristics of an Overseas Chinese business enterprise include *an autocratic, centralized style of management*. Authoritarianism is a primary value in Eastern cultures in general (Sitaram and Cogdell, 1976, p. 191). The Overseas Chinese management style is both a function of the family character of management (which will be discussed several times in this chapter) and a response to the hostility so often experienced in the external environment:

> The overwhelming power of the state in most Asian societies means that all important business decisions require a consensus at the highest levels of government. The need for absolute discretion during this delicate process and the risk of leaks or blackmail, for example, make it impossible to include the lower echelons of the enterprise in decision-making. Large-scale decision-making is generally executed and controlled from above (Lasserre and Schütte, 1995, p. 105).

The Chinese type of culture implies (Hofstede, 1984, p. 92):

- managers are seen as making decisions autocratically and paternalistically;
- employees fear to disagree with their boss;
- weaker perceived work ethic; more frequent belief that people dislike work;

- employees reluctant to trust each other.

Hierarchy is a primary value in Eastern cultures (Sitaram and Cogdell, 1976, p. 191). In the Chinese type of culture, this means greater centralization and tall organization pyramids (Hofstede, 1984, p. 107; Trompenaars, 1995, p. 144).

Some say that the typified Chinese organization structure is informal (Jansson, 1987, p. 28; Lasserre and Schütte, 1995, p. 105). 'Informal' is probably not the right word here, at least not in the sense of 'unconventional' and 'unconstrained', nor is the Chinese organization formal in the sense of 'planned' and 'impersonal'. The proper word for a Chinese business organization is rather *personalized*. There are conventions as well as constraints, which are not planned or impersonal, and these are given by the person in the centre of the organization (the owner or his or her representative). These conventions and constraints may change at very short notice – if the boss so decides (and the business so requires)! (The term 'formal informality' could possibly be used here – compare my discussion in Chapter 5 about Arabs.)

Another related conceptual problem is that Chinese organizations are not personnel bureaucracies (where people, but not their procedures, are controlled), nor are they work flow bureaucracies (that is, procedures but not people are controlled), as is claimed by Redding (1993, p. 176)! Personnel as well as work-flow are controlled in a typified Chinese organization, but not as fully, consistently and impersonally as in Weber's original model. In line with the above, personalized bureaucracy would be a better term to characterize Chinese organizations and management style.

Unlike Western firms that are supposed to concentrate on 'core competencies', in Chinese firms managers want to have a hand in most things connected with their business ('How to conquer ...', 17 June, 1995, p. 27). The Chinese way is to control everything ('Asia's new giants', 27 November, 1995, p. 31). And everybody who is not a key individual (a member of the extended family, functioning more on trust) is supervised (Redding, 1993, p. 217). 'Chinese leaders are control freaks' ('Information anxiety', 9 June, 1997, p. 52):

> The search for control was held by a number of people (interviewed) to be a basic instinct, somehow a natural part of being Chinese (Redding, 1993, p. 88).

Other aspects of the Chinese type of management include (Hofstede, 1984, pp. 92, 107):

- formal employee participation possible without informal consultation;
- large proportion of supervisory personnel;
- managers more satisfied with directive and persuasive superior;

● close supervision positively evaluated by subordinates.

Paternalistic family leadership is a characteristic of young enterprises all over the world. Overseas Chinese enterprises, however, appear to have a tendency to retain this patriarchal character, or extended family structure, even if they grow (Lasserre and Schütte, 1995, p. 103). The patriarchal founder owner in a Chinese enterprise is generally surrounded by an internal network of clan members who occupy all key positions (the Chinese family business will be discussed later in this chapter). Paternalistic behaviour in business leadership is common across Asia. In some societies, women are virtually absent from higher managerial levels. Korea is an extreme example of this (ibid., p. 270).

The idealistic image of this is that superiors should behave benevolently. A top Asian social value, according to Naisbitt (1995, p. 167), is 'accountability of public officials'. However, theory and principles are one thing, practice may be another. Power easily corrupts. In reality, Chinese managers may show less consideration and the extended family concept often turns into nepotism (Jansson, 1987, p. 28; Lasserre and Schütte, 1995, p. 276). One commentator claims that corruption and stultification is very much part of Chinese culture (Yang, 1991, p. 110), another that China is governed by Man, not by Law (Hofstede, 1984, p. 217). This can easily lead to gerontocracy, as is commonly the case in China itself. One Southeast Asian country notably free of corruption in business is Singapore. The Singaporean government is also proud to run what they call a meritocracy.

One characteristic of the Chinese business leaders is that their power rests on high flexibility, adaptability (Jansson, 1987, p. 28) and political pragmatism (Seagrave, 1996, p. 17). (Adaptive, flexible and pragmatic Chinese businesses will be discussed later in this chapter.) In general, the Chinese have a pragmatic view on how to get things done (scruples or no scruples) by considering each situation on its own merits, not following general guidelines. Directness combined with a lack of the Western world type of abstract thinking (more details of this will be discussed later) are shown, among other places, at the negotiation table as a focus on the immediate transaction and as an immunity to logic (Jansson, 1987, p. 27).

The Chinese are fast adapters when it may lead to business advantages (Seagrave, 1996, p. 17) and Asians in general have a high respect for learning and an openness to new ideas (Naisbitt, 1995, p. 73).

> The common thread running through all this is a willingness, one way or another, to be hooked into the outside world and judged according to its standards. And behind this willingness lies probably the deepest and most important characteristic of modern Asia: its passion for discipline, for change, and for the future (Rohwer, 1995, p. 78).

Willingness to learn and to change should *not*, generally, be taken as creativity and innovativeness here:

> Chinese culture tends to suppress individual initiative and often tames the spirit of the most resourceful individuals, rather than encouraging the sometimes erratic fire of creativity (Chu, 1991, p. 190).

The Asian insistence on the authority of parents and other seniors (Confucianism) may discourage creativity, competition and innovation. There is much concern in several Asian governments today about the lack of creativity, for instance, in its schooling system. So far, the Chinese business logic has, even if it contains many personalized characteristics as noted above, been based mainly on imitation (Lasserre and Schütte, 1995, p. 135), to imitate rather than to lead. This may 'take the form of illegal copying, counterfeiting of trademarks or simply attempts to replicate the success of a competitor by adopting the same product or service concept, or by entering the same market' (ibid., p. 135). Asians 'may regard Western technologies as part of the environment, like fruit on a tree, which wise people pick and incorporate into themselves' (Trompenaars, 1995, p. 130).

By being politically pragmatic (often corrupt in Western eyes) and sometimes by copying (occasionally illegal in the same eyes), many Chinese business millionaires (sometimes billionaires) have started from a humble trading position or an intermediary background (not very innovative professions), building up conglomerates concentrating on businesses such as property, shipping, hotels and telecoms. Because they find it hard to separate management from ownership, they tend to 'avoid industries that require the complex integration of many different skills, such as car making or aerospace' ('Fissiparous fortunes and ...', 30 November, 1996, p. 70).

This might change. Many of Asia's business empires have begun to outgrow the ability of their founders to manage them, as they become ever more complicated to run ('Fissiparous fortunes and ...', 30 November, 1996, p. 70). Megadeals are coming to an end ('Time for a ...', 2 December, 1996, p. 45): 'the days are gone when big deals were done on the basis of nothing more than a common birthplace or ancestor' (Rohwer, 1995, p. 238). Another network, that of the second-generation American-educated Chinese MBAs, is beginning to overlay the first. There is also generally more pressure to import professional management from outside the family.

## POWER AND MATERIALISM

The theme of authoritarianism is discussed further in this section. Authority is very important to a Chinese (Jansson, 1987, p. 15). In a study reported by

Naisbitt (1995, p. 73), respect for authority was a top Asian societal value. In his critical analysis of Chinese culture, Yang claims that it is 'racked by the politics of enslavement' and ingrained by an 'irrational worship of authority' (1991, pp. 110–111). Respect for authority in the Chinese culture follows a respect for seniority:

> Age is not only supposed to bring wisdom, but also gives a natural right to command. Respect for seniority is one of the basic principles of the Confucian philosophy. Islamic and Chinese cultures also accord high respect to the aged. Local personnel would be more comfortable in dealing with mature, middle-aged superiors than with younger ones (Lasserre and Schütte, 1995, p. 274).

Respect for elders is a primary value in Eastern cultures in general (Sitaram and Cogdell, 1976, p. 191), and with respect for age follows respect for hierarchical position (Hoon-Halbauer, 1994, p. 85).

*The Chinese culture is a very power-centred culture.* The Chinese-dominated countries in Southeast Asia score high in power distance (Hofstede, 1984, p. 77). Power distance connotes the differences in values and role models between higher- and lower-status individuals in a given culture. If these differences are substantial – if they call for materially different behaviour – the power distance is long. The more stratified a society, the greater are the feelings of inequality and the lesser are social interactions between people in different strata. Hofstede (ibid., pp. 94, 107) characterizes a long power distance culture like the Chinese and the Arab, among other things, as follows:

- Power is a basic fact of society which antedates good or evil. Its legitimacy is irrelevant.
- Hierarchy means existential inequality.
- There should be an order of inequality in this world in which everyone has his or her rightful place; high and low are protected by this order.
- A few should be independent; most should be dependent.
- Other people are a potential threat to a person's power and rarely can be trusted.
- The way to change a social system is by dethroning those in power.
- Low qualifications of lower strata.
- Large wage differentials.
- White-collar jobs valued more than blue-collar jobs.

There were four classes in traditional Chinese society: the scholar class occupied the highest position, followed by the farmer, labourer and merchant classes. This class membership was largely hereditary but one important

*Business leadership and culture*

possibility to move upwards was through an examination system. Even if today class distinctions are becoming somewhat blurred and classes are no longer ranked in the traditional order, the very idea of class is an ingrained part of Chinese life (Chu, 1991, pp. 185–186). Identity is based on a social class system concept and (materially based) status symbols are important (this will be discussed again later in this chapter).

A top Asian societal value is an orderly society (Naisbitt, 1995, p. 73), presumably (at least in the eyes of the power-holders) in the existing order. A few more characteristics of a long power distance society are (Hofstede, 1984, p. 92):

- parents put high value on children's obedience;
- students put high value on conformity;
- higher – and lower – educated employees show similar values about authority.

The Chinese leader is definitely a power player. Dependence on 'class' and importance of power is shown in many different ways among the Chinese. One is a general lack of communication across positions, particularly in a vertical downward direction (Chu, 1991, p. 194).

> The leadership style is authoritarian and can be best described by the word 'didactic'. In order to maintain his power, the boss controls information and transmits it piecemeal to subordinates so that they become dependent and unable to outperform him. The amount of information given to a specific subordinate depends on the degree of trust that the leader has for that individual. With the control of information, the subordinates frequently have to ask the leader for instructions (Chen, 1995, p. 88).

Withholding information to gain or maintain power is acceptable among the Chinese (Hodgetts and Luthans, 1991, p. 41). Openness is, in fact, often considered to be a sign of weakness in the Chinese culture (Samovar *et al.*, 1981, p. 41). I have personally seen examples of this in Chinese-based societies: doctors withholding information about patients leading to wrong treatment at the nurses' level; notices about unpopular changes to be made arriving the day after they are actually being effected and so on. One commentator even claims that the Chinese often prefer and feel more comfortable in a side-to-side arrangement and may feel uncomfortable when placed face to face (ibid., p. 53).

One way to show 'class' is through money and material possessions. The Chinese culture is generally very *materialistic*. The old Chinese principle of avoiding excesses to keep a proper balance between the opposite forces of Yin and Yang often seem to be neglected in our modern times. The Chinese have difficulties in letting go of money (Jansson, 1987, p. 26); there is a worship of power and money according to some (Yang, 1991, p. 111). It is not greed, however, that drives the Overseas Chinese to be so money-oriented; it is fear – and the yearning for the protection that money will give you ('A survey of business in Asia', 9 March, 1996b, p. 12).

> The work ethic of the Overseas Chinese rests on two principles: the obsessive pursuit of individual wealth is respectable because it benefits your family and your community; and it is honourable to protect personal wealth from confiscation by moving it offshore. Today it is estimated that 60 per cent of the world's money is in hiding offshore. A lot of it is Overseas Chinese money (Seagrave, 1996, p. 17).

> It is a frequent object of bemused curiosity among Westerners in Hong Kong to find Cantonese people so completely ingenuous over the topic of money. To be asked at a cocktail party how much you paid for your suit, or what you are paying your caterers, is for them perfectly normal and not something to be whispered out of earshot. It is as if many other cultures felt the need to cover the very basic fact of their personal wealth with a veil of symbols, leaving the inquisitive to interpret their meaning. Enhanced by the sensitivity to face, this technique is also embraced by the Chinese, especially the affluent, and especially via brand names with a cachet, but at the same time they show no embarrassment in probing down to the basics of what, in cash terms, will indicate your worth.
> This frankness suggests that the money itself has become for them an especially potent symbol, around which much meaning circulates (Redding, 1993, p. 39).

The materialistic orientation in a Chinese society is shown, for instance, in Singapore by such formulae for success as:

*One* wife
*Two* children
*Three* bedroom flat
*Four* wheels

Cash
Credit card
Condominium
Car
Country Club membership

Another aspect of the Chinese interest in worldly matters is that herbal medicine and aphrodisiacs is big business in their communities.

In a Chinese type of culture, achievement is defined in terms of recognition and wealth (Hofstede, 1984, p. 200).

## SALES AND QUICK RETURN

As previously pointed out, the Chinese are very secretive. They like to keep information to themselves; they do not want to expose anything about their business outside the inner family circle (this will be discussed further later in this chapter) and, as outsiders, people only have a rudimentary knowledge of Chinese management, but slowly more is being gained.

*Success is measured by numbers and marketing is limited to sales.* Such Western inventions as advertising and sales promotion hardly exist at all (except in the networking sense). The Chinese seem to deliberately avoid entering the world of mass marketing and brand name goods (Redding, 1993, p. 229). They have also no sense of after-sales service. Once a deal is done, it is done, and the nearest to anything we can call point-of-sales service would be the common Chinese practice of 'mooching'.

> Mooching among the Chinese is a popular and accepted form of behavior. If a Chinese person purchases a few eggs and some greens at the market, it is expected that the vegetable seller will throw in some green onions or a few carrots. A peddler who does not do so will not remain in business very long.
>
> This expectation of a little something extra extends to international trade. The Chinese often expect something to be tossed in for free when they buy goods. When dealing with the Chinese, it is important to build a small contingency into your price to cover the costs of mooching.
>
> The Chinese also like to discount a seller's price. The Westerner may think a professional should set a fair price and stick to it. In China, however, everyone, from early childhood on, is trained to bargain. The Chinese sometimes bargain, simply for the sake of bargaining. A British plastics dealer told me that he always adds 2 to 3 percent to the price of his goods. That way, when the bargaining begins, he can give this margin to the Chinese, allowing them to save face (Chu, 1991, p. 190).

Endless bargaining and a seemingly never-ending list, added to as the bargaining goes on, of 'that little something extra' has given the impression to outsiders that the Chinese are among the toughest negotiators in the world (Harris and Moran, 1979, p. 232). The Chinese may appear obsessed and unreasonable, even ruthless, in negotiations. There is a Chinese expression for this behaviour when it is at its extreme, that is, to have 'a thick face and a black heart', to pursue one's own ends without considering the effect of one's actions on others, and not showing any emotion in the meantime (Chu, 1991, p. 77).

Concentrating so much on sales and sales numbers may occasionally mean that quality becomes of less significance. Lack of quality control is also often a problem in the Chinese workplace.

Chinese enterprises may often appear impressive in terms of market capitalization and growth. However, looking under the hood, management may look like a mess in Western eyes (Hoon-Halbauer, 1994, p. 298; 'Fissiparous fortunes and ...', 30 November, 1996, p. 45). There is often no formalized personnel management to speak of (Hoon-Halbauer, 1994, p. 298), and constant supervision of staff is, as mentioned previously, common, and employees expect it. This is also experienced by Western expatriates working in China itself:

> Some managers spend up to half their time on staff supervision. 'We can't relax for a moment,' says a general manager at a factory in Shenzhen. 'We have to limit workers' responsibility, because there is no loyalty or trust on their part. I literally spend six hours a day doing detective work on what the staff are up to.' ('Managing in China ...', May, 1994, p. 25).

The one thing the Chinese are good at, however, is *financial business management*. Chinese entrepreneurs 'have an excellent mastery of financial levers' (Lasserre and Schütte, 1995, p. 106), and in their daily business dealing, they pay close attention to cash management. In order to always have cash available to be ready for any profitable deal that may turn up can lead a Chinese to selling his or her goods at a lower price (even at a loss) in order to move money faster and even to borrowing money in a bank and then saving it in the *same* bank again to increase his or her assurance of access to ready cash, even if the bank is changing its credit policy (Limlingan, 1986, pp. 86–91).

> Most Overseas Chinese firms are small, and all tend to be hawkeyed about cost control and financial efficiency. This is a natural result of the family-firm structure, but there is more to it than that. Whether in the majority or the minority in a given country, the Chinese rarely 'enjoyed' the sort of access to subsidized bank credit that was made available in other parts of Asia or to other ethnic groups. The Chinese lent and borrowed through a single informal market for capital that stretched throughout their diaspora, including North America and other remote outposts. The market rates of interest at which they lent (together with low taxes) encouraged their prodigious capital accumulation. The market rate at which they borrowed encouraged the efficient use of capital and the proliferation of small, labor-intensive firms (Rohwer, 1995, p. 233).

> The reader may remember that the Chinese predilection for low-margin, high-turnover business impressed an observer, Bishop Salazar of Manila, as far back as the sixteenth century. Four hundred years later, this characteristically Chinese *modus operandi* is still noticeable. A study worth citing is that of George Hicks and Gordon Redding, which looks at the largest enterprises in the Philippines and compares the ones owned by ethnic Chinese with the ones owned by Filipinos, Spaniards and Americans. The authors are interested to know how a people representing only two per cent of the population have managed to control fifty-eight per cent of the commerce, and they find, using measures such as income to sales ratio and days of accounts receivable, that, in the commercial sector especially, Chinese firms are more efficient, maintaining tougher financial control, and

that they make do with lower margins, suggesting an 'ability to persevere on the basis of a steady accumulation of small returns' (Pan, 1991, p. 241).

As long as the Chinese make money, they feel that time is on their side. On the other hand, thinking in terms of sales and financial outcome makes the Chinese prone to short-term thinking (Jansson, 1987, p. 23; Lasserre and Schütte, 1995, p. 131). However, foreign firms trying to do business with the Chinese should not think short term. A lot of time is involved in acquiring experience and cultivating relationships for an outsider. Laboriously established connections can easily break down. The point is not to work with the Chinese in the sense of a complete strategic package, but accumulating trust, one step at a time. Time is not equal to money for the Chinese, as it tends to be in the West. In the Chinese culture, time is time, and money is money.

The Chinese are patient and impatient at the same time. They can be very patient in hammering out a business deal and discussing business in general, but they often lack patience in their daily lives (Chu, 1991, p. 195). It shows in their behaviour in queues, getting on and off a bus, in traffic in general or when boarding and disembarking an aeroplane, just to mention a few examples.

The Chinese have also mixed attitudes towards time and worry:

> The Chinese feel that if you don't worry about the future, trouble will quickly descend upon you. Most Chinese would rather worry about the possibility of trouble in their future than enjoy the present and deal with trouble if and when the time comes. They 'worry now' in hopes that they will have no worries in the future. This contrasts sharply with their acceptance of fate once it arrives (Chu, 1991, p. 196).

So, the Chinese are running a tight ship and they replace strategic thinking by *flexibility*. Whether this should be called strategy or not is arguable:

> It is common observation that Overseas Chinese organizations are flexible and that this is a great strength. They can switch products quickly, chief executives can act decisively, the economies which contain them can display over time smooth transitions from one type to another: from, for instance, a concentration on semi-skilled assembly of consumer expendables to skilled manufacture of durable industrial components; from low tech to high tech; from commerce to manufacturing; from plastic flowers to wigs, to toys, to printed circuit boards. Each of these large-scale shifts of emphasis in an economy is the aggregate result of myriad strategic changes by single companies carried out without crisis, with little bankruptcy, and with often complex internal adjustments such as those of technology and labor skills. Such organizations are patently some of the world's most adaptive.
>
> There are a number of fundamental structural features of the Chinese family business which are conducive to strategic flexibility. The first of these is its small scale, and the second is the simple decision-making structure. A related factor connected with smallness of scale is the common tendency to avoid being committed by technology to one product market (Redding, 1993, pp. 221–222).

# FAMILISM

Asian tradition puts the rights of the group ahead of those of any individual (Seagrave, 1996, p. 367). In Asian cultures, individuals have a very deep attachment and sense of belonging to social groups (Hoon-Halbauer, 1994, p. 85; Lasserre and Schütte, 1995, p. 270). Asian countries score very low on individualism (Hofstede, 1984, p. 158).

At the same time, if an attempt is made to put together a coherent picture of Chinese culture in relation to harmony, conflicts and cooperation, it seems rather mixed. *On one hand* it has been stated that a top Asian societal value is harmony (Naisbitt, 1995, p. 73). A Chinese wants to be in harmony with nature (Harris and Moran, 1979, p. 313) and 'the Chinese have never been warlike' (Chu, 1991, p. 188). There is a doctrine in Chinese culture stressing tradition, continuity and links with the past. Avoiding conflicts is one Chinese way to keep the social harmony (Jansson, 1987, p. 27; Lasserre and Schütte, 1995, pp. 272–273). The Confucian tradition has emphasized cooperation. According to some reports, the Chinese is a fair person (Harris and Moran, 1979, p. 311) and a top Asian personal value is honesty (Naisbitt, 1995, p. 73).

*On the other hand* it has been stated that the Chinese are suspicious and do not trust others (Jansson, 1987, p. 14). They lack unity (Chu, 1991, p. 193) and they are unable to cooperate among themselves (Yang, 1991, pp. 14, 110). The Chinese are inclined to avoid involvement (Chu, 1991, pp. 191–192), especially with government and its interferences (Rohwer, 1995, p. 231).

An answer to these contradictions if two things are kept in mind could be:

1. Harmony and tradition are aspects of Confucian teachings, which have been stressed by governments and the élite more or less throughout the centuries to foster the ideal of conformity. As has been said previously, it is not to be taken for granted that these values are honoured in other social classes or at the grassroots level.
2. The societal unit in Chinese culture is *the family*. In the Chinese type of culture individuals are born into extended families or clans which protect them in exchange for loyalty (Hofstede, 1984, p. 17). An individual in Asia is not an individual in the Western sense of a person in isolation, but includes also his or her relations (Jansson, 1987, p. 8; Bjerke, 1998). Chinese values are based more on personal obligations than individual rights. Confidence *is* important to a Chinese, but it stays within the family. There is little or no trust beyond this unit – and also no cooperation (Chau, 1991, p. 165). Bickering and squabbling (even fist fights) are not an unusual scene on the streets in Chinese societies, but in most cases they do not take place among members of the same family or

*Business leadership and culture*

clan. Finally, the Chinese do not want to work alone but in groups. However, the group should not be too big – the size of a family is about right.

The importance of the family and of strong family ties among Asians in general and maybe particularly so for the Chinese is certified by many (Harris and Moran, 1979, p. 311; Chau, 1991, p. 161; Chu, 1991, pp. 200–201; Hoon-Halbauer, 1994, p. 89).

> In Asia, the maintenance and development of a person's membership in a group – whether a family or a firm – takes priority over the assertion of individual identity. Compliance with group norms is expected and individualistic behaviour is discouraged and sometimes condemned outright. Individual transactions are often based on membership of groups or networks. This particular and deeply ingrained trait has important implications for human resource management. Expatriate managers who encourage one-on-one competition between their local managers, or reward individual performance rather than group or team performance, may encounter resistance. This does not mean that individual performance should be left unrewarded. In Hong Kong and Singapore, individual performance is expected to earn a pay-off. The difference lies in the way in which the reward is granted; in general, individual rewards (or punishments) should be handled in private, while team rewards are always public and ceremonial. These categories are mutually reinforcing; in Asia, even the most self-centred and ambitious person will still do things on behalf of his or her team or organisation (Lasserre and Schütte, 1995, pp. 271–272).

One reason why the Chinese family system is so important is that it provides security in an insecure world (Jansson, 1987, p. 27). Motherhood is a primary value in Eastern cultures (Sitaram and Cogdell, 1976, p. 191). McCaffrey and Hafner (1985) tell the story of a question posed to groups of Asian and American businesspeople: 'If you were on a sinking ship with your wife, your child, and your mother who could not swim, which one would you save if you could rescue only one?' In the USA about 60 per cent chose the child and about 40 per cent the wife, with none choosing the mother. All the Asians chose the mother. With husbands often away from home on business, women as mothers are the de facto authority for their children (Wong, 1995, p. 141).

'Asian values' (a concept which was mentioned previously) include a strong feeling of familism. The former Singaporean prime minister, Lee Kuan Yew, has said repeatedly that the family is the bedrock of the society. On the other hand, Chinese families (like their businesses) are typically ruled very autocratically. This can be understood from surveys carried out in China finding that 90 per cent of children are discontented with their parents and 80 per cent are regularly beaten. At the same time, 'Chinese men ... adopt the posture that real men are wife-fearing' (Chu, 1991, pp. 202–203).

Families are not only the bedrock of the Chinese society, they are also the bedrock of Chinese business ('Fissiparous fortunes and ...', 30 November, 1996, p. 69). A Chinese firm is almost always a family firm (Jansson, 1987, p. 27). This is especially so in the Overseas Chinese business system (Chen, 1995, p. 84; Rohwer, 1995, p. 232). Peter Drucker has expressed it such that 'the secret of Japan consists in Japan's ability to make a family out of modern corporation. The secret of Chinese management may well consist in the ability of the Chinese to make the family into a modern corporation' (Drucker and Nakauchi, 1997, p. 7). Comparing Japanese and Chinese management, it can also be said that Japanese-style management may be described as 'head-office-oriented', while Chinese-style management may be characterized as 'family-oriented' (Tanaka *et al.*, 1992, p. 18). However, as mentioned previously, a 'family' may for a Chinese include the same ethnic background and even birthplace. Kinship terms (such as 'uncle' and 'auntie') are widely used in social interaction, even if not genealogically related (Wong, 1995, p. 141). The Overseas Chinese have built up their strength, among other factors, on an unusual ethnic solidarity (Seagrave, 1996, p. 17).

The implicit model of the Chinese organization is the family. This is supported by several researchers (Hofstede, 1984, pp. 215–217; Jansson, 1987, p. 8; Lasserre and Schütte, 1995, pp. 129–131). The senior manager/owner has a patriarchal relationship with his subordinates and decisions are made in the best interest of 'the family' (Jansson, 1987, p. 27). Characteristics of Chinese firms include (Hofstede, 1984, pp. 166–167, 171, 173–174; Trompenaars, 1995, pp. 85–86; Lasserre and Schütte, 1995, pp. 135–136):

- managers rate having security in their position more important;
- managers aspire to conformity and orderliness;
- managers endorse 'traditional' points of view, not supporting employee initiative and group activity;
- promotion from inside and on seniority;
- expertise, order, duty, security provided by organization or clan, in China even housing (not in Singapore);
- business logic is reliance on personal commitment in organic business entities;
- more importance attached to training and use of skills in jobs, rather than to individual self-fulfilment.

It was mentioned earlier that Chinese business orientation is, in a way, short term. One reason for this could be the approach taken to inheritance and succession in the Chinese business firm. After the death of the business founder, each legitimate son by birthright is entitled to a share of the property and other economic resources of the deceased (*coparcenary*). In contrast, in

Japan, a father is succeeded by one male heir only (*primogeniture*) (Chau, 1991, pp. 162–164). The former can easily lead to fragmentation of economic resources and lack of corporate longevity. Also, the door is open to family feuds and succession squabbles, which is a threat to some Asian family-run conglomerates today ('Fissiparous fortunes and ...', 30 November, 1996, p. 70).

There is tremendous strength in the family tradition in Chinese conglomerates, but several problems are obvious today (Redding, 1993, p. 135; Chen, 1995, pp. 91–93; Drucker, 1995, pp. 179–180):

- The founders who still run the groups are, in the majority of cases, getting old. The successors to the founders have grown up in a very different world, and many are Western-educated. What will be the consequences of a generation shift?
- In order for many of these conglomerates to grow, they will have to go into joint ventures with all kinds of foreigners. Will they be able to do that?
- Many conglomerates will have to import experts in various fields, that is, give information to nonfamily members. Problems?
- To run a business as family can never be entirely rational. A brother may not be the best manager and a cousin may not provide the best supplies. Does this mean a slow change of identity in Chinese conglomerates if they want to become more effective?

The optimist will say that as Chinese enterprises get increasingly absorbed into the international capitalist pattern, they will lose their distinctiveness, their tribal loyalties will no longer remain primitively uppermost, and the us-them demarcations that so bedevil race relations will blur. By his membership in the worldwide society of capitalists, the modern Chinese magnate will feel happier in the company of those who operate on the same urbane, cosmopolitan scale, whether they are Chinese or not, than among those who earn a living selling Hainanese Chicken Rice or hawking ice-cream. His social circle, overlapping with his business one, is more likely to be built up from contacts made through membership of the Rotary and Golf Clubs than through those of clan halls and dialect associations. At this end of the business scale, it is not so much being Hokkien or Cantonese that matters as class (Pan, 1991, p. 241).

Family businesses dominate in the economies of many countries, of course (Braadbaart, 1995, pp. 179–180). Boswell found that the boards of nearly two out of three medium-size British manufacturing enterprises (25–500 employees) were family-dominated (Boswell, 1973, p. 248); according to one estimate, 80 to 90 per cent of all Dutch businesses are family-owned (*Sociaal Economische Raad*, 1990); Pollack reports that 'family farm products accounted for 67.6 percent of the value of farm products sold in the U.S.

in 1974' (Pollack, 1985, p. 591); comparable findings have been reported for rural agricultural and industrial enterprises in India (Upadhya, 1988, pp. 1,376–1,382, 1,433–1,442). However, the 'family' in a Chinese 'family firm' is a much stronger unit than in most other cases. There is, for instance, a strict line between family and nonfamily among Chinese both in attitude and behaviour. Also, growth in Chinese business is commonly achieved not by expanding the same firm too far (then possibly losing the family control), but by adding another family unit, run by a relative.

## *GUAN-XI*

The Asian business environment can be best described as a series of interlocked networks (Lasserre and Schütte, 1995, p. 124). It is a key element of Chinese business (Hoon-Halbauer, 1994, p. 85). The distinctive feature of the Overseas Chinese model has never been the individual firm, but the network of them (Rohwer, 1995, pp. 240–241). In Chinese this is called *guan-xi*, which can be translated as 'relationships' or 'connections'.

Everywhere in the business world contacts are needed, but their importance must be magnified many times to understand *guan-xi* (Chu, 1991, p. 199). Hundreds of books have been written about *guan-xi*, but it takes a lifetime to master. Every society in Asia is built around relationships and it is more than a matter of degree compared with the West. The Chinese include their relationships as part of understanding themselves as individuals. This philosophy has deep roots:

> *Guanxi* grew out of an agricultural society in which people swapped favours with neighbours, relatives and friends of friends. Like fishermen, Chinese make nets of *guanxi* in which knots are tied with marriage, school, clubs, secret societies, both forward and backward in time. You can collect *guanxi* built up by your mother or grandfather. It can be inherited or conveyed. Under communism, business was not arranged for profit but for *guanxi*, a different kind of collateral that bypasses official channels. *Guanxi* eases pain. It stops bullets. Feuds are ended by calling in someone obliged by *guanxi* to both parties, who negotiates a settlement. Some Chinese keep records of *guanxi* in ledgers. A Singapore programmer has developed software to keep track of *guanxi* (Seagrave, 1996, p. 341).

In the West there is networking as only an aspect of ongoing business; in Asia, there is networking before a business is started and then networking takes a leading role again in further promoting the business ('And never the ...', 29 March, 1997, p. 73).

*Guan-xi* is based on mutual obligations. In an extended family, members are mutually obligated to help one another; a wealthy member helps a poor one. Also, in business organizations, it is rather common for members of a family to use their family connections to try to obtain jobs or other benefits (Hoon-Halbauer, 1994, p. 88).

However, *guan-xi*, which tends to be more utilitarian than emotional, goes beyond the biological family. It is also relevant to other ties, such as clan, shared surname, home village, region, education or other shared experience (Hoon-Halbauer, 1994, p. 88). Good *guan-xi* both inside and outside the firm is a guarantee of success at the personal as well as at the professional level (ibid., p. 89).

The Overseas Chinese found that dialect, kinship or common origin in a clan or a village gave a more sure footing of trust to a business deal conducted even at a great distance (Rohwer, 1995, p. 233). In fact, Overseas Chinese power rests on an underground network. Regional identity is important to a Chinese everywhere in the world. Same-native-place ties can play a crucial role:

> A Hokkien firm is one city did not export goods to a Teochiu firm in another. As merchants travelled in search of goods and markets, members of the same clan or guild could draw upon a line of credit wherever they went. To default on such a loan was rare, for that would jeopardize the *shinyung*, or personal trust, that provides the only social security in Chinese life (Seagrave, 1996, pp. 173–174).

For the Chinese, networking is a natural thing to do (Seagrave, 1996, p. 341). It is a natural tendency for a Chinese manager (as well as for an Arab) to focus on the person who can best resolve the particular problem or clinch the deal (Lasserre and Schütte, 1995, p. 124). Business with a Chinese over and above simple buying and selling is to a large extent based on trust. Chinese business boils down to contacts. Trust does not, however, exist naturally between people for a Chinese and it may take a long time to establish, if commonality does not exist, for example, in dialect or birthplace. Trust is intimately associated with obligation and duty for a Chinese. 'A common business interest' is itself not enough for him or her to trust somebody else.

The importance of influential contacts is characteristic of all Asian societies (Chu, 1991, p. 200), but more so in some societies than in others. *Guan-xi* is more important in China, the Philippines and Indonesia than, for instance, in Singapore (Lasserre and Schütte, 1995, p. 127). The Chinese society is neither individual-based nor society-based, but rather relation-based (Liang, 1974, p. 95). In fact, moving around and doing business in China is almost impossible without *guan-xi* (Chu, 1991, p. 199).

> *Guanxi* is the only way business can be conducted inside China. It gives you the best ventures, the best choices, the best prices. *Guanxi* is vital in places where there have been few, if any, legal controls. In such a place, you are completely adrift without *guanxi* (Seagrave, 1996, pp. 341–342).

In order to get things done in China, a person must cultivate the right connections, but do it carefully, trying to avoid 'those who are likely to fall out of favour' (Hoon-Halbauer, 1994, p. 88).

The Chinese network of networks is a new paradigm, a new formulation within the framework of the world's economy. It is, according to Naisbitt (1995, p. 7), the organizational model for the twenty-first century. Its importance and power rest on several characteristics (Lasserre and Schütte, 1995, p. 106; Naisbitt, 1995, pp. 5–7; Rohwer, 1995, p. 234; Seagrave, 1996, p. 17):

- It links a multitude of autocratic owner-managed firms intimately and instantaneously together, which means fast decision-making and acute sensitivity.
- Everybody can be in the centre (their own centre) and be their own boss, which is what the Chinese want. The Internet can be used as a model: it is very decentralized and no one is in charge, except the market.
- The participants are intensely competitive among themselves and exclude outsiders, but when necessary they will close ranks and cooperate.
- Individual members can function effectively, nimbly and speedily, they can test their own information in the network and they can get access to exceptional information from others.
- The network has made it possible for the Chinese to enter a variety of business ventures with a variety of local partners.

These networks also have several consequences (Jansson, 1987, p. 5; Chu, 1991, pp. 158–159; Hoon-Halbauer, 1994, pp. 88–89; Lasserre and Schütte, 1995, p. xvi):

- The man at the top does not have to be the boss; seniority and connections carry more weight. To be a good manager, a Chinese must be good at 'connectionology'; knowing the business and having management skills come second. Also, a well-connected manager is more likely to be less controlled by his superiors.
- Different networks are needed for different purposes, for example, one network for supplies, one for getting the appropriate signatures, one for securing distribution, and so on.
- Relationships count more than market efficiency and groups and networks matter more than individuals – the model of *homo economicus* must be questioned in the Chinese business setting.

Westerners tend to shrink away from the *guan-xi* system and associate it too quickly with bribery ('And never the ...', 29 March, 1997, p. 73). They find it cumbersome and difficult to understand (Lasserre and Schütte, 1995, p. 126). In the West, the cultivation of relationships is often equated with corruption. However, in Asia, what most Westerners define as corrupt is sometimes considered both acceptable and even indispensable. There are also fewer social sanctions on it (ibid., p. 128). It will take years before Asian markets become as transparent as in the West, if they ever will (or want); in the meantime, *guan-xi* and good local partners is what counts ('And never the ...', 29 March, 1997, p. 74).

The aggregate impact of Chinese family-owned firms depends on their network. These firms may not be impressive individually, but in a big network, they can have a role to play even on the world business stage. This is happening today, partly because China itself is joining these networks (Naisbitt, 1995, p. 7; Rohwer, 1995, p. 234).

Without *guan-xi*, you are nothing; with *guan-xi*, you cannot do wrong (Chu, 1991, p. 199). Friendship in a network means a lot to a Chinese. For example (ibid., pp. 154–155):

- When you are ill, your doctor friend will treat you without charge.
- Your lawyer friend will always help you with your legal problems without charge.
- If you must go on an extended trip, a friend will care for your children at his or her own expense, even if you are gone for a year or more.
- Your merchant friend will sell his or her goods to you at a substantial discount. If he or she is a very good friend, he or she will sell at or below cost.
- If a friend is travelling to an area where you have relatives or other friends, he or she will deliver anything from messages to furniture for you.

Also, the Chinese are not strangers to interpreting the law creatively through friends. Trompenaars (1995, pp. 33–35, 38–39) reports on two studies, where the Chinese expect to be tipped off by friends for inside confidential information and where they expect friends to testify that they behaved legally (even if they did not).

## FACE AND PRESTIGE

Cultures may stress various parts of the body. For a Westerner, the 'heart' is important (that is where our feelings are supposed to be); for a Japanese, it is the 'stomach' (the centre of harmony). An important aspect of Chinese culture is 'face' (Hoon-Halbauer, 1994, p. 85).

The Chinese concept of face has two meanings (Hofstede, 1984, p. 151; Jansson, 1987, pp. 9–10; Hoon-Halbauer, 1994, p. 87). One (*li-an*) concerns a person's moral character and honour, the other (*mian-zi*) connotes reputation and prestige. Both are important in social interactions considering the importance of recognition by others in Chinese culture. They are often mixed when the Chinese interact with each other to protect, save, add, give, exchange or even borrow 'face'. *Mian-zi*, however, 'enters more into everyday transactions as a form of social currency' (Redding and Ng, 1982, p. 207).

The Chinese fear of losing face is the fear of having their ego and prestige deflated. It can be caused by a broad range of things: having an expected promotion fall through; a child failing an examination; a daughter marrying a poor man; a brother working in a lowly position; receiving an inexpensive gift and so on. (Chu, 1991, p. 197).

The logical counterpart to 'losing' face is 'gaining' face. The prestige of a Chinese may be inflated by working in a large company, by being surrounded by influential 'friends', by showing off materially and so on.

*Asian cultures stress 'shame' and Western cultures stress 'guilt'.* Shame is associated with public disgrace and loss of prestige and guilt carries a sense of individual responsibility and conscience (Lasserre and Schütte, 1995, p. 273). The importance of shame for a Chinese makes it difficult for him or her to admit a mistake (Jansson, 1987, p. 17; Yang, 1991, p. 14) or to ask for help (Lasserre and Schütte, 1995, p. 273). Also, they are not happy to be told how to do things, especially in public (Jansson, 1987, p. 17).

The importance of 'face' in Chinese society is well caught by the Hokkien term *kiasu*, which can be translated as 'afraid to lose out'. This is used in some Chinese societies to describe the Chinese fear of being left out or left behind, which to Westerners can sometimes give the impression that the Chinese do not want to miss any opportunity which someone else is taking (even if none of them gains anything).

Face is important in business as well, of course (Jansson, 1987, pp. 19–20):

- Gaining 'face' leads to strong feelings of satisfaction, pride and confidence. Losing 'face' brings negative feelings, which are equally strong.
- 'Face' is justified primarily for pragmatic reasons, and it is instrumental in reaching several goals and has many effects. It is difficult to understand this complex of 'facial effects'; it requires conscious measures as well as instinct.
- 'Face' is mutual. What is given should be returned; it becomes a delicate social balancing act.
- 'Face' is mainly of relevance in social relations between colleagues, but also in business relations in, for example, purchasing, banking and

personal sales. In relations with public institutions it is of less importance, probably because these contacts are more official and
bureaucratic.
- Even if 'face' is important in hierarchical vertical relations within
companies, it is more important in horizontal social relations.
- Status is important when gaining 'face'.

Associated with face and prestige are some Chinese 'specialities' (not unrelated to each other):

- The Chinese have always held themselves in high esteem. The name of
their country translates as 'middle kingdom', implying the centre of
human civilization. This attitude continued until modern times, when
the Chinese met Europeans and Americans and the Chinese expected
respect and understanding as a prerequisite for working and doing
business with them (Harris and Moran, 1979, p. 308).
- The Chinese may make a practice of emphasizing and de-emphasizing
cultural differences between Asia and the West. It is important for
foreign businesspeople to understand which situations are the result of
true cultural differences and which are just manipulation strategies
(Chu, 1991, p. 164).
- The Chinese may speak deceptively (Yang, 1991, p. 111). It is common for them to criticize someone who is not present, but through
subtle hints indicate that the criticism is also meant to apply to someone who is (Chu, 1991, p. 67). The Chinese also often speak in
euphemisms and by circumlocution. This is especially true when they
speak humbly. They may not want to advertise their qualifications even
though they feel they have them (ibid., p. 194).

## SUPERSTITIOUS AND DARING

Most Asians are *superstitious*. When the Chinese are faced with an important
decision, they may seek auspicious signs or consult oracular books or for-
tune-tellers. They may also give special significance to colour, generally
favouring red (for life) and gold (for prosperity) (Chu, 1991, pp. 162–163).
Being superstitious is one way to 'cushion oneself' against failure in the face
of risk (Wong, 1995, p. 144).

The prevalence of certain traditional mystical or superstitious practices in China
and South-East Asia may come as a surprise to the unprepared Western manager.
Even in the more industrialised and Westernised Chinese societies, notably Hong

Kong, Taiwan and Singapore, certain traditional practices still prevail and should not be overlooked. To cite one example: geomancy, also known as *feng shui*, or the divination and interpretation of certain landscape features and sacred sites, is still widely practiced in the Chinese world. In practical terms this means that real-estate purchases and building sites must first be approved by a geomancer. Whether Western expatriate managers approve of this process or not, they should not disregard the fact that their Asian staff and colleagues will consider it an important procedure (Lasserre and Schütte, 1995, p. 276).

Chinese thinking is also somewhat fatalistic and very direct (Jansson, 1987, p. 11; Weidenbaum and Hughes, 1996, pp. 57–58). The Chinese may, in fact, have problems thinking in abstract terms as these terms are understood in the West, that is, to mentally experiment with a symbolic model and think of events and objects as something to be manipulated in hypothetical experiments (Jansson, 1987, p. 21). Furthermore, having a circular sense of time, they believe that much of what is going on happens as a result of fate (Chu, 1991, p. 189).

One example of the Chinese lack of abstract thinking (the way Westerners look at it) is that they do not look at their companies calculatively, as impersonal and purposive, but much more as parts of themselves, even existential. Also, the striking lack of abstracts in the Chinese language leads to different thought processes from those normal in Indo-European languages (Redding, 1993, p. 141). The Chinese think about problems as deeply embedded in a context, out of which explanations cannot be torn (ibid., p. 77).

On the other hand, taking decisions directly, relationally and specifically as the Chinese often do, gives them a trust in themselves and in common sense, plus a high willingness to take risks and an ability to face uncertainty. The Chinese score low on uncertainty avoidance (Hofstede, 1984, p. 122) and *they excel in risk-taking* (Jansson, 1987, p. 22; Chen, 1995, p. 108).

Low uncertainty avoidance may include less hesitation to change employer (Hofstede, 1984, p. 132). In fact, job-hopping has become a problem in an advanced, mature society like Singapore. The Overseas Chinese would not have been so successful without their boldness in risk-taking. The Chinese are also well known to be compulsive gamblers.

## LOCALISM

The Chinese are different. In this last section on Chinese culture I have put together some examples of Chinese behaviour which we can read about in various publications and which I have experienced myself, behaviour which may seem 'peculiar' and 'strange' to a Westerner at first:

- The Chinese are proud of being what they are to the extent that, throughout much of their long history, they have maintained a self-imposed isolation (as did the Japanese). This was not out of fear of the outside world, but out of a sense that there could not be much of interest to learn from it. Today, the Chinese still feel an innate sense of cultural superiority to all other people. They call foreigners *lao wai*, a term of denigration that translates literally as 'outsider' (Chu, 1991, pp. 165–166). This feeling of superiority has made them very culture-patriotic.

  The Chinese want to feel distinct and convey a feeling of 'Chineseness', which is not always pushy, but which may be deep and influential (Jansson, 1987, p. 27). They regard it as natural to feel that their race, their nation, their province, their city and their family are better than ours. A Westerner would call it 'racism', which is an ugly word in English, even though it often only expresses the common weakness of humanity to believe that 'mine is better than yours' (Chu, 1991, p. 8).

  The Chinese have a strong sense of history, and events during this last century have created a distrust of foreigners in some of them (this is understandable due to many humiliations that the Chinese have experienced from encounters with foreigners during this period). The Chinese also describe the Americans with the term *tean-zen*, which means 'childlike'. They feel that American history is simple, uncomplicated, short, peaceful and rather pleasant (Chu, 1991, p. 172).

  Western businesspeople would be wise to recognize the shadow cast by the past 150 years of mistreatment that the Chinese have suffered, not to impose on them their own norms and be patient, even if persistent, showing sensitivity and respect (Harris and Moran, 1979, p. 328).

  One consequence of the Chinese interest in being distinct is that they have not been very good (and maybe not even interested) in building successful multinational corporations outside their own region.

- A Chinese wants to assert him- or herself to the extent that he or she may behave selfishly (this may be the result of the realities of survival; unselfishness is a virtue most often practised where there is enough for everyone). In his brutally frank analysis of Chinese culture, Yang (1991) claims that this is because the Chinese feels basically very insecure and he characterizes them in terms like 'overbearing selfishness', 'self-centred world view' and 'arrogance and carelessness' (ibid., p. 111). The Chinese have a tendency to be judgemental (Chu, 1991, p. 198) and, as previously mentioned, they do not hesitate to further themselves through contacts (Ralston *et al.*, 1993, p. 160).

- The Chinese are very relaxed when it comes to work, and they take time to gossip and talk about basic amenities while drinking tea.

However, as previously stated, they put in long hours each day and generally work six days per week with only one major holiday per year, that is, the Chinese New Year (Harris and Moran, 1979, p. 325).

- The Chinese are fond of gossiping and are always interested in what their neighbours are doing (Chu, 1991, p. 198; Yang, 1991, p. 111). The Chinese believe they have a greater capacity for jealousy than Westerners but, strangely, there is an unspoken rule that their jealousy be directed towards each other and not towards foreigners (Chu, 1991, p. 195). Remember the term *kiasu*, which was mentioned earlier.

- The Chinese seem to have a lack of regard for public property:

The selfish attitude of the Chinese has led to a total disregard for public property. The extent of damage inflicted upon public buildings in China by abuse and neglect is extreme. Even relatively new buildings are in such a state as to cause disbelief among Westerners.

Littering and spitting in public places are examples of the Chinese disregard for public property. Even a Chinese official will tidy up the interior of his car by throwing trash into the street. Although it is not done in hotels and restaurants that Westerners frequent, in Chinese restaurants patrons think nothing of spitting and throwing trash on the floors (Chu, 1991, p. 193).

Some of the characteristics of the Chinese described above, and in particular in this section, may seem unpleasant to an outsider. However, remember that others should not be judged by our own criteria and standards. To reiterate, *all cultures are different and Asians and Westerners think as differently as they speak*. China is one of the most high-contextual cultures there is (Ferraro, 1994, p. 51). On one hand, the Chinese have a high regard for the written word, as seen in their poetry and paintings (Harris and Moran, 1979, p. 312), but this does not, on the other hand, stop them from having a creative attitude to the texts of laws as well as contracts. Those engaging in business with the Chinese should not be surprised to experience changes in Chinese requests at any phase of a project, even long after the contract has been signed and work has begun (Chu, 1991, p. 197). This is because the Chinese (as well as the Japanese) negotiate a relationship more than a contract *per se* (Chen, 1995, pp. 237–238).

## A TYPIFIED INTERPRETATION OF CHINESE BUSINESS LEADERS

The Chinese culture has been discussed focusing on certain themes. These are summarized in Table 6.3. Based on these themes, it is possible to give a typified interpretation of Chinese business leaders as follows:

*Table 6.3    The Chinese culture themes*

---

- Philosophy, strategy and future
- Autocracy and tradition
- Power and materialism
- Sales and quick return
- Familism
- *Guan-xi*
- Face and prestige
- Superstitious and daring
- Localism

---

- They belong to a very old civilization with many of its values still preserved; have many compatriots; have their roots in China; feel strong ties to blood and geography.
- They operate in, and dominate, a part of the world which has been booming until recently, where a sense of optimism has been common and shared; have been part of a growth pattern which was unprecedented in history.
- They have learnt to endure hardship and have self-discipline; put in many hours of work; value thriftiness, obedience, patience and perseverance in business, but may be very impatient in private life; are highly flexible, adaptable and pragmatic; have creative attitudes to the letter of laws and contracts; are willing to initiate and to learn, but not to innovate.
- They may have started as traders or as other intermediaries and are good (even ruthless) negotiators; probably run a family business and see the family as very important, a safe harbour in an unruly world.
- They are extremely good at networking, use it to the fullest and operate in networks as extended families, defined by ethnicity, geography and other kinds of common background of members, strictly closed to outsiders; find friends within the networks but are reluctant to trust outsiders; are very secretive and do not want any interference in their businesses from outside.
- They are proud and have a strong sense of identity; are self-reliant (even selfish) but honour (and use) obligations in their networks of contacts; have respect for education, but are direct and practical; are very superstitious but willing to take risks.
- They are at least half philosophers, but look at phenomena in relation to their context rather than in abstract and isolated terms; are not fond

of strategic planning as a separate, isolated thinking process, but rather build up their firms as flexible and adaptive mechanisms.

- They are autocratic and paternalistic (in business as well as within the family) and use a centralized style of management with tight control of employees; are power-centred, have respect for seniority and for traditional hierarchical relationships and prefer order; enjoy their status, money and material wealth.
- They judge success in their business ventures mainly by sales figures; may neglect (and find irrelevant) the more subtle aspects of management and service; are very good at finance and particularly cash management; are always willing to discuss a deal.
- They grow by establishing new units like 'mushrooms through an underground mycelium', opened up by relatives, rather than expanding the existing unit beyond family control.
- They look at honour, reputation, shame and prestige as very important (and guilt and conscience as less important); want to gain 'face', not lose it.

# 7.   Japanese culture

## INTRODUCTION

There are many myths about Japan:

> Our myths arise from the fact that we are a group of narrow islands off the coast of Asia, coming only sporadically into contact with our continental neighbours down through the years. We take comfort in our homogeneity, in our capacity to absorb influences from the mainland at our own pace, in timespans measured by centuries rather than decades. For us, much more than for Britain, 'the jungle begins at Calais' – in our case, the Korea Strait. In essence, we see ourselves as a cosy village society where consensus is the norm and where we all live by unspoken rules to make life tolerable in a green but crowded land with few national resources ('The third opening', 9 March, 1996a, p. 19).

The first challenge to Japan came in 1853 when an American fleet dropped anchor in Tokyo (then known as Edo) Bay and demanded that Japan open its door to trade with the world. Until then, the Shoguns had kept the country closed for 250 years. The reform that came with the collapse of the Shogunate and the establishment of a reform-minded government under Emperor Meiji is known today as 'the first opening of Japan'.

Japan's surrender in 1945 and the sweeping reforms brought about during the occupation by American forces constitute what is called 'the second opening of Japan'. This opening, like the first, began as a result of conflict with foreigners. Reforms that followed were genuinely popular with voters and included: land reform, dissolution of *zaibatsu* (giant financial and industrial trusts), freedom of speech, free trade unions and a new constitution ('The third opening', 9 March, 1996a, pp. 19–20). Under the impetus of these reforms, Japan concentrated single-mindedly on economic recovery and growth and became known to the world as an economic superpower.

Thus, much of what we today regard as the unique Japanese industrial system was forced by necessity in the turmoil of the post-World War II days, even if it was built on a solid bed of basic cultural values (Ohmae, 1982, p. 217). In fact, the trauma of the war and post-war years so affected the Japanese economy that it may be considered to have been *reborn in the post-war years* (Humes, 1993, p. 273).

Late industrialisation helped to spur Japan's economy to grow at rates that were never possible in the West. Until about 1970, Japan applied technologies invented elsewhere, then sold the results to consumers enriched by earlier industrial revolutions. And fast growth, in turn, was a big reason for Japan's distinctive habits and institutions. It encouraged high investment and exports, holding down consumption. It also meant that managers needed special tools. They had to have a guaranteed supply of labour, so they invented life-time employment. They needed a completely reliable supply of parts, so they fostered long-term relationships with subcontractors. And they wanted access to capital, which they secured through long-term relationships with banks. Links with banks and subcontractors were cemented by another distinctive feature: Japan's system of cross-shareholdings ('A survey of Japan', 9 July, 1994, p. 17).

The Japanese became known as 'the world's most prominent borrowers from other cultures of everything from management to technology' (Johnson, 1988, p. 41). Managers were new to the challenge of running modern factories, so they had few fixed ideas. They learnt bit by bit by discussing each step with shop-floor workers. However, it was easier to import industrial technology than new social attitudes. The resulting mix of modern industry with old feudal ideas was quality circles, excellent industrial relations, teamwork and governmental administrative guidance, just to mention a few characteristics of manifestations of Japanese culture today.

The Japanese made the development and use of technology a backbone in economic growth, stressing commercialization of technology as opposed to its creation. And even if only a small portion of its GNP is exported, the whole economy is designed towards what is happening on the international markets (Bjerke, 1989, p. 35). The Japanese have proved their talent for turning technological know-how into world-beating products ('A survey of Japanese technology', 2 December, 1989, p. 5). The result has been super-efficient manufacturers, but also lingering weak spots, for example, in financial services ('A survey of Japanese finance', 8 December, 1990).

The Japanese corporations followed suit, skilfully sequencing the improvement of functional competence, starting by investing money and people in manufacturing in the 1950s, later concentrating on quality control and product design and gradually moving into basic research and marketing today (Figure 7.1) (Ohmae, 1982, pp. 112–114).

Many Western commentators and even many Japanese assert that the economy of Japan is run by dedicated collectives. They also doubt that Japan has the necessary individualism to overcome the country's relative lack of original research shown in the fact, for instance, that the number of Japanese Nobel Prize winners in natural sciences is very low (Bjerke, 1989, p. 40).

There is a historical explanation for this, related to what has been said earlier in this chapter. The Japanese emphasis on applied research, above all

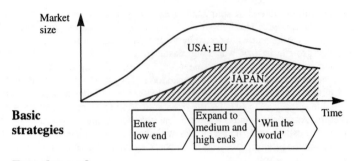

## Enter low end
*Strategic emphases*
- Market analysis
- Production technology
- Southeast Asia
  (experimentally, USA)
- Trading firms

*Representative products*
- Computers
- Gas turbines
- Compressors
- Construction equipment
- Large-scale integrated circuits
- Colour film

## Expand to medium and high ends
*Strategic emphases*
- Economies of scale
- World market
- 'High class' image orientation
- OEM or own brands

*Representative products*
- Turbines/generators
- Plain paper copiers
- Pianos
- Automobiles
- Telecommunication equipment

## 'Win the world'
*Strategic emphases*
- Global brands (more
  than two companies)
- Nonprice competitiveness
- Overseas production
- Continued innovation
  (prolong life cycle)

*Representative products*
- Cameras
- Stereo equipment
- Tape decks
- Personal calculators
- Motorcycles
- Watches
- Steel

*Source*:   Ohmae (1982, pp. 112–113).

*Figure 7.1   Evolution of Japanese 'win' strategies*

during the post-World War II period, was influenced by the country's relative
economic backwardness, lack of capital to finance independent research institutes and lack of immigrating scientists that could train and inspire
researchers. In one sense, modernization of Japan took place in the opposite
order to the West's: the industrial revolution came before the intellectual one.
Individualism is now slowly catching up ('A survey of Japan', 9 July, 1994,
p. 5). Japan's traditional emphasis on applied research has been gradually

changing towards a greater emphasis on basic research (Namiki and Sethi, 1988, p. 74).

To be fair, Japan is not a newcomer in innovation. Its tradition goes back a long way. In materials research, for instance, it is known that Japanese porcelain and sword blades were invented hundreds of years ago (Hoover, 1988, p. 46) and, in modern times, low-friction ball-screws and compounds for coating machine tools ('A survey of Japanese technology', 2 December, 1989, p. 5).

Some characteristics of Japanese innovation are (ibid., pp. 5–6, 9, 17–18):

- It is common to hail the Japanese government for assisting industry (more details will be discussed in the next section). However, the real driving force behind Japan's technological juggernaut is not the nudging or cajoling by government, but massive private investment.
- Western companies frequently act as though industrial innovation is a matter of bursting through a series of technological barriers. Japanese engineers have never deluded themselves about how tough it is to bring an innovation to fruition. They have always believed that innovation is driven by demand, not supply.
- The Japanese are convinced that investment, in research and development (R&D) as well as plant and equipment, is a matter of corporate life and death.
- Confronted with problems, Japanese engineers try to ignore the obstacles and press on, allowing for nothing but attack, seemingly moving by the spirit of *bushido*, the warrior code, where retreat or surrender meant unmentionable shame.
- The warrior approach to technology presents one problem. It leaves little room for curiosity, frivolity and tinkering – behaviour that seems to be the real mother of invention.

One source (Wee *et al.*, 1991, pp. 6–7) claims that, in the process of entering world markets, the Japanese have followed the product development strategy and manufacturing processes of the '5Is':

1. *Imitators*  They started by copying others, commonly remanufacturing foreign products using cheaper materials, parts and labour. Japanese products were known to be cheap and of poor quality at that time.
2. *Improvers*  The second stage meant making minor improvements to products they originally copied. Japanese products began to gain acceptance.
3. *Improvisers*  This stage marked the beginning of local ingenuity in making better products with distinctive features and quality.

4.  *Innovators*  Japanese products started to show superiority over many similar products made by the West. This stage started in the mid-1970s.
5.  *Inventors*  Today, the Japanese have embarked upon the final phase of their economic conquest, inventing new products, for example, super-computers, artificial intelligence and biotechnology.

This leads to an important question: how much is Japan changing today?

At the macroeconomic level, Japan was able for many years to avoid many of the difficulties that beset the other industrialized nations, notably, their inability to achieve a low level of unemployment even in booms ('A survey of Japanese economy', 6 March, 1993, p. 3). At the business and management level, the systems employed were well suited to the Japanese cultural and socio-political context (Namiki and Sethi, 1988, p. 89). During the 1970s and 1980s most of Japan's industries had to cope with economic shocks as bad as, if not worse than, those affecting the rest of the world; but they adapted so well that in many cases they emerged even stronger than before. Many Japanese manufacturing corporations were able to capture a large share of world markets, and Japan became a major financial centre in the world. All of this also took place without any change in Japan's basic values and structure. Why should the pattern be different this time?

There are two reasons why it may be ('A survey of Japanese economy', 6 March, 1993, p. 3):

1.  the nature of the present economic slowdown;
2.  the social side-effects of the previous spectacular performance.

Currently, there are several signs of turbulent times in Japan:

- the burst of the real-estate speculation bubble;
- the financial system creaking under a burden of bad loans;
- major banking and political scandals with loss of confidence in leaders;
- unemployment at a post-war high;
- unstable yen;
- major earthquakes including one that devastated the city of Kobe;
- terrorist attacks in Tokyo's subways;
- reduction of job security, cutbacks in jobs for women and no longer a guarantee of jobs for new university graduates.

Japan has been locked into recession for several years. It is interesting to see that many people trace Japan's present economic failure, as in the case of Southeast Asia, back to the same roots that once provided a model of superiority – in the case of Japan, close links between firms, banks and government officials, managers sheltered from impatient shareholders and from foreign competition ('Japan's economic plight', 20 June, 1998, p. 19).

Nevertheless, past success has led to environmental destruction and ignorance of consumer protection and worker safety and health, which have only been partially remedied. The standard of living is now high and the expectations of the population have risen, especially those of the younger generation. The social contract that has acted as a binding agent is fraying. Japan is shifting priorities from industrial advancement and international competitiveness to a better quality of life, although extremely slowly.

Thus, Japan may have to modify its distinctive model, to deregulate and to embark on structural reform ('creative destruction'), but that is not easy to do where the structure is so deeply embedded in traditions, where incumbents expect to be supported even in bad times, where outright failure is not tolerated and where politicians play only a ritual role.

However, when talking about change of a society, differences between fundamental, mostly implicit, values (my definition of culture) and manifestations of these values again have to be made clear. Manifestations may vary without values doing so, as previously mentioned.

One Japanese prime minister, Kiichi Miyazawa, once characterized his fellow country people as 'very practical' and 'ready to adapt' ('A survey of Japan', 9 July, 1994, p. 5). The famous Japanese dedication includes dedication to change! However, traditional Japanese change takes place in procedures and practice, while its fundamental structure and basic values, at least in the short run, remain intact.

> The Japanese have been able to absorb foreign knowhow without its underlying thought process and cultural values, and thus have maintained intact their principal values. So strong are the alliances among Japanese companies ... that though foreigners may become 'semi-insiders', the Japanese ... will never truly open ('Why success won't ... ', 31 December, 1990, p. 10).

As previously noted, foreign products may occasionally sell well in Japan suggesting luxury, prestige or status (Koontz and Weihrich, 1988, p. 238). However, at a deeper level, Japan has a largely homogeneous society and a stable set of values (Namiki and Sethi, 1988, p. 91). Already in 1984, about 90 per cent of the Japanese population thought they belonged to the middle class (Kosai and Ogino, 1984, pp. 108–109).

At the true cultural level, the Japanese may not even want to change. Its citizens' consciousness of being Japanese is strong ('Why can't little ... ', 21 April, 1990, p. 20). The Japanese type of culture is very nationalistic (Hofstede, 1984, p. 140) and Japanese statements claiming a connection between their economy and culture could be understood as political expressions of neonationalism (Johnson, 1988, p. 41). The Japanese culture raises an almost invisible – yet often unscalable – wall against all *gaijin* ('foreigners') (Koontz and Weihrich, 1988, p. 238). Japan is reluctant to throw itself too far open to the outside world, fearing it would change their picture of themselves and alter their sense of identity. Fewer people are prepared to live abroad in the Japanese type of culture (Hofstede, 1984, p. 133) and if Japanese do, 'they tend to isolate themselves from the local culture and care little to learn anything about it because they become outsiders to the Japanese home office if they are too identified with the local culture' (Sethi, 1983, p. 14). Only a few foreign (mainly American) universities are counted as a merit for the Japanese to visit, and I have met Japanese at universities outside Japan claiming they came there basically only to learn another language.

The first two openings of Japan may be followed by a third, but if that is the case, it will take time ('The compass swings', 13 July, 1996d, p. 4). It is fair to say that the interpretation of the Japanese culture in this chapter is valid for Japan of today. As in the case of the Chinese in the last chapter, the present economic plight in Japan does not alter its culture in the sense that culture is understood in this study.

A lot of research has been done on Japan, but there are also *many contradictions surrounding the subject of Japanese management*. These contradictions are exacerbated by exaggerated claims of consultants and pundits, by overgeneralizations of research results, but also by the tendency of many Japanese not to be candid with foreigners about their own methods (Johnson, 1988, p. 35).

Theories to account for Japan's success and failure also come in all shapes and sizes. Economists, sociologists, political scientists and social anthropologists all want their say ('A survey of Japanese economy', 6 March, 1993, p. 4). I don't intend to enter this discussion, partly because (as mentioned in Chapter 3) this book is not about judging good or bad cultural habits.

Japan *is* different. When discussing cultural clusters, it is normally placed on its own as independent (Ronen and Shenkar, 1985, p. 449). But success of Japanese methods abroad proves they are not totally culture-bound (Johnson, 1988, p. 40). However, again, remember the difference between culture as fundamental values on one hand and manifestations of these values on the other. The real barriers in Japan are attitudinal, institutional and cultural (as values). They cannot be negotiated away by trading partners, trying to break Japanese markets more open ('Why success won't ...', 31 December, 31, 1990, p. 15).

Even with its economy in a downturn, Japan is still one of the most interesting cultures on earth from a business leadership point of view.

## GOVERNMENT–BUSINESS CONNECTIONS

The 'core' of Japan is the bureaucracy, parliament and big business. On top of that, there is *a high degree of cooperation between Japanese business and government*. Figure 7.2 shows typical processes for the formation of public policy and the roles of governmental agencies, political parties and other economic and social groups (Sethi, 1975, p. 33). It will be further explained throughout the remainder of this chapter.

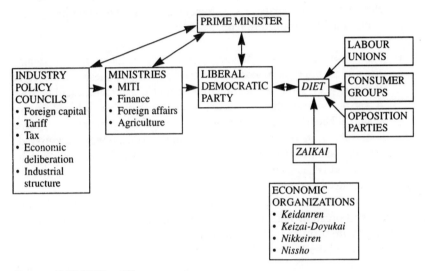

*Source:* Sethi (1975, p. 33).

*Figure 7.2  Major influences on central policy-making in Japan*

This close relationship has deep historical roots and has been going on for a long time (Namiki and Sethi, 1988, p. 61).

> Government and business representatives tend to work and plan closely together. Objectives are usually formed by the two groups in collaboration. When the government makes a policy statement, business has had a hand in formulating it.
> The large trading companies are economic leaders and work directly with the government in setting economic policy. The Bank of Japan reviews the impact of any agreements that might influence the domestic economy. Their evaluation and recommendation are then sent to other concerned government agencies. Government involvement is essential in any major negotiations that affect either the national interest or those of an entire industry.
> It is prudent to be aware of appropriate government channels, as the achievement of national objectives is a mutual aim of both business and government. Both the Economic Planning Agency and the Ministry of International Trade and

Industry (MITI) establish guidelines for all international transactions. Guidelines are enforced not by the agencies themselves, but by individual agents who act as intermediaries between the public and private sector.

Yet it would be wrong to assume that business and government in Japan have a single compatible goal in mind at all times. Conflict does arise, both within different government ministries, as well as between competing economic sectors. Unlike many Western nations, the Japanese government enjoys a proportionately small ownership of industry. Thus private industry maintains a very powerful voice in Japan's economic direction (Moran, 1988, p. 44).

Characteristics of the Japanese government and business community and their relations are (Johnson, 1985, pp. 59–63):

- The Japanese state bureaucracy, particularly in the economic ministries, is an intrinsic meritocracy. Service in any of these ministries is the most prestigious occupation in the country, and recruitment is from a narrow source, that is, mainly from the best law schools in the country. These men originate virtually all national policies. They have a similarity in outlook because of similar educational background, because of lack of pronounced class, ethnic, or religious divisions in Japan and because of a widespread awareness of Japan's vulnerability and its need to trade.
- The parliament of Japan (known as the *Diet*) is constitutionally the highest organ of state power, but in practice one of the weakest parliaments in advanced industrial democracies. The bureaucracy makes policy and the *Diet* merely rubber-stamps it.
- The oligopolistic organization of Japanese big business into bank- and trading-company-based conglomerates or industrial groups (these *keiretsu* will be discussed later in this section) means that profit is less important than market share, capital formation, research and development and long-term market penetration.
- Big business kept the Liberal Democratic Party in power uninterruptedly from 1948 until 1993 by supplying enormous funds to the leaders of conservative factions. The bureaucracy supports big business because it is interested in securing the economic welfare and economic defence of Japan as a whole.
- Japan's enterprises obtain most of their capital via bank lending rather than the sale of equity shares. This means that Japanese managers are much more influenced by the government, in particular by the monetary policies of the central bank, than in other systems.
- The history and norms of Japanese labour relations result in intense enterprise loyalties, an almost total absence of interfirm transfers but very extensive intrafirm transfers, enterprise unionism and norms of

consensus in both governmental and enterprise decision-making (this will be discussed again later in the chapter).

It could be claimed without exaggeration that Japan is a planned economy ('A survey of Japanese economy', 6 March, 1993, p. 12). Japan Inc. is actually an expansion of the corporate culture idea on a national scale (Deal and Kennedy, 1988, p. 5). Today's bureaucracy at senior levels in Japan is like the old political class from its history in a new guise – 'leadership by an intelligent élite with moral obligation to guide the people' ('Hidden Japan', 26 August, 1991, p. 18).

The network between politicians and business leaders is very tight in Japan. The primary influence of business on government is through the *zaikai* ('business world'), defined as 'a politico-economic group of wealthy financial and big business leaders who can exert tremendous influence on government and politics' (Sethi, 1975, p. 34). No legislation strongly opposed by the *zaikai* is introduced by the government or passed by the *Diet* (Namiki and Sethi, 1988, p. 66). Nowhere are the tight links between government and business more evident than in the phenomenon called *amakudari* or 'descent from heaven' ('Hidden Japan', 26 August, 1991, pp. 11–12). This means that, in order to stay plugged into the ministries, most banks and brokers offer government officials senior jobs upon retirement. These officials serve as a kind of double agent; conveying their employers' wishes to government bureaucrats at the same time as keeping the government informed about their companies' activities.

Bureaucrats, on the other hand, having ambitions to achieve cabinet posts, need business support for running an election campaign. Thus, money is another strong link between business and politics. In Japan it is perhaps more prevalent, pervasive and openly practised than in most industrialized nations (Namiki and Sethi, 1988, p. 64). Scandals reported in the media expose how politicians, bureaucrats, big business and sometimes even gangsters work hand in glove to keep the economic engine primed ('Hidden Japan', 26 August, 1991, p. 14). There is a long tradition of favours and bribes in Japan (ibid., p. 18).

However, the government's role in Japanese business should not be exaggerated. It acts more as a coach than as a captain (Ohmae, 1982, p. 216). With the exception of certain political sacred cows, such as railroads and rice farmers, the economic bureaucracy tries to avoid subsidies, preferring instead to use loans, seed money, tax breaks and *ad hoc* benefits as promotional policies (Johnson, 1985, pp. 61–62).

The most well-known government institution for an outsider is probably the Ministry of International Trade and Industry (MITI). The Japanese economy has been developing under its protection and guidance. In the broadest sense, the MITI does four things (ibid., pp. 66–68):

1.  It makes medium-term forecasts concerning the development of the Japanese industrial structure and sets up goals and plans which are necessary for the private sector to achieve if Japan is to remain competitive.
2.  It arranges for the allocation of capital to selected strategic industries.
3.  It targets those industries it believes Japan must develop in the future and creates packages of policy measures to promote such development.
4.  It is actively involved with formulating industrial policies for structurally recessed industries.

However, that is not the whole story. No one thinks today that MITI can steer the private sector as it once did. Companies are simply too big, too prosperous and too independent for that ('What's good for ...', 23 September, 1991, p. 8). MITI is still a force, but not that strong anymore. Now that Japan is no longer a follower, the bureaucrats' advice has even often proved disastrous ('A survey of Japan', 9 July, 1994, p. 16).

There are also all sorts of interfirm networks in Japan. The four major business federations are *keidanren* (Japanese Federation of Economic Organizations; the élite of Japan's corporate world), *keizai-doyukai* (Japan's Association of Corporate Executives, or Committee for Economic Development), Japan Chamber of Commerce and Industry, and *nikkeiren* (Japan's Federation of Employers' Association). Alliances take many different forms. Japan is well known for its huge oligopolistic groups called *keiretsu* (some of which are based on the pre-war *zaibatsu*).

A traditional *keiretsu* was organized around a general trading company, or a *sogo shosha*. There are approximately 4000 trading companies in Japan, with over 9000 branch offices around the world (Chen, 1995, p. 250). The nine largest general trading companies account for some 60 per cent of the country's imports and 40 per cent of its exports, down from 70 per cent 25 years ago ('Japan's trading companies ...', 11 February, 1995, p. 63). These nine *sogo shosha* include Mitsubishi, Mitsui and Sumitomo ('A survey of Japanese economy', 6 March, 1993, pp. 14–15).

Together, Japanese general trading companies have a number of functions (Yoshino and Lifson, 1986, pp. 57–78). The first one is trade, especially the import of raw materials and energy, as well as the export of manufactured products of the heavy and chemical industries. The second one is to finance trade. The third is information collection from offices all over the world. The fourth function is overseas investment, periodically constituting up to one-third of Japan's overseas investment.

The Japanese *sogo shosha* could be called *financial keiretsu*, because they include a main bank. Another type is a *production keiretsu* (exemplified by Toyota), which is best thought of as a web of interlocking long-term relationships between a big manufacturer and its main suppliers ('A Japanese buddy

...', 14 October, 1991, p. 11). In such a *keiretsu*, no single company predomi-nates. The group members compete fiercely in the market and with each other ('Mighty Mitsubishi is ...', 24 September, 1990, p. 40). On the other hand, companies in the *keiretsu* enjoy a family safety net that encourages long-term investments and high-tech risk-taking (ibid.). An example of dependency between manufacturer and suppliers can be found in the *kanban* or the just-in-time (JIT) system that is employed by the Toyota Motor Company. *Keiretsu* in Japan constitute almost one-third of the total economy of the country (Chen, 1995, p. 156).

It should not be forgotten that Japanese companies are sometimes strik-ingly different (Humes, 1993, p. 118). Nor that the Japanese economy has a dual structure because large-size companies coexist with numerous small companies and there are wide gaps, for example, in wages, between the two groups (Sasaki, 1981, p. 20). Small- and medium-sized firms not only serve as subcontractors for the giants, they also account for over half the nation's workforce (Moran, 1988, p. 54). They are, in a way, the basis of the Japanese economy. Competition to introduce new products is fierce, and the tough, live-or-die mentality in its corporate world helps Japan's free economy re-main healthy in spite of some disturbing signs over the last few years.

## FEUDALISM, RANK AND WORK

Japan remains at heart a *feudal* society ('A survey of Japanese finance', 8 December, 1990, p. 11). This is, for instance, shown in the fact that democ-racy is practised more in form than in substance (Namiki and Sethi, 1988, p. 64). Japanese are highly *rank-conscious*. Higher-ranking persons expect respect from those below (At-Twaijri, 1989b, p. 35). Because the position and status of a person play such a big role in Japan, the Japanese have developed a complicated system to draw attention to such matters (Pascale and Athos, 1982, p. 120).

The Japanese show respect not only for hierarchical position but also for age (Moran, 1988, p. 43). In Japan respect for elders is a primary value but equality of women only a secondary one (Sitaram and Cogdell, 1976, p. 191). The Japanese encourage deference to authority but also stress consensus as a style of management (this will be discussed further later).

> Japanese ... business culture [is] embedded in [its] national culture. ... Managers have functioned within an interlocking system of personal relationships in which individuality, at least in the Western sense, is repressed. ... The corporate loyalty exacted by [Japanese] multinationals has provided an organizational glue some-what comparable to that once owed to feudal lords (Humes, 1993, p. 116).

Part of this picture is what was hinted at before, that is, Japanese companies are very conservative in their hiring of graduates. Many firms recruit only from a few famous universities in the country, so an entire career may hang on getting into the right university (Moore, 1982, p. 529; 'Why can't little …', 21 April, 1990, p. 20).

Japanese organization triangles are very steep (Trompenaars, 1995, p. 144). They are supposed to be a copy from Western organizations but only in form; the substance remains Japanese, or communal (Ohmae, 1982, p. 221). Formal organizational structure is only secondary in importance in Japanese firms. The fact is that most Japanese corporations lack even a reasonable approxi-mation of an organization chart (ibid., p. 220). The vertical system of personal relationships, plus a need to belong, are the main bases for the formation of subgroups and cliques within a larger group. There may be so much group participation in a Japanese firm (especially in middle- and low-level deci-sions) that individual responsibility ceases to exist (Moore, 1982, p. 530).

The combination of feudal history and modern participation is the reason why Japan scores only medium in power distance (Hofstede, 1984, p. 77). In one respect Japanese firms are 'thin-cultured'. At the overall company level culture is expressed as a few general principles: to strive for quality, to be a market leader and so on. However, within the company these principles provide for a flexibility strong enough to survive even the harshest and most adverse external conditions ('Culturing change', 7 July, 1990, p. 65). This is inciden-tally typical of 'excellent' companies according to Peters and Waterman (1984).

Returning to education again, but not only in the context of hiring gradu-ates, the Japanese are unusually rich in the qualities that make good industrial workers. The education that turns out such people is 'a monumental victory for any nation's educational system' (Ohmae, 1982, p. 228) or even 'one of the wonders of the modern world' ('Why can't little …', 21 April, 1990, p. 19). And education might be everything:

'There are two things in Japan that determine one's life', explains Taizo Koto, a professor of sociology at Waseda University. 'One is marriage and the other is the college entrance examination'.
   Passing is everything. A good score justifies the nearly round-the-clock routine of study that begins in grade school; the result is a ticket into the highest levels of industry, finance or government. Failure spells abject humiliation for the family and the likelihood of a dismal career ('Tokyo's power club', 8 July, 1991, p. 14).

Maybe Japan's greatest strength is *loyal, hardworking people*. It has been referred to as its 'only national resource' (Peters and Waterman, 1984, p. 39). Japanese culture inspires workers to excel (Waterman, 1982, p. 70), and this type of culture has strong superegos and an inner urge to work hard (Hofstede, 1984, p. 140).

Japan scores highest among all 40 countries in Hofstede's study in masculinity (Hofstede, 1984, p. 189). Characteristics of a high masculinity culture include (ibid., pp. 200–201, 205, 207–208):

- greater work centrality;
- greater social role attributed to corporations;
- larger organizations more attractive;
- managers less attracted by service role;
- more sex-role differentiation;
- money and things orientation;
- live to work;
- young expect to make a career; those who do not see themselves as failures;
- fewer women in more qualified and better-paid jobs.

## SCARCITY AND QUALITY

The Japanese have learnt to live with *scarcity*. Physical and geographic density in Japan has made its people not only reinforce groupism, interdependence and a sense of debt and obligation, but also to excel in material handling, transportation, quality control, cutting out waste, energy conservation and convertibility (McMillan, 1985, pp. 20–21).

There is an age-old passion in Japan for smallness and craftsmanship. The folding fan, miniature gardening, the tea ceremony and other ritual staples of Japanese life all stem from this (Peters, 1989, p. 15). Its emphasis on *quality* fits nicely with its skills, in particular its bent for craft (nonspecialized) labour and its use of the worker as the primary means of adding value to a product (ibid., p. 13). The repertoire of Japanese management practices generally includes quality circles (QCs) and zero defect movements fully implemented (Johnson, 1988, p. 35). And the Japanese understanding of quality is all-inclusive (Nadler, 1984, pp. 50–51):

- quality of the product;
- quality of management;
- quality of the community relations;
- quality of the company's performance;
- quality of the company image in society;
- quality of the work environment.

Flow of work and material in export industries in Japan is determined in detail thereby eliminating unnecessary movements and time (Shinoda, 1973,

p. 393). In spite of having a synchronic view of time (as mentioned in Chapter 4), the Japanese do not want to waste time in their manufacturing (even if they are generous with their own personal time), because more time means cost and loss of competitiveness. A typified Japanese firm has a JIT system of inventory reduction in place.

## DOMINATION AND *KARMA*

Even if looking at business long term, the Japanese do not use the word 'strategy' the way it is understood in the West. They have, rather, a method of coevolving with customers (Trompenaars, 1995, p. 174). This means, also, that 'decision-making' as an act at a specific point in time does not make sense in the Japanese culture. Decision process and implementation overlap without any precise moment of decision in between (Söderman, 1983, p. 8). The Japanese language does not even have an equivalent for 'decision-making' (Hofstede, 1984, p. 27).

> The Westerner and the Japanese man mean something different when they talk of 'making a decision'. In the West, all the emphasis is on the *answer* to the question. Indeed, our books on decision making try to develop systematic approaches to giving an answer. To the Japanese, however, the important element in decision making is *defining the question*. The important and crucial steps are to decide whether there is a need for a decision and what the decision is about. And it is in that step that the Japanese aim at attaining consensus. Indeed, it is this step that, to the Japanese, is the essence of decision. The answer to the question (what the West considers the decision) follows from its definition. During the process that precedes the decision, no mention is made of what the answer might be. ... Thus the whole process is focused on finding out what the decision is really about, not what the decision should be (Drucker, 1974, pp. 466–467).

It could be said that the Japanese are *more process-oriented than result or objective-oriented* (Pascale and Athos, 1982, p. 95). Furthermore, Japanese managers value caution highly (Davis and Rasool, 1988, p. 17). They feel it is far more risky to announce intentions too early than to declare a change which, by and large, is happening (Pascale and Athos, 1982, pp. 92–93). Japanese managers' attitude to the 'decision process' allows them to follow the development much longer before action is taken. They want to learn more and not rush. The Japanese opinion about a good manager is someone who can resist the temptation to act until he or she really knows what is required (ibid., p. 111).

Generally, the Japanese have a mixed attitude to the future. On one hand, they hate uncertainty; they score very high on uncertainty avoidance (Hofstede, 1984, p. 122). There is more worry about the future in the Japanese type of culture and uncertainty in life is felt as a constant threat to be fought:

On the uncertainty-avoidance dimension, Japanese tend to have high uncertainty-avoidance orientation. For example, the practices of lifetime employment and seniority-based wage and promotion are designed to reduce uncertainty in life and promote security. Conflict and competition are avoided, and group consensus and compromise are emphasized. They also value conservatism (that is, law and order) and do not tolerate persons who deviate from the social norms and mores (Namiki and Sethi, 1988, p. 61).

However, on the other hand, the Japanese can accept more uncertainty, ambiguity and incompleteness. Certain things simply *are* and should be accepted as such (Pascale and Athos, 1982, p. 88). The Japanese do not think, for instance, that it is worth trying to control nature (Trompenaars, 1995, pp. 126–127).

What complicates the picture is that the Japanese commonly believe in *karma* (Sanskrit = 'deed'), which is a Buddhist understanding that the sum of a person's acts is a link between his or her different existences in the wheel of reincarnation. These acts are not given from outside. There is, at least partly, a choice.

In the context of business, Japanese see the future as full of complications and the idea is not to explore possibilities, but to solve problems (Sallivan and Nonaka, 1988, pp. 7–8). This can be explained historically. Some of Japan's worst disasters are constant reminders of the link between geography and nature's perils (McMillan, 1985, p. 24). The idea is not to create the future, as in American culture, but to *dominate* a selected section of it, to prepare the battleground through a thorough information intelligence operation (Dedijer, 1991).

It is a known fact that Japanese military thought and strategies have tremendous influence on Japanese management practice (Wee *et al.*, 1991, p. 4).

The Japanese conquest of world markets is very much like a well-directed military campaign, and they take a 'big think' approach (Boulton, 1984, pp. 168–170). In fact, Japanese business can, occasionally, be quite ruthless ('Tokyo's power club', 8 July, 1991, p. 15).

Since the late 1950s, Japanese manufacturers have become some of the fiercest competitors in the world. Initially, Japanese companies made textile goods and cheap mass-assembly products, then they made cars, electronic goods, and other high-quality and high-tech products that swamped Western markets. Japanese companies have consistently underpriced their Western competitors by 20 to 30 percent for equivalent products. The result has been the collapse and closing of many Western industries, such as the British motorcycle industry, which used to be the best in the world. Western businesses, panting under these throat-cutting pricing strategies, have universally directed various charges against the Japanese companies, such as 'kamikaze bidding', and 'predatory tactics'. To some extent, these charges seem to be supported by Japanese strategies, as evidenced by a 1985

Hitachi sales presentation that stressed the 'win at any cost' spirit by saying 'Quote 10 percent below competition; if they requote, bid 10 percent under again; the bidding stops when Hitachi wins' (Chen, 1995, p. 197).

## SENSITIVITY AND TACTFULNESS

Several studies show that Japanese culture is one of the most high-contextual cultures there is (competing with the Chinese and Arabs for this position) (Czinkota *et al.*, 1994, p. 231; Ferraro, 1994, pp. 51–52). Verbal communication in Japan is *implicative*, that is, comprehending the subject of communication through linkages to its environment or other events, relying on analogies, symbolisms and indirect statements. To announce something is for the Japanese only half the truth. The other half is who is the announcer and what is going on behind the stage (Pascale and Athos, 1982, p. 92).

Environment is part of yourself for a Japanese. He is trained to look at the space between objects not as nothing, but as a link between these objects:

> In Zen [Japanese Buddhism], ... dualistic reasoning, subject–object duality, and attachment to form are all considered to hinder a free experiencing of reality by their constricting effects on awareness and openness to experience (Samovar *et al.*, 1981, p. 102).

This means experiencing reality intuitively and directly. In a study by Schwind and Peterson (1985, p. 71), Japanese managers showed a preference for intuition over logical thinking more than American MBA students and even Japanese management trainees did (intuition comes with experience and age). The Japanese are, in general, suspicious of too much logic. They have a word, *rikutsupoi*, which means 'too logical' and which is used in a derogatory sense (Pascale and Athos, 1982, p. 96).

> Japan's old mistrust of reason owes much to its history. In Europe, as the middle ages ended, feudal loyalties gave ground to reason, and Luther declared that the individual's interpretation of the Bible mattered more than allegiance to the Roman Catholic church's teachings. The triumph of reason over inherited ideas spurred scientific advance, and led to the industrial revolution. Rational individualism plus growing wealth laid the foundation for democracy.
>
> Japan's revolutions have come in a different order. Feudalism lived on into the 19th century, when a nationalist clique imported the technologies necessary to modernise industry. The import of democracy and reason were postponed, with the result that Japan is now a mature industrial power, but immature politically ... and intellectually ('Japan's intellectual revolution', 30 April, 1994, p. 22).

The weak position of reason and logic in Japan shows itself in many ways, for instance:

- schools cram students with facts, not with argument skills;
- several unscientific views are held, for instance, Japanese snow and stomachs are different, making the imports of skis and beef impossible;
- actions come after establishing what the majority feels, not after a logical analysis;
- no matter how misguided the boss is, his subordinates still believe they owe him loyalty.

It could also be said that the Japanese apply 'a logic of the situation', always considering context, and like the Arabs and Chinese, Japanese culture encourages the ability to understand nonverbal behaviour. The Japanese are also known to be good listeners and develop group commitment in finding solutions (Boulton, 1984, p. 170).

The Japanese appreciate mild, undemonstrative and humble attitudes. They are extremely anxious to avoid unpleasantness or confrontation, like the Chinese, 'saving face' is a key concept (Pascale and Athos, 1982, p. 99; Moran, 1988, p. 43). Exhibiting emotion is not acceptable in Japan (Trompenaars, 1995, pp. 63–64). Aggressiveness is a tertiary value (Sitaram and Cogdell, 1976, p. 191). The psychiatrist, Tadeo Doi, claims in his book, *The Anatomy of Dependence*, that shyness (*hitomishiri*) is so common among Japanese, there is reason to denote shyness a Japanese cultural trait (1971, p. 106).

The Japanese are also not likely to say 'no' directly lest it offends someone. With the Japanese, too, a 'yes' at first is not to be taken as a firm 'yes'. It may be just a polite 'yes' which keeps the door open for further discussions, which later on may lead to 'no' (Moore, 1982, p. 538). A 'yes' (or rather a non-'no') may contribute to a pleasant atmosphere (Kawasaki, 1984, p. 6). So a 'yes' can mean many things and should be interpreted contextually (Ferraro, 1994, pp. 52–53).

Along the same lines, how something is said could be more important than what is said in Japan. Tactfulness and indirectness are highly valued. Frankness may not be appreciated (Sitaram and Cogdell, 1976, p. 191). Also, even the Japanese use of English words can mean something of their own, stressing compromise and harmony. For example (Moran, 1988, p. 48):

- the word 'yes' often means 'I understand' or 'I agree'; it can sometimes mean 'no';
- the expressions 'I understand' or 'I see' can mean 'I will carry that out' or 'I agree'. They can also mean 'no';
- the word 'problem' can be used to avoid saying 'no'.

A dialogue keeps the possibilities open for an agreement or a compromise and aims at reducing the chances of emotional escalation towards a direct personal confrontation. Furthermore, the verbs in a Japanese sentence come last and may, therefore, be changed depending on the facial expression of the discussion partner (Pascale and Athos, 1982, pp. 95–96). A Japanese discussion moves in circles according to the self-esteem of the participants.

With regard to circles, the Japanese looks at his relations to other people as 'concentric circles'. In the inner circle you will find the Japanese himself together with his closest friends and relatives (most Westerners would place themselves only in the inner circle). The next circle includes others to whom he relates regularly and on whom he depends, for instance at work. Gifts are commonly given to those people who are within these two circles. Gratefulness is also a primary value in Japan (Sitaram and Cogdell, 1976, p. 191). However, if a Japanese has no relationship with a person (that person is not within any circle), anything goes. A foreigner may, therefore, experience a Japanese as very rude, a pushy person (usually in a group) who will use knees, elbows and thumbs to force his (their) way from one place to another (Moran, 1988, p. 51).

It is an established understanding that the Japanese are formal and ritualistic, which is a common manifestation in this type of culture (Hofstede, 1984, p. 143). They are also conservative in dress and behaviour (Moran, 1988, pp. 45–46). There are rules for foreigners in a business meeting. There are rules from the moment they arrive until the moment they leave (and even before and after) (Hodgetts and Luthans, 1991, p. 39).

## GROUPISM AND HARMONY

A Japanese has relations with many different kinds of group with strict roles to be played and well-defined obligations in each, that is, the household instils the sense of ordered hierarchy where the father and eldest son are very close; the group guided by a mentor transmits loyalty and attachment or the rice paddy community with its collective norms of obligations and status (McMillan, 1985, p. 37). Japanese *groupism* originated in the strong tradition of the household – motherhood is a primary value in Eastern cultures (Sitaram and Cogdell, 1976, p. 191) – but the term has a broader meaning in Japan, relates to any context and is social in orientation (Nakane, 1967, 1972). Thus, when a Japanese faces an outside group, he establishes his point of reference not in terms of who he is as an individual but what group he belongs to (Namiki and Sethi, 1988, p. 57). Westerners try to develop and sustain a separate identity against external influences. A Japanese, on the other hand, has a tendency to develop an 'inclusive identity' which contains those in which he confides (Pascale and Athos, 1982, p. 119). Individualism is only of tertiary value in the Japanese type of culture (Sitaram and Cogdell, 1976, p. 191). In fact, the individual as a single person is so inseparable from an individual as a member of a group for a Japanese that it may explain why he scores only medium on Hofstede's scale of individualism–collectivism which attempts to separate the two (Hofstede, 1984, p. 158).

Trompenaars (1995, pp. 139–142) refers to such a culture as the Japanese as 'a family culture'. The characteristics of a family culture include:

- It is personal, with close face-to-face relationships, but also hierarchical in the sense that the 'father' has experience and authority greatly exceeding those of his 'children'. Many relations are by obligation rather than by choice (Schwind and Peterson, 1985, p. 71).
- The power exerted is essentially intimate and (hopefully) benign. The work is commonly carried out in an atmosphere that in many respects mimics the home. In a typified Japanese firm, there are afterwork drinks with fellow employees to build company loyalty and allow gripes to be aired informally, and there are company outings and re-treats for all members of an employee's family (Johnson, 1988, p. 36).
- The group is the basic unit at work (Pascale and Athos, 1982, p. 123; Humes, 1993, p. 112; Trompenaars, 1995, pp. 51–52). The group takes decisions, assumes responsibility, does the job and is rewarded (Arvonen, 1989, p. 132). There is lower ambition for individual achievement in the Japanese type of culture (Hofstede, 1984, p. 132), team responsi-bility more than individual responsibility (Bjerke, 1989, p. 41; Trompenaars, 1995, pp. 52–54), group and organizational success more than personal and individual success (Schwind and Peterson, 1985, p. 71). Spectacular individual achievements are not praised loudly, but modesty and self-restraint are valued highly (Sitaram and Cogdell, 1976, p. 171; Pascale and Athos, 1982, p. 127).
- A large part of the reason for working is the potential pleasure derived from relationships in a group. To please the superior (or elder brother or father) is a reward in itself. While the affection may not be visible to outsiders (it is known that the Japanese are very restrained emotion-ally), it is nevertheless there. The expected reward is esteem and punishment is disappointment.
- The general happiness and welfare of all employees is regarded as the concern of the corporation and the corporation may even assist in family matters. Care of others is more important than individual freedom.

The family is important in the Chinese culture as well as in the Japanese culture. However, in the Chinese system, family ethics are always based on relationships between particular individuals such as father and son, brothers and sisters, husband and wife, while in Japan they are always based on the collective group, that is, members of a household, not on the relationship between individuals (Nakane, 1972, pp. 1–2).

The extended image of the individual comes so naturally to a Japanese that he may not be willing to discuss delicate matters unless he feels that these are problems for the group (Koontz and Weihrich, 1988, p. 238). Daun (1989, p. 97) tells the story about a Japanese student who was horrified when she found out that she was to have a room of her own as an exchange student in Sweden. Adopting new information technology, in particular e-mail (where you meet with a computer screen rather than with a human being), is something of a revolution in Japan ('Second time around', 12 August, 1995, p. 57).

Japanese people not only value a group more highly than its individual members, but also order and harmony among persons in a group more than the characteristics or idiosyncrasies of any member (Harris and Moran, 1987, p. 27). The consequences of Japanese reverence for *harmony*, or *wa*, in a corporation may be that all are dressed in identical uniforms, all are tirelessly punctual and all trust each other like brothers ('A survey of Japan', 9 July, 1994, p. 6). Another general consequence in Japan at large is that cases of conflict are rarely taken to court as this would imply open confrontation and a breakdown in harmony. When serious complications arise, an arbiter is commonly used to resolve the difficulty (Moran, 1988, p. 44). And many bonds tie members of a group together in Japan. One is *giri*, which refers to a bond of moral obligation and debt that must be repaid 'with mathematical equivalence to the favor received, and there are time limits' (Yanaga, 1965, p. 58). Another is the common practice of consensus in a group before action is taken (this will be discussed again later in this chapter).

## ORGANIZATIONS AS PEOPLE AND FACILITATING LEADERS

To the Japanese businessman, organization *really* means people (Ohmae, 1982, p. 216):

> In Japan, the individual employee is utilized to the fullest extent of his or her creative and productive capacity through such participative methods as suggestion boxes, quality circles, and value analysis-value engineering contests. The whole organization looks organic and entrepreneurial, as opposed to mechanistic and bureaucratic. It is less planned, less rigid, but more vision- or mission-driven than the Western organization. The basic difference is that the Japanese company starts with people, or individual constituents, trusting their capabilities and potential (Ohmae, 1982, pp. 224–225).

When the Japanese say that organization is people, they really mean it. They know that a great many contemporary corporate problems fall outside the scope of organization or planning in a paperwork sense. Only active and alert organization members, working as an integrated team, can properly address and resolve them (ibid., p. 227).

Another way to express the fact that Japanese organizations really mean people is to say that Japanese companies are run for the benefit of their employees – *of*, *by* and *for* its people ('How Japan puts ...', 11 November, 1991, p. 11):

- *Of the employees* To never forget that a business organization is made of people and can function no better than they do.
- *By the employees* To organize the firm into teams, from the executive suite to the factory floor; to encourage workers to make on-the-spot contributions rather than use their brains at the superior's door.
- *For the employees* To have a natural cooperation between management and workers, because everybody's welfare is tied up with that of the company.

It could be said that, in Japan, the organization is its people, not its shareholders. This is 'management capitalism', not 'shareholder capitalism' ('Why success won't ...', 31 December, 1990, p. 10).

One major advantage that Japanese executives have over their American counterparts in managing their companies lies in their relationship with shareholders. The Japanese corporate system is competitive because its managers can devote themselves to compete with other companies both at home and abroad, without having to worry too much about satisfying the parasitic interests of shareholders (Chen, 1995, p. 181).

According to Matsumoto (1991, p. 200), 'the superiority of the Japanese corporate system is that it keeps managerial autonomy, once the core of capitalism, intact'. American shareholders expect to receive a good share of profits in the form of a dividend payment. Managers are given incentives, such as stock options and other profit-related bonus plans, to work in the interests of the shareholders in the USA. The situation in Japanese companies is quite different (Chen, 1995, pp. 182–184). The dividends are paid not as a percentage of earnings but as a percentage of the par value of shares of the company, that is, they are constant and not dependent on profit. Furthermore, due to the fact that the board of directors in a Japanese company mainly consists of the senior executives of the same company, Japanese shareholders have very little power to meddle in the company's affairs. This practice 'is a de facto total separation of management from the wishes of the owners'

(Matsumoto, 1991, p. 6). Management does not have to worry about the interference of the shareholders, and thereby enjoys a high degree of autonomy.

One consequence of the Japanese system of managerial autonomy is that Japanese executives are able to plan well into the future of the company, worrying less about any short-term influences from the owners.

Rather than regarding labour as a separate factor of production, as Western textbooks show, the Japanese regard labour as a form of capital – human capital 'that is cultivated and developed within a firm as carefully as any proprietary trade secret' (Johnson, 1988, p. 44).

It could also be said that the Japanese apply textbook management principles in everyday work life (Bjerke, 1989, p. 35). On the other hand, if it is true that people are the only natural resource Japan has, care must be taken to treat them well. Even if autocratic leadership style or top-down decision-making has slowly become more popular, due to rapidly changing environments and more open and fiercely competed international markets, Japanese business leaders traditionally keep a low profile and operate as *facilitators*.

> Many Japanese chief executives, when asked what they consider their main responsibility, will say that they work for the well-being of their people. Stockholders do not rank much higher than bankers in their list of concerns. Most Japanese chief executive officers (CEOs) are in fact employed in much the same way as factory workers, having climbed the corporate ladder starting in their early twenties and having been members of the company union before becoming *kacho* (section chiefs) in their mid-thirties (Ohmae, 1982, p. 219).

Japanese managers are of the opinion that it is *their* task to pay more attention to the individual as a whole, not leaving it to other extra-firm institutions. And they mean that it is only when individuals' needs are satisfied as part of the corporate culture that the latter can be released for productive work (Pascale and Athos, 1982, p. 82). The most important characteristic of Japanese managers is that they are accepted by the group and only a small part of this is related to their formal professional merits (ibid., p. 123).

At the same time as Japanese managers are very practically oriented (Davis and Rasool, 1988, p. 15), they are prioritizing the market and long-term development of the firm (Japanese long-termism will be discussed further in the next section).

Takeo Fujisawa, one of the founders of the Honda Motor Company, stated once that 'Japanese and American management are identical to 95 per cent and differ in all important aspects' (Pascale and Athos, 1982, p. 82).

# LONG-TERMISM

As a consequence of (but also a cause of) Japanese groupism, dedication and synchronous view of time, they have a *long-term view* (Humes, 1993, p. 112). (Part of this story is also that Japanese managers do not have to bother too much about shareholders when thinking about the future.) They are also very loyal to their employer:

> Two very fundamental values rule behaviour [in Japanese business]. The first is absolute loyalty to the company employer. Work is honourable and a privilege. The second is an overwhelming identification with the place of employment. Japanese are hired at a young age from school and most will remain with the company throughout their lives. A high premium is placed on company loyalty and the team concept. Employees are expected to defer to group over individual interests (Moran, 1988, p. 43).

In Japan, individuals are subordinated to their companies. Among Japanese managers, commitment to company is more than commitment to job and even commitment to self (Schwind and Peterson, 1985, p. 71). There is also a lower turnover of labour and a tendency to stay with the same employer in the Japanese type of culture (Hofstede, 1984, pp. 132, 143).

The clannishness among the Japanese may explain, among other things, why they feel a far keener commitment and loyalty than most other people to the place where they work. Religion does not:

> It is different in the world of Buddhism and Confucianism and Shinto. For people brought up in such a culture, gods are a collection of relatively vague beings on the misty edge of life. What really matters in the ordering of people's conduct is the concept of the family. It is the family that gives a sense of continuity, as you pay your respects to the ancestors who shaped your children's bodies. Out of family come the rules of what you may and may not do. And the family is not just father, mother, a couple of children and the hovering presence of those ancestors. It extends to a wider sort of family, once the feudal lord and his dutiful followers, now the captain of industry and his assiduous workforce ('The compass swings', 13 July, 1996d, p. 21).

Supporting a Japanese's concept of his or her company as a family (Arvonen, 1989, p. 102), as a social group (Trompenaars, 1995, pp. 17–18), or as a commune or village (Ohmae, 1982, pp. 217–219) may certainly mean such daily activities as wearing the same company uniform and morning physical exercise for all employees and morning pep talks by supervisors (Johnson, 1988, p. 35), but more that the Japanese have made an institution of the *sempai-kohai* (mentor–worker) relation, which generates emotional as well as functional links between seniors and juniors, comparable with godfather–

protégé ties, for example in the Italian culture (Pascale and Athos, 1982, p. 134; Chen, 1995, p. 189).

Labour unions are usually organized on a company basis in Japan (Namiki and Sethi, 1988, p. 88; Arvonen, 1989, p. 102; Chen, 1995, p. 191). This brings a long-term interest to the union as well as the interest to keep the welfare of the employer, not the profession, first in mind in negotiations.

Japan is also known for its slow evaluation and promotion system (Bjerke, 1989, p. 41). Wages, promotion and status are based on seniority (Boulton, 1984, p. 169; Hofstede, 1984, p. 132; Schwind and Peterson, 1985, p. 71; Arvonen, 1989, p. 102). The apparent drawback of the seniority-based wage and promotion system is the difficulty of rewarding creativity and performance (Namiki and Sethi, 1988, p. 84).

One of the most controversial aspects of Japan which is much noted, commented on and often misunderstood by foreigners is *lifetime employment*. First, a few points should be clarified (Johnson, 1988, pp. 38–39):

- Lifetime employment in Japan does not extend to everybody. Mass lay-offs may still be rare in Japan, but only about a fifth of Japanese workers, most of them core workers and managers in big companies, enjoy solid lifetime job security ('A survey of management ...', 2 March, 1991, p. 23).
- It does not last for life. The mandatory retirement age in Japanese industry is also normally lower than in the West.
- It is not an aspect of old Japanese culture. It is also not practised in other parts of the Confucian culture area, such as Korea and Taiwan. It grew out of the enormous insecurities found by Japanese workers during the late 1940s and 1950s and it did not become a prominent feature of Japanese management until the 1960s. It has continued to the present time above all because the Japanese tax system favours large lump-sum payments at the time of mandatory retirement which virtually all Japanese companies offer their employees in lieu of pensions. If a worker resigns prematurely, he or she gets only a fraction of it.

At any rate, lifetime employment creates a bond between employer and employee and encourages loyalty. It is part of the long-term orientation in Japan in general and the 'people as investment' policy. The success of the lifetime employment system depends on the fulfilment of a dual set of expectations that are deeply rooted in Japanese traditions and cultural norms:

> For the worker there is the expectation that he will be able to stay with his chosen firm and intends to do so. This intention is conditioned by the fact that he will be

within the norm of Japanese occupational life and that he has a good deal to gain financially by staying on. For the employer there is the expectation that the worker will stay, provided that he is offered standard wages and conditions of employment. Social conditions and cultural norms impose a sense of obligation on the employer, who is expected to provide work for his employees and take care of them. Moreover, he stands to face a tremendous loss of worker morale, not to mention union resistance, government pressure, and public ill, if he deviates significantly from the social norm (Dore, 1967, p. 35).

There are several *positive aspects* of lifetime employment:

- A company is able to invest heavily in on-the-job training and further education without fearing that employees will leave.
- The employee has no interest in opposing technological innovations, even if they are labour-saving.
- The worker can become a generalist and learn a broader range of skills.
- Knowledge will be more socially shared and corporate culture will be more pervasive.

The *negative aspects* include:

- New employees are not taken on lightly.
- Business upswings are met by longer working hours first of all (possibly by more subcontracting); downturns by reduced working hours (possibly with reduced bonus pay as a consequence).

The tradition of lifetime employment suited big firms in Japan in growth, but is today a liability to many ('A survey of Japan', 9 July, 1994, p. 12).


# CONSENSUS

The Japanese approach to business has stressed harmony and cooperation more than speed (Humes, 1993, p. 117). There is a strong need for agreement among the Japanese and decisions are commonly not made by formal leaders, but built up by growing *consensus* called the *ringi* system. Akio Morito, the Sony chairman, has noted:

The concept of consensus is natural to the Japanese, but it does not necessarily mean that every decision comes out of spontaneous group impulse. Gaining consensus in a Japanese company often means spending time preparing the groundwork for it, and very often the consensus is formed from the top down, not from the bottom up, as some observers of Japan have written (Morita, 1986, p. 198).

Decision-making by consensus encourages initiatives for change from the lower rather than the upper management, diffuses a sense of responsibility to all members involved, and makes top management delegate its authority to the group. Middle managers perform an essential role in the *ringi* system, of course. The system is effective only if the middle management is competent in bridging the gap between lower and higher levels of management. In Japanese firms middle managers acquire this skill partly through a system of job rotation from one function to another (Namiki and Sethi, 1988, pp. 79–80).

Rationality for a Japanese is to find strategies which can be implemented. The Japanese are happy to discuss the consequences of many alternatives to clarify which of them has the highest possibility of success (Pascale and Athos, 1982, p. 109). The *ringi* system can cover for absent individuals and it hides individual mistakes and makes available skills and knowledge acquired and required in many different situations (Nonaka and Johansson, 1985, pp. 184–185). It can also recognize interface issues without inter-department turf fights (Ohmae, 1982, p. 223).

> Decisions thus reached can be carried out most efficiently. One tendency is to describe all Western companies' decision-making as an individual process while all decision-making in Japanese companies is a group process. Japan certainly has its own share of one-man companies, in which decisions are quickly made by one or two top leaders. Another tendency is to idealize the consensus process as truly democratic and optimal, though much evidence points to the opposite conclusion (Chen, 1995, p. 184).

Due to all group pressure and orientation in Japan, performance appraisals are not very common there. If they exist, they are implicit and infrequent.

## A TYPIFIED INTERPRETATION OF JAPANESE BUSINESS LEADERS

The Japanese culture has been discussed focusing on certain themes. These are summarized in Table 7.1. Based on these themes, it is possible to give a typified interpretation of Japanese business leaders as follows:

- They are males.
- They are citizens of a young economic superpower; live in a country with few natural resources.
- They belong to a very homogeneous and pervasive culture, which is changing only slowly; have gone from being imitators and technological followers to become more of innovators and technological leaders;

*Table 7.1  The Japanese culture themes*

- Government–business connections
- Feudalism, rank and work
- Scarcity and quality
- Domination and *karma*
- Sensitivity and tactfulness
- Groupism and harmony
- Organizations as people and facilitating leaders
- Long-termism
- Consensus

worry about the future and look at it as full of problems to be solved, not as opportunities to exploit; do not want to create the future, but to dominate the battleground; value caution but want to be market leaders; coevolve with customers and believe that innovation is driven by demand; are loyal to and subordinated to their companies.

- They have connections with each other, with business vendors and with the government in tightly knit networks; have long-term and close relations with a bank; belong to several interest groups; have a sense of obligation and debt, if given a hand when needed, and know that their contacts and confidants feel the same.
- They use a language full of analogies, symbolisms and indirect statements; take care of how to express themselves; do not want to disappoint anybody; are not likely to say 'no' directly to avoid the risk of offending somebody; are formal, ritualistic and conservative in dress and behaviour, but flexible and pragmatic in intent.
- They belong to a family-type culture, even at work; look at their companies as families, as social groups, as communes or villages; have never seen an organizational chart of their organization; work in organic organizations where people come first – and last.
- They are dedicated to their roles – and to their country; are export-oriented; live to work; are committed to their job but, above all, to their fellow businesspeople, colleagues and co-workers.
- They have an extended view of themselves as links in social webs; identify themselves primarily as members of a group, not as isolated individuals (inclusive identity); operate daily in many subgroups and cliques; experience pleasure from groupwork.
- They are highly rank-conscious but operate more as coaches and facilitators than captains; work as mentors to juniors, whom they consider to be their protégés; work hard to be accepted by their groups;

take responsibility as members of groups, not as individuals; enjoy excellent industrial relations with long-term fellow employees.

- They are shy, mild, undemonstrative and humble; do not exhibit emotion.
- They stress compromise, harmony and consensus more than speed; do not engage themselves in inter-departmental turf fights.
- They work in companies that are super-efficient manufacturers; have a passion for smallness and craftsmanship; emphasize quality in a wide sense; are process-oriented; apply quality circles, zero defect and JIT programmes.
- They look forward to being slowly evaluated and promoted but to having guaranteed long-term employment; are generalists and good learners; are intuitive more than logical thinkers, and base this on experience.

# 8.  Scandinavian culture

## INTRODUCTION

The European Nordic countries usually refer to Denmark, Norway, Sweden, Iceland and Finland. When discussing Scandinavian countries, this usually means only Denmark, Norway and Sweden even though, from a geographical point of view, Denmark is not situated on the Scandinavian peninsula. When Scandinavian culture is discussed in this study, this refers, by and large, to Denmark, Norway and Sweden. Some of the viewpoints are also valid for Finland (being so close to the Scandinavian countries in history and traditions) but true to the thesis (which has been stated previously in this study) that language is a mirror of culture, Finland does not belong to the Scandinavian culture. The Finnish language is not a member of the Scandinavian language group. However, approximately 7 per cent of Finns have Swedish as their mother tongue.

Even then, the Scandinavians may oppose being lumped together in *one* culture group. A Swede may say that he or she is different, for instance, from a Dane, but remember that I, as mentioned earlier, paint with a broad brush and that cultures do not refer to single individuals. Furthermore, a Saudi Arab may even be more justified in claiming that he or she is different from an Egyptian, or a Hokkien Chinese that he or she is different from a Hakka. In a global perspective, Sweden, Denmark, Norway and Finland are often combined into one cultural group (Ronen and Shenkar, 1985, p. 449).

A widespread belief about business in Scandinavia is that it consists of export-bent multinationals ('A survey of business in Europe', 23 November, 1996, p. 5) and this is an impression among many foreigners (Lawrence and Spybey, 1986, pp. 48–49). Scandinavian economic life is both insular and internationalist at the same time (ibid., p. 55). Scandinavians retain a tremendous pride in their countries, which is also a strong feature of their educational system, and they are still reluctant to promote nonnationals to the top of the corporate ladder, even though this is changing ('The elusive Euro-manager', 7 November, 1992, p. 81), but they are persistently searching for new markets or business opportunities; and they have 'an enlightened interest in new applications' (Lawrence and Spybey, 1986, p. 49).

The strong export orientation exhibited by Scandinavian management could be counted as one factor behind its success. The fact is that among Global 1000 on *Business Week*'s list for 1998 ('The Global 1000', 13 July, 1998, pp. 40 ff), 32 of them come from Sweden, Denmark or Norway, behind only Britain, France and Germany in Europe. Approximately 18 million people live in Scandinavia and because their own markets are so small (Lindkvist, 1988, p. 35), they are dependent on export and must continue to export to keep the living standard high.

To what extent the three Scandinavian countries, as far as business culture is concerned, will be influenced by their different attitudes to the European Union (EU), can only be speculated (Denmark has been a member of the EU the longest, Sweden is a newcomer and Norway has opted to stay outside).

At any rate, Scandinavia has many cultural traits in common with northern Europe in general.

## EGALITARIAN AND DEMOCRATIC

Scandinavians live in very *egalitarian* countries, where there is equality among sexes, among professions, among generations – among anything (Phillips-Martinsson, 1992, p. 19). They score very low in power distance (Hofstede, 1984, p. 77). The societal norm in the Scandinavian type of culture is that inequality in society should be minimized (ibid., p. 94). There are no generally recognized social classes; one even has 'to work hard to "spot the differences"' among people there (Lawrence and Spybey, 1986, p. 58). There are also smaller generation gaps. Kinship is relatively weak and parents put less value on children's obedience.

However, there is not only a feeling of egalitarianism in Scandinavia. There is also justice for all, a 'passion for equality', which goes far back in history (Andersen, 1984, p. 110). All should have equal rights, and laws and rules apply to all; privileges are not considered acceptable (Hofstede, 1984, pp. 94, 259). In modern terms, it can be said that there is *a strong commitment to democratic values* in the Scandinavian countries (Lindkvist, 1988, p. 53), and 'a strong feeling of fair play' (ibid., p. 3).

Scandinavian countries score on the individualism side (Hofstede, 1984, p. 158), which means, for example (ibid., pp. 167–168, 171):

- more importance attached to freedom and challenge in jobs (than to training and use of skills);
- need to make specific friendships (not predetermined in terms of in-groups);

- autonomy, variety, pleasure and individual financial security (not expertise, order, duty, security provided by organization or clan);
- value standards should apply to all (not differ for in-groups and out-groups).

However, Scandinavians do not score extremely low in individualism. They can accept rules and regulations (as long as they are fair) (Daun, 1989, p. 129).

> The researchers and management consultants interviewed find that the Nordic management culture, as a result of our history and religion, among other things, rests on equality and consensus. Cooperation between individuals is deeply rooted within the Nordic social democratic parties. Strong cooperation and high degree of unionization have framed our society. Within the Nordic countries a higher degree of altruism exists than is the case in the USA for example. But, at the same time, no affiliations with the clan exist as they do in Japan and Southern Europe. Thus, the conclusion is that the Nordic countries are characterized by *collective individualism* (Lindkvist, 1988, p. 27).

In the Scandinavian type of culture, hierarchy means inequality of roles which are established for convenience only. There is more vertical communication in organizations and employees are less afraid of disagreeing with their boss (Hofstede, 1984, pp. 92, 94). Egalitarianism means co-determination at work in Scandinavian firms (Lawrence and Spybey, 1986, p. 123), and a democratic decision-making style. Industrial democracy fits well with the Scandinavian type of culture (Hofstede, 1984, pp. 268–269). The deeply entrenched egalitarianism of the Scandinavian culture has made it easier to introduce less formal, more delegating styles of management ('Europe's new managers ...', 24 May, 1982, p. 79). It also means less centralization and flatter organization pyramids (Hofstede, 1984, p. 107; Trompenaars, 1995, p. 144).

Other aspects of the Scandinavian appreciation of egalitarianism and democracy include (Hofstede, 1984, pp. 94, 132–133, 140, 259; Steinberg and Åkerblom, 1992, pp. 39–40; Trompenaars, 1995, pp. 94–95, 159–161):

- There is a rank-dependent, not class-dependent, social status of managers; the respect they gain does not depend on family background. Leadership is achieved, not ascribed, and managers are not selected on seniority and can be younger.
- The ideal superior is a loyal democrat and status is achieved by individuals exemplifying creativity and growth.
- Leadership is nonauthoritative, status differences are suppressed and status symbols should be played down.

- Authorities should serve the people and citizens are optimistic about their ability to control politicians.
- Use of power should be legitimate. If something goes wrong the system is to blame and the way to change is to redistribute power.

Equality in Scandinavia has also led to a high level of sexual equality. There are more women in qualified and better-paid jobs than in most other countries. Scandinavia has, in fact, the highest proportion of working women in the industrialized world ('Home sweet home', 9 September, 1995, pp. 21–22).

Scandinavian governments have played a significant role in developing equality among their citizens. All countries have a huge public sector and widespread social welfare, even if the latter has been reduced in the last few years. Small wage differentials are also a result of high income taxes, and social democratic parties have governed for most of the post-war years.

The relatively large public sector in the Scandinavian countries is partly a result of their active participation in various social issues, for example, egalitarianism, but such a large sector also has a say in various industrial issues. There are some critical voices claiming that Scandinavian industry depends too much on government and, also, that there are too many government industrial institutions or, at least, that they are not as coordinated as, for instance, in Japan (Söderman, 1983, p. 27; Lindkvist, 1988, p. 40).

## ORDERED AND HONEST

It was mentioned in the last section that Scandinavians can easily accept general rules and regulations. There are many – some say too many – *rules and regulations* in Scandinavia. There are those who say that co-determination (governed by many laws, rules and regulations) slows down decision-making (Lawrence and Spybey, 1986, pp. 123–124). Also governments have been late to adopt such widespread financial options as allowing a firm to buy its own shares and to allow share-option schemes in general ('European business', 13 July, 1996b, p. 21). On the other hand, Scandinavians have an ingrained respect for rules, unlike, for instance, the Chinese (Yang, 1991, pp. 28–29). It does not mean that there is less crime in Scandinavia than elsewhere, only that the severity of legal punishment is not the main deterrent to breaking the law, cultural training is. This might be *one* reason why, in an international comparison, legal penalties are relatively mild in Scandinavia:

> As part of its initial backwardness, [Scandinavia] missed out on the feudal system and the economic structure that went with it. The peasants were never suppressed to the degree that they were in the rest of Europe, and to a large part were owners,

under the Crown, of their own land (Tomasson, 1970). On this basis they were consistently represented in the parliaments called by the King. It is difficult to avoid the impression that this was a solid foundation for the high level of involvement in and enthusiasm for government, engendering an ingrained respect for the law for which [Scandinavia] has become so renowned (Lawrence and Spybey, 1986, p. 2).

In one study (Phillips-Martinsson, 1992, p. 19), Scandinavians (in this case Swedes) describe themselves as 'well organized' and 'structured'. Scandinavians love tidiness and cleanliness, but are also described as 'dull' (Lawrence and Spybey, 1986, pp. 20–21). Some call them 'uniform', 'inflexible', 'rigid' and 'bureaucratic' (Phillips-Martinsson, 1992, pp. 60, 62–63, 75).

In the same study (ibid., p. 19), Scandinavians also describe themselves as 'reliable', 'honest', 'ethical', 'loyal' and 'correct'. *Honesty* among Scandinavians is certified by others as well (Lindkvist, 1988, p. 29; Daun, 1989, p. 56). A related concept, that is, frankness, is valued highly among Scandinavians as well as among Americans (Sitaram and Cogdell, 1976, p. 191). It is even difficult for a Scandinavian to play the role of 'devil's advocate', to pretend to have certain opinions just for the sake of discussion. Critical views are also seen as 'honest' expressions of a dissentient attitude (Daun, 1989, p. 131). Another example of how seriously Scandinavians can take 'honesty': I once had a friend from Sweden visit me in a Chinese country. She fell sick the very first evening, because she had to spend the whole day haggling over prices when she was out shopping – and consequently felt (as a Scandinavian) constantly 'cheated'!

Scandinavians are also very punctual, some say pedantically and rigidly so. This goes for business life as well as for social and private life.


## PRIVACY

Scandinavians adore *privacy*. Privacy is a prime feature of the Scandinavian character (Tomasson, 1970). People do not 'drop in' on each other (unless you are very good friends) and there is a strong preference for a private office among white-collar workers (Lawrence and Spybey, 1986, p. 25) as well as among students in their accommodation (Daun, 1989, p. 100).

The Scandinavian style of leadership does not include being responsible for the employees' private sphere (Steinberg and Åkerblom, 1992, pp. 38–39). Four characteristics of the Scandinavian type of culture are (Hofstede, 1984, pp. 171, 200–201):

● everyone has a right to a private life and opinion;
● company interference in private life is rejected;

- work is less central;
- people prefer shorter working hours to more pay.

The strict line put up by Scandinavians between work and private life can be a handicap in contact with or working with other cultures, where this line is less clear. On the other hand, a Scandinavian can be described as independent (Daun, 1989, p. 56). A successful upbringing in this culture leads to responsible and independent young men and women, who will take their place in the collective (Sjögren, 1985, pp. 40 ff), that is, this collective individualist that was mentioned before.

One aspect of the connection between working life and private life for a Scandinavian is that, from a practical point of view, families have no maid, both sexes participate in housework, both parents have a legal right to take time off as a parent when a baby is born, either parent can stay at home when the children are sick and so on. Such a tight private schedule may, of course, have consequences for working life.

Another aspect of privacy is that Scandinavians are not very extrovert (Daun, 1989, p. 217). A Scandinavian manager is not supposed to publicly reveal his or her feelings – and if he or she does, it should be separated from 'objective' and 'rational' decisions (Trompenaars, 1995, p. 66). This means, among other things, that Scandinavians are commonly described as 'serious' (Brewster *et al.*, 1993, p. 113). Scandinavian businesspeople describe themselves, among other characteristics, as (Phillips-Martinsson, 1992, pp. 19–20):

- serious;
- inhibited;
- sensible;
- silent;
- polite;
- reserved.

As a Scandinavian, you are not supposed to speak, unless you have something to say. In general, northern Europeans have a low-touch culture and they do not gaze at each other (Ferraro, 1994, pp. 75, 80). Scandinavians have even been described as shy (Daun, 1989, p. 56); they are less willing to talk, but there is nothing negative in their culture associated with being shy – rather the opposite (ibid., pp. 65–66). Related to this is that you are not supposed to show off as a Scandinavian (this will be discussed in the next section). The frequent use of 'Thank you' in Scandinavian culture has been interpreted as a sign of insecurity and shyness (ibid., p. 75). Scandinavians have even been characterized as difficult to cooperate with, formal, slow and self-righteous (Phillips-Martinsson, 1992, p. 59).

# NOT STICKING OUT

One aspect of the 'collective' part of the Scandinavian collective individualist is that, among themselves, individual Scandinavians are *not supposed to stand out in a crowd*. It is not socially tolerated to be uppity as a Scandinavian; this is very much frowned upon. The important thing is to have got what it takes but not more. This is also the case when they publicly discuss themselves in comparison with other countries. Scandinavians do not like to present themselves as set above others – that is something they shrink away from; yet they privately (and among themselves) retain a tremendous pride in their countries, as mentioned in the introduction.

The widespread Scandinavian social norm that you should not think of yourself as being better than anyone else is known, at least within Scandinavia, as the Jante Law. This 'law' was formulated by the Norwegian author, Aksel Sandemose, but he was talking about Denmark. It could have been Sweden as well (Klausen, 1984). Levelling, that is, not trying to be better than others, is a general characteristic of the Scandinavian type of culture (Hofstede, 1984, p. 205).

> It is bad to act 'uppity', to set yourself apart from others; displays of wealth are frowned upon, and styles tend to be national rather than segmented or stratified. Associated with the egalitarian norm is the norm of accessibility, bureaucrats, politicians and public office holders are expected to be accessible. If you recognise the minister of transport in the airport lounge you can complain to him about the delay (Lawrence and Spybey, 1986, p. 59).

Associated with the norm of not standing out is also the Scandinavian's moderation – people are supposed to take and use just enough of what they need, but not more (Phillips-Martinsson, 1992, pp. 19–20).

The Scandinavian disposition to reasonableness, tolerance compromise and modesty also has a negative aspect in that some would argue that a person can discern forces that might work against initiative, risk-taking and, in extension, keep down entrepreneurialism. A hot public discussion is going on in all Scandinavian countries about whether the business venturing spirit has disappeared when the welfare system is so elaborated and so generous (several foreigners also participate in this discussion, sometimes for their own domestic political reasons). It is sometimes claimed that too many regulations, a large public sector associated with generous social security and high taxes, the norms of corporate solidarity and, perhaps, a toning down of individualism, have a negative influence on this spirit. The Scandinavians' avoidance of setting themselves above others *may* be interpreted as a failure to assert themselves as individuals. To be tolerant and to show solidarity may, on the other hand, of course, lead to successful compromises (Lawrence and Spybey, 1986, pp. 124–126).

The following quotation is valid for Scandinavia as well:

> To the American observer, the rigour of European industry's efforts to restructure might be concealed by a difference in management style. Europe does not breed business heroes along the lines of Jack Welch, who gained a reputation for ruthless efficiency at America's General Electric. Yet, Lennart Ribohn, of Electrolux, a Swedish maker of domestic appliances, which has been radically revamped, thinks that this is partly a question of rhetoric. American shareholders reward tough managers. But in Europe, where politicians and workers have more power, macho management is usually self-defeating. French managers, including Guy Dollé, of Usinor Sacilor, a steel maker, claim that they can cut just as ruthlessly as their American counterparts – though it costs more and takes longer ('The lesson in ...', 27 January, 1996, pp. 59–60).

## CAREFUL AND SLOW

It is a general impression among foreigners that Scandinavian decision-making is *slow* (Lawrence and Spybey, 1986, p. 50; Lindkvist, 1988, p. 55; Phillips-Martinsson, 1992, p. 59; Brewster *et al.*, 1993, p. 30). There are several reasons for this:

- Scandinavians do not rush in a meeting; they find it appropriate to wait for an answer, not to force it. Scandinavians are not, as mentioned earlier, supposed to speak unless they have something to say. The silence, while a Scandinavian is contemplating an answer, can be unbearable for some other cultures.
- An obvious cause is the effect of the co-determination system and the workers' right to negotiation. To this might be added that one manifestation of Scandinavian perfectionism is the search for the perfect compromise!
- The Scandinavian egalitarianism, which tends to value everyone's commitment and consent equally, makes decision-making naturally participative, even if less so than in Japan. It is, therefore, natural for a Scandinavian manager to consult his or her subordinates, and not just to consult them cosmetically.
- Institutions outside companies are sometimes involved in decision-making in Scandinavia to such an extent that occasionally it could be better called 'collective' rather than 'participative' decision-making.
- Scandinavians prefer systematic, rational and detailed problem-solving (this will be discussed in the next section), where decisions may not necessarily come fast, but where problems are well penetrated when the decisions are taken.

There are also critical voices heard about the Scandinavian style of decision-making. Some say that Scandinavian managers are indecisive (Brewster *et al.*, 1993, p. 30), that they are *excessively careful* (Phillips-Martinsson, 1992, p. 59), that they are scared of the decision-making limelight due to a 'natural' shyness and afraid of 'acting uppity' (Lawrence and Spybey, 1986, p. 50), or that they do not feel comfortable taking risks ('A survey of business in Europe', 23 November, 1996, p. 16).

Unwilling to take risks may sound contradictory to Hofstede's (1984, p. 140) conclusion that people embracing the Scandinavian type of culture have more willingness to take risks. My interpretation is that a Scandinavian business leader is not the stereotypical bold American loner and dare-devil who does not even hesitate to break into uncharted lands, or the cunning Chinese who concludes a multi-million-dollar business with a handshake. The Scandinavian manager may be slow in details, but he or she (and other Scandinavians) is certainly not unwilling to change and to experiment (see the section 'Process, continuity and change' later in the chapter). In 'Showing Europe's firms ...' (13 July, 1996a, p. 13) there is a section on the 'European model' as entrepreneurs being unwilling to risk bankruptcy, because their personal reputation is so important. However, in these violent economic times and open economic systems of today, even Scandinavians are forced to manage the hard way – by making tough decisions sometimes.

It may, of course, be counted as an advantage to let many voices be heard and many stakeholders be involved in a decision (this will be discussed again later in this chapter). Also, there are developed networks between companies and between them and other interest groups, such as the government, public institutions, trade unions and environmentalists in Scandinavia. This may ensure that decisions being made are also implemented as intended, that is, without being delayed and blocked 'at the end'.

## RATIONAL AND PRACTICAL

The *rationality and practicality* of a Lutheran background comes through in present-day Scandinavia:

> What emerges from any consideration of the development of [Scandinavia] is a strong impression of the commitment to secular rationality. A Weberian view, linking the 'spirit of capitalism' and associated scientific and technological advancement with the 'protestant ethic', would associate this with the early establishment of the Lutheran Church as the universal state church in [Scandinavia]. This must in turn be linked with the characteristic of the [Scandinavians] ... to put less emphasis on the individual whilst producing a secure social structure that enables the individual to go out and do things (Lawrence and Spybey, 1986, p. 39).

Scandinavians appreciate sensibility and matter-of-factness (Daun, 1989, pp. 162–163). Managers see themselves as practical in the Scandinavian type of culture (Hofstede, 1984, p. 92), and Scandinavian businesspeople describe themselves as 'efficient' and 'rational' (Phillips-Martinsson, 1992, p. 19). The strict emphasis on matter-of-factness may give an impression of a lack of feeling among Scandinavians, but is closely related to the importance of reasonableness and moderation in their culture, which was mentioned earlier.

Top managers in Scandinavia impress some foreigners that they seem to know what they are doing, not in the simple sense of being resolute rather than indecisive, but in the broader sense of having a knowledge of the practical side of business (Lawrence and Spybey, 1986, p. 49). There is a high degree of product-mindedness in Scandinavian companies (ibid.) and a high amount of service in the sense of applying technical systems to satisfy customers' needs, such as the right to return products bought or cancel a hire-purchase agreement (if customers change their mind) and unconditional warranties (Lindkvist, 1988, p. 44).

This practical orientation is also shown in research in Scandinavia. In many cases, management research within the Scandinavian countries has a direct influence on the practical level. Researchers have succeeded in putting their theories into action there. A close Scandinavian cooperation between universities, business schools, management institutes and companies also exists:

> Cooperation and confidence between managers and researchers within the Nordic countries have led to a unique access to research objectives. This implies that we are often much more empirically based than the Americans. The Nordic research tradition is more oriented toward field and case studies, the aim being to increase the understanding and development of conceptual ideas. In the Nordic countries there is a tradition of clinical research ... and action research ..., where the researchers not only state certain discrepancies but also actively participate in changing them. In the USA, experience and research are kept much further apart. The method for field studies does not have the same legitimacy. Researchers are caught up in something like a positivistic straitjacket. In the USA, the discussion is instead focused on management science in the sense of a scientific research ideal. The differences in methods applied are also connected to the American academic career system, where articles must be published each year ('Publish or Perish'). The result is that most researchers find that they have neither the time nor the possibility for engaging themselves in long and risky procedural field studies (Lindkvist, 1988, p. 64).

When comparing American and Scandinavian management development programmes, it is also found that the latter use outside resource persons much more, and evolve much more around discussions based on practical experience (Lindkvist, 1988, pp. 61–62).

There are many factors behind the rational and practical orientation in the Scandinavian culture. Two more basic factors are:

1.  Scandinavian culture is a low-contextual culture;
2.  there is a strong emphasis on education in Scandinavia.

Scandinavians have a low-contextual culture (Ferraro, 1994, pp. 50–52). This means, for instance, that people are what they seem to be; paradoxes and surprises are few, and there is no great need to interpret other people, their thoughts, purposes and so on. The spoken and written word is enough to understand each other. The Scandinavian low-contextual culture also shows in the fact that Scandinavians, when talking, are quite reserved in using their hands and maintain a good amount of personal space.

Management systems develop more from a logical and economic ground in low-contextual cultures. There is less ritual behaviour at work. However, entering a Scandinavian's private space may involve many ceremonies, such as buying flowers when invited to their home, being strictly on time, thanking the host before leaving and so on. Its low context also means that Scandinavians are not everyday good psychologists or skilled judges of human nature, nor are they effective networkers compared to many other cultures.

Education is highly valued in Scandinavia (Lindkvist, 1988, p. 53). There is even what may be called 'a cult of competence' in the Scandinavian culture (Lawrence and Spybey, 1986, p. 61). Lower strata in the society are also highly qualified and managers characterize themselves, and are charac-terized by others, as 'better trained and educated' (Brewster *et al.*, 1993, p. 113).

Europeans have typically focused on 'traditional markets, emphasizing engineering and production, and downgrading marketing and general man-agement skills' ('Europe's new managers ...', 24 May, 1982, p. 78). The high education of Scandinavian managers is caused by, but also leads to, egalitari-anism, high standard of industry and often a product orientation of the man or woman at the top of a firm (Lawrence and Spybey, 1986, pp. 51–52). Addi-tionally, there are many consultants and public institutions acting as experts in various business fields (ibid., 1986, p. 21).

Manifestations of the rational and practical mentality of Scandinavians abound: 'Everything follows the logic of planning', according to the British journalist, Jan Morris (1984, p. 129). The importance of planning among Scandinavian managers is certified by Brewster *et al.* (1993, p. 113). Govern-ment bodies also have 'a voracious appetite for data' in Scandinavia (Lawrence and Spybey, 1986, pp. 21–22). Like the Americans and the Dutch, Scandinavians perceive time as passing in a straight line, a sequence of disparate events to plan (Trompenaars, 1995, p. 10). If the Americans have a short-term orientation and the Japanese have a long-term orientation, Scandinavians have a medium-term orientation (Humes, 1993, p. 112).

## PROCESS, CONTINUITY AND CHANGE

Scandinavians are not only serious, they also take their job very seriously. Those who get to the top must want to be there for intrinsic rather than extrinsic reasons. They are less likely to be there for money. Financial incentives are quite low in Scandinavian companies by international standards. Also, taxes are high and there are hardly any fringe benefits, so there must be factors other than remuneration motivating Scandinavian managers. One such factor could be to be a more central part of the process of learning and of progress. These are important values to a Scandinavian.

In Scandinavia, greater importance is attached to turning leadership into a *process* and a matter of cooperation, rather than a role or a quality (Lindkvist, 1988, p. 63). Scandinavians do not like aggression and confrontation (this will be discussed again later in this chapter), but they accept the fact that conflict in organizations is natural and try to use it constructively. All employees expect to have a say and the organization is viewed as a political environment with possible power struggles, potential conflicts and processes of influence, but also as an organism for creativity and innovation. It can be a most significant and intense experience to be part of such an environment, referred to by Trompenaars (1995, p. 157) as an *incubator*. An incubator at its best 'can be ruthlessly honest, effective, nurturant, therapeutic and exciting, depending as it does on face-to-face relationships and working intimacies' (ibid., p. 158).

Management development programmes suitable for incubators and consequently for the Scandinavian culture would be based on the following elements (Lindkvist, 1988, pp. 61–62):

- The leaders of the programmes are seen as actors in a cooperative ongoing process with the participants.
- The participating organization is seen as a political environment more than as a hierarchy.
- There is an interaction between objectives and means of the programmes rather than just objectives being determined beforehand.
- There is learning through a genuine dialogue.
- The skills required to participate should include an ability to learn and to adjust.
- The process of the programmes, that is, the way they are run, is seen as more important than their result *per se*.

Scandinavians do not look at loyalty to an employer as a virtue in itself. They attribute a greater social role to institutions outside work and they do not hesitate to change employer if they feel it will enhance their individual self-fulfilment (Hofstede, 1984, pp. 132, 200). At the same time, however, they look at companies not simply as instruments for creating wealth; a company is not a temporary organization (ibid., p. 154), but 'an institution with its own history, values and traditions' ('A survey of business in Europe', 23 November, 1996, p. 18). Companies are a means for producing continuity and stability:

> Even some Americans hold up the European way of doing business as an alternative to American capitalism. At least in northern Europe, most countries emphasise continuity, consensus and training. European capitalism, argue its defenders, has been good at building skills and businesses for the long term, and at avoiding the financial and social excesses of corporate America.
>
> [S]ome see Europe's emphasis on 'continuity' as a strength. Pointing to the hollowing out of middle management in America, they argue that American firms rush from one management fad to the next. European companies, they argue, are more measured and less destructive ('A survey of business in Europe', 23 November, 1996, pp. 4, 18).

Scandinavians are very *much for learning*, and very interested in the learning process itself. Belief in progress has characterized much of the development of the Scandinavian countries (Lawrence and Spybey, 1986, p. 35).

Part of the picture of having a positive attitude to learning is that all the Scandinavian countries score low in uncertainty avoidance (Hofstede, 1984, p. 122). This means (ibid., pp. 133, 140):

- to have a preference for broad guidelines;
- to expect rules to be broken for pragmatic reasons;
- to be prepared to live abroad if necessary;
- not to feel deviance as threatening;
- to be tolerant.

Scandinavia has a remarkable record of innovations. It has also since World War II gained an international reputation as a 'shop' for social experiments. Scandinavian managers are change-centred (Brewster *et al.*, 1993, p. 113). Scandinavians are, in general, extremely willing to accept change (Frykman, 1987) as long as change will not jeopardize their national values and the feeling of security (Daun, 1989, p. 166). As mentioned above, the Scandinavian way of thinking and learning is characterized by a focus on the learning process as such, creativity, being *ad hoc*, and inspirational (Trompenaars, 1995, p. 159). Even the problem itself is open to redefinition. Ways of changing are by improvising and attuning (ibid.). Creativity should, in the eyes of a

Scandinavian, be guided by some kind of practical purpose, however, not running completely out of control.

Scandinavians are recognized as being good at problem-solving and they like to experiment (Lawrence and Spybey, 1986, pp. 27–28). They have a strong belief in learning through experimentation (Lindkvist, 1988, p. 53). This is possible within companies because there is an optimism about people's initiative, ambition and leadership skills (Hofstede, 1984, p. 133), and employees are interested and involved in innovations (Lindkvist, 1988, p. 53). One author, Fons Trompenaars, has characterized relationships between employees in the Scandinavian type of organizations as 'diffuse, spontaneous relationships growing out of a shared creative process' (1995, p. 160).

Organizational theories in northern Europe focus on *change*, not on general principles or on efficiency in existing structures (Hofstede, 1984, p. 218). Also, values ruling in this part of the world support research on new forms of social and organizational arrangements.

Stakeholders in Scandinavian firms may have different opinions about which changes are needed, of course. In the uncertain and volatile times of today, Scandinavian unions want more investments and managers want deregulation:

> Trade unions and managers in Europe are set on a collision course. European firms have already taken the easy steps to cut their labour costs by shifting labour-intensive work abroad. If they want to continue operating in their countries of origin, they will have to renegotiate rights that their workers value highly. Where sectoral bargaining breaks down, as it is beginning to in Germany and Sweden, costly and bitter disputes are almost certain.
>
> Union leaders think that the solution to Europe's problems is investment, not deregulation. They strongly resist lowering industry's nonwage costs by cutting benefits and reducing employment protection. The unions are in favour of flexibility, but they want it to be negotiated centrally in minute detail. With membership falling, and industries shifting from manufacturing to services, the unions are not as strong as they were. Their nightmare is that the setting of pay and conditions will become so flexible as to make their central organisations redundant ('A survey of business in Europe', 23 November, 1996, p. 17).

## NO AGGRESSION OR CONFRONTATION

Egalitarianism leads to patience, restraint, moderation and emotional control, which are all seen as Scandinavian virtues. In spite of interest in change and experimentation, however, Scandinavians *do not like direct confrontation and forceful interpersonal challenges*. In their opinion, problems should be solved by open discussions leading to a compromise, not by force (Lawrence and

Spybey, 1986, p. 59). It is, for instance, very rare to hear drivers using their car horns 'in anger' in Scandinavian cities, unlike most other places in the world. Aggressive behaviour is frowned upon in the Scandinavian type of culture (Hofstede, 1984, p. 140). Even the term 'aggressiveness' has negative connotations in Scandinavian languages.

Evading conflicts can be understood as a tendency to stay away from direct confrontation. Typical for many Scandinavians engaged in a discussion is that they try not to raise topics which are strongly emotional and where opinions may differ widely (Daun, 1989, p. 102). This is a clear tendency in Scandinavian companies as well (Forss *et al.*, 1984, p. 15; Steinberg and Åkerblom, 1992, p. 36).

> [C]omparing Swedish managers within the public sector with similar managers in Great Britain, Germany, Italy, Holland and the USA, [we can say that] Swedes [are] characterised by pragmatism and evasion of conflict. ... [T]his may be caused by the mentality of the Swedish public servant, who, because Sweden is a small country, takes the necessity of cooperation into account. An example of this attitude is the Swedish 'remissförfarande', the process through which one administrative department seeks advice from another department and aspires to reach mutual agreement on various decisions. ... [T]he Swedish recruitment policy, apart from formal qualifications, emphasizes the employees' ability to interact socially and to adapt (Lindkvist, 1988, pp. 53–54).

The Scandinavian tendency to avoid open conflicts should be clearly understood:

1. Evading aggression and conflict is a cultural norm, not necessarily a characteristic of the personality of individual Scandinavians.
2. Where friendliness is sanctioned, say at work, this cultural norm is the rule. Conformistic colleagues are then treated favourably. However, as mentioned previously, a Scandinavian draws a strict line between work and private life. Privately, Scandinavians can be very aggressive and confronting. They may simply need instances where they can 'blow up'. It is a common opinion among foreigners (a myth?) that Scandinavians become different when influenced by alcohol. If this is so, it may be related to their need to loosen up from time to time from their *cultural* norm of being moderate, restrained and emotionally controlled.
3. Some institutional situations, for instance, political discussions in public media, and some roles, for instance, business leadership, require that dissentient opinions are brought into the open and, in the case of business leadership, become constructively managed. A successful Scandinavian business leader must, as other leaders, be able to handle

confrontations when they exist, and allow differences and criticism in approach and attitude in the name of progress.

One thing is true, however. Prolonged conflicts and deep social breaches are not part of the Scandinavian culture:

> It is this consensus approach that has helped these four Nordic countries come closer than any other country to what the Norwegian playwright Henrik Ibsen saw as the ideal: an unusual combination of socialism and individualism, not the individualism of selfishness but the individualism of self-fulfilment. It has provided Finland, Norway, Denmark and Sweden with a great comparative advantage: the ability to solve social problems peaceably (Lindkvist, 1988, p. 33).

One aspect of Scandinavian business of special interest to the topic of this study is that Scandinavian businesspeople describe themselves as 'diplomatic' (Phillips-Martinsson, 1992, p. 19), 'flexible' and 'adaptable to foreign cultures and people' (Lindkvist, 1988, p. 58). This may be so. Let me, however, point out what has been mentioned several times previously in this study: there is a big difference between having the technical knowledge of other countries, willingness to accept differences among people and an international outlook in general, on the one hand (*factual* knowledge), and the intellectual and emotional understanding of how cultures operate at the level of implicit values, on the other (*interpretive* knowledge).

## STAKEHOLDER CAPITALISM

As much as Scandinavians dislike clashes and confrontations, they like negotiation and compromise (Lawrence and Spybey, 1986, p. 93). The reaction of a Scandinavian to uncertainty is to negotiate, not to lean on hierarchy or to refer to procedures (Hofstede, 1984, pp. 216–217). Negotiations are also easier in long-term relations, which become stronger with every new process of negotiation:

> In most continental European countries, strong business relationships are highly valued; the 'European model' fosters long-term ties between managers, owners and workers. In contrast, in America and Britain, firms are more influenced by shareholders who rely not on personal ties but on published accounts, straightforward ownership structures and clear goals for managers. The spread of such practices is no small matter. ('Le Défi Américain ...', 13 July, 1996c, p. 25).

Lindkvist (1988, p. 40) has compared American and European managerial style. Some of his findings are shown in Table 8.1.

*Table 8.1    Comparison of American and European managerial style*

| Managerial dimensions | USA | Europe |
|---|---|---|
| Type of cooperation | Competition | Cooperation |
| Initiative | Personal initiative and decision-making | Collective decision-making |
| Rights | Individual rights | Collective (employees') rights |
| Role of company | To promote personal goals | To promote societal goals |

*Stakeholder capitalism* rules in Scandinavia as well as in many other parts of Europe:

> Stakeholder capitalism is often blamed for Europe's reluctance to change, for managers' discomfort when faced with difficult decisions and for their failure to heed warnings sounded by poor profitability. But this is as much of an exaggeration as blaming 'shareholder values' in America for social decay, exploitation of workers and counter-productive short-termism. The values at the heart of stakeholder capitalism can help create a motivated and loyal workforce. The best European companies can combine the professionalism of American management, its discipline and flexibility, with a thoroughly European commitment to consensus and continuity. Europe's adaptation will be slow, and come in fits and starts. Yet as long as European companies are flexible and open to change, they will take strength from the past ('A survey of business in Europe', 23 November, 1996, p. 22).

The typified Scandinavian business leader is a *negotiator*. Scandinavian top managers stress that their most important ability is to obtain results in cooperation with the employees' combined with their ability to negotiate. The future Scandinavian managers' most important task is to be able to choose the right employees and motivate, involve and stimulate them (Lindkvist, 1988, pp. 43–44). The determination of the appropriate balance between competing demands remains the most critical function of senior management in Europe. This was already pointed out more than 15 years ago ('Facing realities', 1981, p. 37).

The Scandinavian model is based on cooperation between employers, employees and politicians (Söderman, 1983, p. 8). This cooperative style is enhanced by a noncompetitive school system, a high degree of unionism and a universal military service. The American sociologist David Popenoe (1988) has said that the reason why Scandinavians say 'yes' so often is not that they cannot say 'no' like the Japanese, but because they always look for agreement.

The main characteristic of the Scandinavian alternative is to strive for consensus. This follows naturally from the Scandinavian tendency to avoid confrontation and to be cautious decision-makers. Hofstede (1984, p. 261) tells the story of a prestigious American consulting firm that was asked to analyse the decision-making processes in a large Scandinavian corporation. In their report, the consultants criticized the corporation's decision-making style, which, among other things, they characterized as 'intuitive' and 'consensus-based'. The consultants did not get very far in the end. As one manager of the corporation put it: 'They looked at us through American spectacles and discovered that we don't operate the American way with fact-based management and fast decisions based on clear responsibilities. What did they expect?'

Characteristics of the Scandinavian type of culture include (Hofstede, 1984, pp. 92, 94):

- managers are more satisfied with participative superiors;
- managers make a decision after consulting;
- subordinates prefer a consultative style in a manager;
- informal employee consultation is possible without formal participation;
- cooperation among the powerless is based on solidarity.

Europeans have their own approach again here. Instead of stressing the individual in the American way, the family in the Chinese way, the clan in the Arab way or the group at large in the Japanese way, they tend to stress the team and personal relations (Humes, 1993, p. 121). In one study, Scandinavian managers saw themselves and were seen by British managers as more 'consultative' than in Britain, where a more autocratic management style is common (Brewster *et al.*, 1993, p. 93).

Scandinavian leadership style is participative. Managers are more interpersonally oriented and keep the role of other people in mind. Trompenaars (1995, p. 160) calls it *management by enthusiasm*: ways of motivating and rewarding to make people feel that they are participating in a process of creating new realities.

In management development programmes there is a democratic process in choosing those who will join (Lindkvist, 1988, p. 63). Furthermore, both managers and employees participate in such programmes and people select themselves instead of being earmarked for them.

Scandinavian organizational structures are often diffuse, sometimes perceived by foreign managers as ambiguous. Hofstede (1984, p. 264) calls these 'implicitly structured' organizations, where neither work processes nor relations between people are rigidly structured. Both personal and egalitarian relations go well with the Scandinavian culture (Trompenaars, 1995, p. 157).

The Scandinavian management style is less formal and less carefully defined (Humes, 1993, p. 121), and relations to subsidiaries in a Scandinavian multinational corporation are less formalized (Lindkvist, 1988, p. 55): they operate as autonomous units with loose affiliations (ibid., pp. 44–45). Scandinavian managers are characterized as 'open/direct/relaxed' (compared to British managers) (Brewster *et al.*, 1993, p. 113) and 'more consistently cooperative, consultative and informal' (ibid., pp. 89–90).

Management as such in Scandinavia is not seen as a well-defined profession as in the USA, but managers are rather 'quasi-generalists loosely and ambiguously defined' (Humes, 1993, p. 112).

European business schools emphasize the 'softer' people skills ('The elusive Euro-manager', 7 November, 1992, p. 81), and European (maybe especially the homogeneous Scandinavian) corporations have never felt the same need as in America to assiduously and consciously develop corporate-wide cultures from the top or from outside (Humes, 1993, p. 121). This is mainly because, as mentioned earlier, Europeans look at culture as something corporations are, not something they have (Schneider and Barsoux, 1997, p. ix).

Egalitarianism in Scandinavia reduces interpersonal friction between managers and workers (Lawrence and Spybey, 1986, p. 62). Personal relationships are also combined with trust in Scandinavia (Humes, 1993, p. 112). The human factor is even often seen as more important than technology (Lindkvist, 1988, pp. 43–44). Models are looked for where initiatives are taken by subordinates (Hofstede, 1984, p. 258). Such initiatives are also encouraged (ibid., p. 167; Brewster *et al.*, 1993, p. 113). The attitude to people is that they are 'co-creators' (Trompenaars, 1995, p. 160).

Two characteristics of the Scandinavian type of culture are (Hofstede, 1984, pp. 92, 94):

- people trust each other across the hierarchy;
- close supervision is evaluated negatively.

However, equality, social justice and 'caring' have not stopped European corporations from restructuring:

> European views on equality and social justice do not fit well with the American style of restructuring. Europe's mixture of job protection and regulation is widely criticised as a drag on business and job creation. But being 'caring' has not stopped European managers getting rid of workers. The magnitude of change shows up in one life-crushing statistic: the 18m Europeans who have no job. And yet, perverse as it might seem, dole queues are a symptom of progress. They show

how much restructuring has gone on ('A survey of business in Europe', 23 November, 1996, p. 4).

Scandinavians score the lowest of all on Hofstede's masculinity index (1984, p. 189). Among other things, this means for the Scandinavian culture:

- achievement is defined in terms of human contacts and a living environment;
- self-expression and self-fulfilment are important;
- feeling part of progress and change is an important motivational factor;
- there is a sympathy for the weak in society.

## A TYPIFIED INTERPRETATION OF SCANDINAVIAN BUSINESS LEADERS

The Scandinavian culture has been discussed focusing on certain themes. These are summarized in Table 8.2. Based on these themes, it is possible to give a typified interpretation of Scandinavian business leaders as follows:

*Table 8.2   The Scandinavian culture themes*

- Egalitarian and democratic
- Ordered and honest
- Privacy
- Not standing out
- Careful and slow
- Rational and practical
- Process, continuity and change
- No aggression or confrontation
- Stakeholder capitalism

- They could be a man or a woman; are well educated, possibly in a technical field; are product-minded and service-oriented.
- They are proud of their country; are strongly committed to democratic values; can easily accept rules and regulations as long as these are 'fair' and they honour them respectfully.
- They work for an export-bent company; are persistently searching for new markets and business opportunities.
- They live in a very egalitarian culture with justice and the same value standards for all; do not belong to a specific social class; are not highly

paid compared with other cultures; do not enjoy privileges or status symbols; are intrinsically rather than extrinsically motivated; want to play a role in the process of progress; are willing to experiment and to change.

- They have good contacts with the government; cooperate with universities and research institutions; work with unions in co-determination schemes.
- They work in less centralized and flat organizational pyramids, which are not charted or in any detail.
- They are not autocratic, but use a delegating and participative style; use power if necessary, but then based on legitimacy; consult their subordinates; look for cooperation, compromises and consensus; are collective individualists.
- They put teams before individuals or before groups at large; support, even encourage, individual initiatives among subordinates; encourage vertical communication; issue broad guidelines and do not want to control subordinates in detail; try to manage by enthusiasm.
- They feel independent, not overattached to their employer, but are serious and look at their organization as having its own history, values and traditions, and a vehicle for producing continuity and stability; attach importance to challenge in jobs.
- They participate together with their colleagues and workers in management development programmes; are interested in learning, in creativity, innovation and growth.
- They are slow decision-makers; are systematic and detailed in their problem-solving; love order, tidiness and cleanliness; are very punctual.
- They are rational and practical; appreciate sensibility and matter-of-factness; are reliable, straightforward, honest and ethical; are not good judges of the character of other people.
- They are emotionally controlled and restrained; do not like direct confrontation and forceful interpersonal challenges; try to evade conflicts, but if they appear, approach them as a negotiator.
- They do not want to show off or be uppity; could be shy; live in moderation.
- They adore privacy; draw a strict line between work and private life; never interfere with the private life of their colleagues or subordinates.

# 9.  A comparative analysis and interpretation

## CULTURE LOOKS AT CULTURE

Five different cultures and some of their manifestations in the context of business leadership have been discussed in some detail. As one illustration of the results of this study the following Table 9.1 could be constructed.

*Table 9.1   Comparative analysis of five different cultures*

|  | Americans | Arabs | Chinese | Japanese | Scandinavians |
|---|---|---|---|---|---|
| Americans | – | (*as*) ritualistic | (*as*) controlling | (*as*) formal | (*as*) careful |
| Arabs | (*as*) work-oriented | – | (*as*) callous | (*as*) consentient | (*as*) egalitarian |
| Chinese | (*as*) patronizing | (*as*) religious | – | (*as*) participative | (*as*) environmental |
| Japanese | (*as*) direct | (*as*) pushy | (*as*) power-centred | – | (*as*) matter-of-fact |
| Scandinavians | (*as*) profit-centred | (*as*) rhetorical | (*as*) secretive | (*as*) sexist | – |

It is important to understand that this table is to be interpreted as a typified picture. For example:

- the Chinese (as a type) look at the Japanese (as a type) as (too) participative;
- Americans (as a type) look at the Arabs as (too) ritualistic, the Chinese as (too) controlling, the Japanese as (too) formal, and the Scandinavians as (too) careful (all as types); or

- Americans look at the Chinese (as a type) as (too) controlling, the Arabs look at them as (too) callous, the Japanese look at them as (too) power-centred, and the Scandinavians look at them as (too) secretive (all as types).

## CULTURE AND CAPITALISM

It is clear that five different types of capitalism rule our five cultures, that is:

1. America = shareholder capitalism
2. Arabia = neo-traditionalist capitalism
3. China = family capitalism
4. Japan = management capitalism
5. Scandinavia = stakeholder capitalism

Financial numbers are the common denominator for business in *America*. Americans emphasize liquidity in the *stockmarket* and shareholders monitor managers through their trading in this market – with share prices acting as a sort of 'approval rating' ('A survey of government ...', 29 January, 1994, pp. 4–5), that is, success or failure of business is measured as a return to the shareholders. Share option is a common means of motivating American managers.

The American obsession with what is measurable and with regular, say quarterly, results, is fostered by American financial markets and business schools' and shareholders' preference for immediate return on their investment.

Mergers, acquisitions and short-termism are a way of American business life.

The *Arab* world did not start to modernize until 20–25 years ago and much of business there is still done in the old traditional way. Many rituals and symbols operate in the Arab business world; Arab managers are less concerned with fashionable management ideas, endorse traditional points of view and do not support employee participation or initiative; Arab business firms are expected to conform with the class structure in the society at large by using discriminatory recruitment and promotion policies (nepotism).

Westernization is not the same thing as modernization in the Arab world and modern Arab management is something of a *mix* of desert cunning and Western sophistication.

Many Arab societies feel, therefore, caught in a conflict with change and they want to modernize without sacrificing the traditions of Islam and Arab culture.

A *Chinese* firm is almost always *family-based*. It is founded in a family, it grows in a family, it is run by a family and it remains in a family.

Asian values, supported by Confucius's teaching, stress the family rather than the individual as the paramount unit of society. However, families are not only the bedrock of Chinese societies, they are also the bedrock of their businesses. The family provides the sole security for a Chinese in a fast-changing, discriminatory and unruly world.

Chinese enterprises tend to retain their family character, even if they grow. Growth, therefore, tends to take place as multiplication and extension of the family network (in a broad meaning of 'family'), in order for each unit not to grow out of the family control.

In *Japan*, the business organization is its people, not its shareholders. There is a de facto separation between owners and managers in Japanese companies. A trusted intermediary – a bank – does the monitoring of the managers on the owners' behalf ('A survey of government ...', 29 January, 1994, pp. 4–5).

Japanese businesses are *head office-oriented* and do not have to worry too much about satisfying the interests of their shareholders.

Even the board of directors of a Japanese company consists mainly of the senior managers of the company itself.

Cooperation is deeply rooted in the *Scandinavian* culture. There is co-determination at work, and many interests are involved in the well-being of the firm.

The Scandinavian model promotes long-term ties between managers, owners, workers and society, where the role of the company includes promotion of goals of society at large.

This involvement of many *stakeholders* in Scandinavian businesses has been blamed for reluctance to change or for slow decision-making processes. It may, on the other hand, create a motivated, dedicated and loyal workforce.

## CULTURE AND BUSINESS LEADERSHIP TYPE

The business leader (as a type) plays different roles in our five cultures. When this role is played at its best (according to its own culture), it produces the following results:

1. American business leader = the foresighted manager
2. Arab business leader = the benevolent autocrat
3. Chinese business leader = the well-connected paternalist
4. Japanese business leader = the participative facilitator
5. Scandinavian business leader = the broad-minded negotiator

*Americans* look at management as a specialist profession, where rational scientific tools are to be applied; managers are to be task-oriented, stress efficiency and take the right decisions; American managers tend to emphasize what is new and young, and to endorse 'modern' management ideas.

American managers are to be *future-oriented*, to place a high value on action and work, to always believe in a better future and to change every situation (including its environment) for the better.

Growth and leadership are seen as virtues in themselves in America; those managers who will acquire leadership apply the 'right' skills, make the risky and hard decisions, and guide their firms with the 'right' foresight, occasionally being a part of creating the future as well.

*Arab* business leaders are dominant individuals who extend their personal control over all phases of the business. Authority is associated exclusively with them. Arab managers also apply *a very personalized style* and their own methods – management by subjectives.

Arab business leaders enjoy power. To give it away is a sign of weakness. Top-down communication is, therefore, dominant in Arab organizations and authoritarianism becomes a primary value.

Arab organizations are supposed to care for their members in more sense than one – all sorts of help and assistance may be asked for. Organizations provide expertise, order, duty and security; and they invade the private life of their members.

*Chinese* business is family business. The implicit model of the Chinese business organization is also the family. The business leader/owner has *a patriarchal relation to subordinates and decisions are made in the best interest of the 'family'.*

The Chinese business environment can be best described as a series of interlocked networks; the business leader is also generally surrounded by an internal network of clan members who occupy all key positions. In the West, it is business first, then networking; in a Chinese society, it is the other way round. The Chinese society is not individual-based, nor group- or clan-based. It is relation-based. In Chinese business, relationships count more than market efficiency and networks matter more than groups or individuals. A successful Chinese businessperson is good at connectionology and, because of this, is highly flexible, adaptable and pragmatic.

The Chinese have problems in letting go of money – and control. They have been characterized as control freaks. Seniority and authority are very important in all aspects of how they run their businesses.

The qualities of *Japanese* business leaders are truly defined by their followers. The most important characteristic of Japanese managers is that they are accepted by the group. To Japanese business leaders, organizations really mean people; the employee is used to the fullest; companies are run of, by and for its people. If the workers' need are satisfied, they can be released for productive work. This attitude goes all the way up to the top in Japanese society. The government acts more as a coach than as a captain in Japanese business.

Japanese business leaders traditionally keep *a low profile and operate as facilitators* of their precious resource – workers. Japanese managers are more process- than result- or objective-oriented. They appreciate caution and do not want to announce intentions too early but follow the development as far as possible first. Good Japanese business leaders should resist the temptation to act until they really know what is required. Also, the Japanese do not subscribe to the model of decision first and then implementation; the two phases overlap.

Ideal business leaders in *Scandinavia* are loyal democrats; macho managers are usually self-defeating. Scandinavian business leaders aim for a 'perfect' compromise and look for *consensus* on the way.

It is a general impression among foreigners that Scandinavian decision-making is slow.

## CULTURE, CULTURAL MANIFESTATIONS AND VARIOUS ASPECTS OF BUSINESS LEADERSHIP STRUCTURE AND PROCESSES

### Analytical Dimensions

I have developed 14 dimensions from the presentations in Chapters 4–8 by which the five cultures can be analysed and compared. These 14 dimensions are:

1. power distance: short or long;
2. uncertainty avoidance: low or high;
3. social orientation: individual or group;
4. time orientation: short or long;
5. attitude to change: stability or change;
6. attitude to trust: no trust or trust;
7. aims: materialistic or idealistic;
8. attitude to environment: exploitative or adaptive;
9. measure of success: self-recognition or position in society;
10. relations: informal or formal;
11. problem-solving: traditional or scientific;
12. power exertion: democratic or autocratic;
13. communication: low-contextual or high-contextual;
14. skills wanted: systems- or people-based.

Most of the remainder of this chapter will be a discussion of the five cultures along these dimensions. It is important that a few points are borne in mind when considering the following:

- These 14 dimensions are *my* choice. Another researcher and writer would most probably have come up with another set of variables.
- I still discuss the cultures as types, of course. This means, for instance, that there are a lot of individual exceptions to whatever is said.
- Even so, placing the five cultures along these 14 dimensions is occasionally a questionable procedure. One reason is that it is sometimes a problem to place them there in the first place (as mentioned earlier, for instance, there were problems in placing the Arab and the Chinese cultures on the informal–formal continuum). These problems will be discussed throughout the remainder of this chapter. Another reason is that the cultures may not give the same meaning to many of the variables, for example, 'power', 'trust' and 'democracy'.
- My placement of the cultures along the dimensions is very subjective. Several pictorial figures have been included in the latter part of this chapter and it should be pointed out that these are not the result of any careful and procedurally correct cardinal measurement whatsoever. *They should rather be seen as impressionistic paintings than strict Cartesian two-dimensional geometric planes!*
- Space allows me to discuss only a few possible combinations among the variables. Other possible combinations exist.
- Concentrating on what is specific in the five cultures and analysing their differences hides and neglects many of their similarities.

## Cultural Positions

Let me start by presenting my impression of how the five cultures are placed along the 14 dimensions above, one at a time (some combinations, two variables at a time, will be discussed later in the chapter).

### Power distance
Power distance relates to what extent inequalities are accepted, even taken as natural, in a culture. A long power distance in a culture means that such inequalities are clear and obvious. The more stratified a society is, the greater are the feelings of inequality and the lesser are social interactions between people in different strata. In American and Scandinavian cultures, the power distance is relatively short, in my interpretation even shorter in Scandinavia than in America. In the latter case, subordinates expect (as in Scandinavia) to be consulted, but they accept autocratic behaviour to some extent, as well as

certain privileges and status symbols. There are no recognized social classes in America or in Scandinavia. However, Scandinavians fight harder than Americans to minimize all kinds of inequalities and there is even more equality among sexes in the former case.

In the Arab as well as in the Chinese culture, power distance is long. My interpretation is that it is longer in the former case than in the latter. Arab culture has a definite class structure, people's position in Arab society depends on their tribe, and Arab firms are expected to honour this tribal class system. Arabs as well as Chinese are very rank-conscious, they respect seniority, and status symbols are important in both cultures. Japanese culture leans towards the short power distance side, but it not easy to place this culture along this scale. Even if Japan is at heart a feudal society and even if the Japanese are highly rank-conscious and show a deep respect for hierarchical position and seniority, there is a lack of pronounced class, ethnic and religious divisions in Japan. There is also a high degree of participation among subordinates in decision-making in Japanese firms.

## Uncertainty avoidance

Uncertainty avoidance relates to people's need for structure. The higher such avoidance, the more there is a need in a culture for a structured life. In an uncertainty-avoiding organization there are many rituals, for example, certain memos and reports, some parts of accounting, much of planning, a considerable part of control systems and occasional reliance on experts (Hofstede, 1984, pp. 116–118). In my opinion the Japanese culture is the highest avoider of uncertainty among the five. The Japanese basically hate uncertainty, and feel it as a threat to be challenged. There are also many steps taken in the Japanese culture to reduce uncertainty, for example, lifetime employment, seniority-based wages and promotion and consensus rituals. The Chinese are rather the opposite. Being direct, relational and specific, they trust themselves and their own judgement and they have a high willingness to take risks and an ability to face uncertainty. Being very superstitious helps and cushions the Chinese in any risky endeavour in the face of uncertainty. The Arabs are close to the Japanese. Even if Arabs have their religion they use a lot of symbolism and formal rules in order to make life predictable. Americans and Scandinavians accept the inherent uncertainty of life. My interpretation is that Scandinavians are more willing than the Americans to do so (but still not as much as the Chinese), at least in business, where the American approach is a bit more structured and predictable than the Scandinavian.

## Social orientation

Some cultures are definitely focused on the individual and on individual free choice, as the Americans; other cultures consist of people who do not even identify themselves as individuals but rather as members of a group, as the Japanese. Americans value the individual way very highly; the self-made individual is a very American phenomenon. Japan, on the other hand, is run by dedicated collectives, individuality is repressed, and harmony, cooperation and consensus are stressed in Japanese firms. Scandinavians are focused more towards the individual side. However, there are levelling tendencies in the Scandinavian culture; rules and regulations are readily accepted (if they are seen as fair). The Arab and the Chinese are both collective cultures where the right of the group is placed before the right of single individuals. My interpretation (even though I know that their meaning of 'group' is different) is that the Chinese are a little more group-oriented than the Arabs. The Chinese ties to their families are definitely stronger than the Arab ties to their clans and tribes.

## Time orientation
A culture can have a shorter or a longer time orientation. I find the Japanese the most long term in their orientation among the five cultures. They have many procedures, such as slow evaluation and promotion, to support this in business. Scandinavians and Arabs are somewhat long term in their orientation. Patience is a virtue in both cultures. They think that acts should be taken when the time is right, not on schedule or by reference to a mechanism. Americans, on the other hand, always seem to be in a hurry. Even if they are future-oriented and work for the future, they want results now. I find the Chinese even more impatient; they worry now about the future; they are not so much strategic thinkers, but extremely versatile and flexible tacticians.

## Attitude to change
Some cultures are more change-oriented than others, for instance, the Americans. Americans find it possible, even mandatory, to improve on the present; they are very action-oriented, accept changes (even embrace what is new and up to date) and think they can control them. They also look at growth in business as a virtue in itself. Scandinavians are also change-oriented, even if not as much as Americans. Scandinavians are willing to learn, believe in progress, like to experiment but they are a bit slow in details, due to a disposition to carefulness, solidarity and compromise. The famous Japanese dedication includes dedication to change (but never in basic cultural values). Like the Scandinavians, however, they want to know what is happening before they set a new course and their full dedication to consensus makes them even slower than the Scandinavians to act.

The Arab culture is definitely not change-centred; they may even be emotionally resistant to change. Departure from tradition is generally presumed to be bad among Arabs until proven otherwise. The Arab value pattern may make process- and person-embodied technology transfer (but not product-embodied technology transfer) into its culture more difficult (Kedia and Bhagat, 1988, pp. 562–563). There are signs of interest in stability as well as change in the Chinese culture (there are certain problems in making the Chinese culture fit a one-dimensional range of change versus no change). Creativity is stifled in this culture. The Chinese are more adapters than innovators; they stress tradition, continuity and links with the past, but they also have a high respect for learning and believe in potential gains from growth and development in a society.

### Attitude to trust

The Japanese, Arabs and Chinese all belong to a no-trust culture, even more so in the case of the Arabs and, especially, among the Chinese. The Japanese are very cooperative among themselves; they may have very close relations to each other, and are very loyal to their companies, but being a *gaijin* ('foreigner') means that you can never really be one of them. Arabs may have mixed feelings about working with other clans or tribes than their own and Arab employees are reluctant to trust each other, even if loyalty and a sense of duty are important in an Arab organization. The Chinese are a suspicious type. There is no real trust beyond the (extended) Chinese family unit, and different Chinese groups may have serious problems in cooperating. Americans and Scandinavians belong to trust cultures. There is a tolerance of deviant behaviour and people are generally trusted. My interpretation is that Scandinavians are even more trusting than Americans, sometimes bordering on naiveté. 'Blue-eyedness' (a common Scandinavian trait) has more than one meaning.

### Aims

Some cultures aim for materialistic gains; others are more idealistic. I consider that the Americans are very materialistic, just ahead of the Japanese. They look at it as almost their right to be materially well off and physically comfortable. However this is nothing compared with the Chinese culture where achievement is measured in terms of wealth; the Chinese use money not only as a pool of security, but also as a sign of success and as a means of asserting themselves. The Japanese (like most cultures) do not say 'no' to material success, but they also stress other needs, such as belonging and so on. The Arabs do even more so, being so religiously oriented in interest and customs. Scandinavians play down status symbols and preach moderation; there are other factors than remuneration motivating Scandinavians in business and management.

### Attitude to environment

Americans believe that the environment is to be controlled and changed for the convenience of man and that it can be subjugated to the human will

(Hodgetts and Luthans, 1991, p. 41). This could be called an exploitative attitude to the environment. Trompenaars (1995, p. 125) refers to it as an inner-directed culture. The Japanese, on the other hand, belong to an outer-directed culture. They have learnt to live with scarcity, they do not think it is worth controlling nature and want to live in harmony with it. In Japan, organizations are seen as a product of nature, owing its development to the nutrients of the environment and to a favourable ecological balance. This could be called an adaptive attitude to the environment. In business this includes really listening to the customer (Delaryd, 1989). I find the Scandinavians adaptive to their environment as well, appreciating a nonpolluted life and being proud of having it, even though they do not take it as so strictly harmonious as the Japanese. Arabs are not far from the Scandinavians in this respect even though, in my interpretation, they may occasionally interfere drastically in the flow and balance of nature by, for instance, desalinating sea water and starting agricultural projects in the middle of the desert. The Chinese are on the exploitative side. One example is their apparent lack of respect for public property.

## Measure of success

Success can be defined on many different dimensions and it may perhaps be thought impossible to reduce it to one dimension. The dimension used here is to look at success as what has been achieved wthin yourself (it could be called 'self-realization') as against what has been achieved in terms of position in society in relation to others (this could partly be ascribed and not necessarily completely achieved). Ignoring the fact that self-realization and societal position are not clearly each other's exact opposites, it could be said that some cultures, like the Scandinavian, nurture a cult of competence, appreciate knowledgeable experts and look at success from a more intrinsic point of view (for example, 'feeling complete' in a 'living' environment). Other cultures, such as the Chinese, overwhelmingly stress position and recognition by others as a sign of success. Most cultures are in between these two extremes. My interpretation is that the Arab and the Japanese cultures tend towards the 'position' pole (success for an Arab is to be loved and respected, to have a good family position and to be well connected, more than to be admired as a separate individual; success for a Japanese is to belong, to be accepted in a group – and to have a good education is just a means to achieve this) and that the American culture tends towards the 'self-actualization' pole (success for an American is recognition, particularly in business, but more importantly, people in America are valued by how they perform and in terms of what they contribute, especially if they do it creatively and constructively).

I sometimes say that in order to feel successful and to stand out from others (on culturally acceptable terms) people should show that they have more of what society is short of, for example, Scandinavians like to be suntanned (showing that they have been in the sun somewhere south; the Scandinavians are short of sun at home). The Japanese associate success with space (they measure their physical life in terms of number of *tatami*, a standard-sized Japanese mat) and like to take vacations where they can find it (for example, in Australia or Canada). The Chinese want to gain respect and recognition after having been discriminately and badly treated by foreigners for so many years. The Arabs love to show off by building fountains all over their cities, splashing around their traditionally scarce resource, that is, water, and Americans are very happy to talk about their history (which is very short, at least in comparison with the other four cultures).

## Relations
Americans are very informal and on the expressive side. They also associate informality with sincerity. Frankness is a primary American value. I consider that the Scandinavians are a little less informal and also not very extrovert, a bit serious and reserved, but at the same time direct and uncomplicated. The Japanese are just the opposite: formal, ritualistic and conservative in dress and behaviour. Exhibiting emotion is not acceptable to the Japanese; some even call them shy. The Arabs and Chinese are in between these two extremes, with the Arabs the more formal of the two, using many rules, rituals and symbols at the same time as they are very expressive; the Chinese are much more formal but can be very lively if you get near enough to their family circle. I have mentioned before that there are problems placing Arabs as well as the Chinese on the formality–informality scale. I have, therefore, referred to the Arabs as 'formally informal' and to the Chinese as 'personalized' in their relations.

## Problem-solving
Some cultures are heavily dominated by tradition; solutions to problems are sought by sifting through past procedures to find the correct, in this case the traditional, solutions. Problems that require new solutions present great difficulty in such cultures. Solutions to such problems come slowly and often after much controversy. The Arab culture is such a culture. In other cultures, logic and scientific methods have been internalized as the means of solving new problems and solutions are then perceived as progress or improvements. The American culture is the archetype of such a culture. The Scandinavian ideal is, in my opinion, close to the American culture, appreciating rationality, practicality, sensibility and matter-of-factness as much as they do. However, the Scandinavians have more of an applied research approach and less of a basic research approach than the Americans have. The Chinese and Japanese cultures are more traditional. My interpretation is that the Japanese are a little

less so, and more open to influences from outside (at least in procedures, even if not in values and basics, as mentioned previously).

## Power exertion

In my opinion the most democratic culture (in the context of business leadership) among the five cultures is the Scandinavian; industrial democracy fits well and is practised there. The ideal superior in Scandinavia is, as discussed previously, the loyal democrat. It is natural for a Scandinavian business leader to consult colleagues and subordinates – and not just cosmetically. The most autocratic culture (in a business leadership context as well, of course) in my view is the Chinese; authoritarianism is a primary value in Eastern cultures in general and in the Chinese culture in particular. The Chinese business leader is definitely a power player. Chinese managers are more satisfied with directive and persuasive superiors, and close supervision is positively evaluated by subordinates. Arab managers also enjoy power and come close to the Chinese ideal of autocracy. The American culture is near the Scandinavian end. Company information should be available to anyone who needs it within the organization (Hodgetts and Luthans, 1991, p. 41), but initiatives for participation should come from above. The Japanese society is a complicated mix of democracy and autocracy (it does not fit very well along this dimension), but in business, I definitely place the Japanese culture on the democratic side.

## Communication

High- and low-contextual cultures are concepts introduced by Hall (1977). If a culture is low-contextual, information can be directly understood by a foreigner without knowing the context or without a specific knowledge of the culture in question. If a culture is high-contextual, it is necessary to know more about the culture itself before a foreigner can understand the real meaning of a message. America and Scandinavia are low-contextual cultures; Arabia, China and Japan are high-contextual cultures. I regard the Scandinavian culture as even more low-contextual than the American. One reason is all the slang and insider jargon that goes on in the latter culture. My interpretation of the ranking order among the high-contextual cultures is that Japan is ranked the highest, China the lowest and Arabia in between. The statement that how something is said is more important than what is said is more valid for the Japanese culture than for the other two, and Arabs have more rituals, symbols and rules in business than the Chinese.

## Skills wanted

My final cultural dimension (with which I struggled a bit) became one where, in one end, system skills are stressed more and where, in the other, people skills are stressed more (it may be questioned, of course, whether system skills and people skills can be seen as opposites to each other or whether they should rather be seen as supplementary to each other). In my interpretation, Japanese stress the people skills more than any of the other four cultures, people being their greatest strength and only natural resource. A company is, on the other hand, more of a system in America than a social group, a system which is characterized by output-oriented control more than self-control by employees (Chen, 1995, p. 297). I place our other three cultures between the Japanese and the American extremes, with the Scandinavian closer to the Japanese and the Arab closer to the American.

## Some More Obvious Relations

Looking at the dimensions in pairs, some relations are found to be rather obvious and direct across the cultures. These relations could be called 'direct unbroken' (see Figure 9.1). Some of these relations are:

1.  Power distance–power exertion    Democratic cultures have a short power distance; autocratic cultures have a long power distance.
2.  Uncertainty avoidance–relations    Informal cultures do not need structure, formal cultures do; expressed differently, unstructured cultures lead to informality, structured cultures to formality.
3.  Social orientation–attitude to trust    Where the social orientation in a culture is individualistic, people trust each other; where the social orientation in a culture is towards groups, this could mean no trust (of outsiders to the group). This could also be phrased such that when individuals tend not to trust each other, they join groups where trust can be found. Another way to put it is to say that closely associated with individualism in a society is equal opportunity and the notion of a 'social contract', unlike a group-oriented society, where people are governed by their position in a hierarchy, high duty-consciousness and sometimes consensus (Lodge and Vogel, 1987, pp. 10–22).
4.  Time orientation–attitude to environment    Short-term-oriented cultures have an exploitative attitude to the environment (they are inner-directed); long-term-oriented cultures have more of an adaptive attitude to the environment (they are outer-directed).
5.  Attitude to change–problem-solving    Cultures interested in change typically take a scientific approach to doing it; cultures interested in stability apply traditional methods. Some traditional methods (in this case the Japanese) may promote change.
6.  Attitude to trust–measure of success    In trusting cultures people feel they have succeeded when they have 'found and realized themselves'; no-trusting cultures look at position in society as a sign of success.

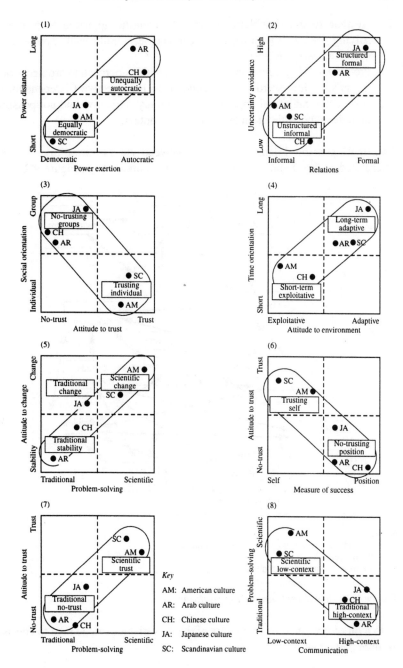

*Figure 9.1   Eight direct, unbroken relations*

7. Attitude to trust–problem-solving  A scientific approach to problem-solving goes well with trust between people; a traditional approach can take place without trust.
8. Problem-solving–communication  A scientific approach to problem-solving is straightforward and is supposed to be objective (independent of context); a traditional approach is commonly subjective and not possible to understand without understanding its context.

Out of 91 possible bilateral relations (between the 14 variables), 32 were interpreted as direct and unbroken. These are summarized in Figure 9.2.

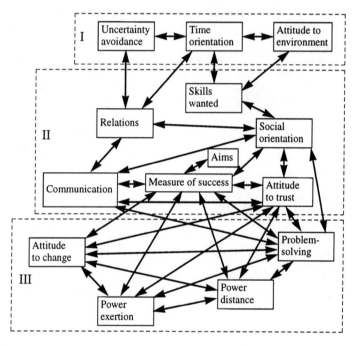

*Notes*:
I:     Attitude to uncertainty, time and environment.
II:    People relations.
III:   Approach to problems and use of power.

*Figure 9.2    My direct, unbroken relations*

With a bit of imagination, this figure of the 14 variables can be read to consist of three parts, that is:

1. attitude to uncertainty, time and environment;

2. people relations;
3. approach to problems and use of power.

Many relations were almost of the above type, but one culture broke the pattern. These relations could be called 'direct broken' (see Figure 9.3). Some of these relations are:

1. Power distance–social orientation   A short power distance is traditionally associated with an individualistic orientation in a culture, and a long power distance with a group orientation. One exception to this is the Japanese culture, which is able to combine a short power distance with a group orientation in business ('we are all the same').

2. Power distance–communication   A short power distance is also typically associated with a low-contextual communication environment, and a long power distance with a high-contextual communication environment. Again, an exception is Japan, which combines a short power distance with a high-contextual business communication environment ('we are different'). This Japanese position can be combined with the one in the former relation and show that the Japanese have a very homogeneous culture, which may take a long time for a foreigner to learn. However, once this is done, the foreigner will find that the Japanese are very similar to each other (this is much less so among the Arabs and the Chinese).

3. Uncertainty avoidance–attitude to trust   A culture where people trust each other does not need a structure; a culture where people do not generally trust each other (and/or outsiders) may have to compensate this with structure. An exception from this 'rule' is the Chinese, who commonly base their existence in business on the unstructured family and do not trust anyone outside this family.

4. Uncertainty avoidance–measure of success   In cultures where people take risks and win, they expect to be rewarded individually by an intrinsic, personal satisfaction of success. On the other hand, in cultures where people avoid risk and live a structured life, success is defined as position in the society. The Chinese diverge from this picture and occasionally take heavy risks with the primary ambition to promote the social standing of their family.

5. Uncertainty avoidance–communication   Lack of structure in a culture and low-contextual communication environment typically go together, and so do structure and a high-contextual communication environment. The exception, again, is the Chinese culture. We can combine this Chinese position with those in the previous two relations and show that the Chinese use a personalized approach to high risk-taking and judge the result by whether their family has gained in social status or not.

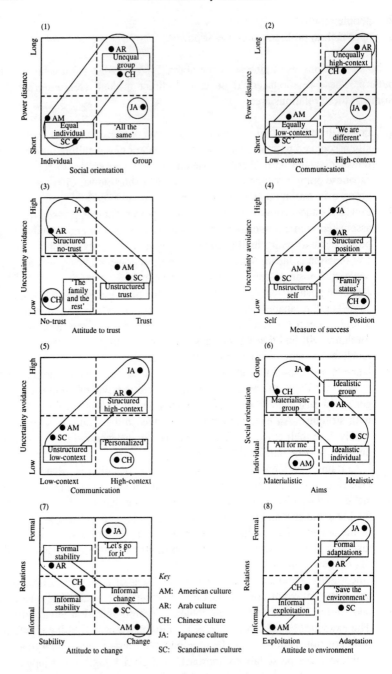

*Figure 9.3   Eight direct, broken relations*

6. **Social orientation–aims** People in group-oriented cultures commonly aim for materialistic gains ('all for us'); and people in individual-oriented cultures often go for idealistic achievements ('me for all'). The exception is the American culture, which is individualistic and materialistic ('all for me') and, to some extent, the Arab culture, which combines idealistic motives with a group orientation ('us for all').
7. **Relations–attitude to change** Here the Japanese attitude to change (and to progress) can be noted. They can go very far, even change drastically, *if* they are united and *if* their basic cultural values are not being altered in the process of change. (It may also be noticed the problem in making the Chinese fit the formality–stability relation here – even if they are characterized by 'informal stability' as in Figure 9.3, they can change, but then under 'personalized' guidance).
8. **Relations–attitude to the environment** It is possible to see the Scandinavian interest in preservation of the environment here. Informal cultures are otherwise generally exploitative (and formal cultures adaptive).

### Cultural Dimensions and Cultural Types

A few examples of relations that give more spread among the five cultures are examined in this section. One is *power distance–uncertainty avoidance* (Figure 9.4).

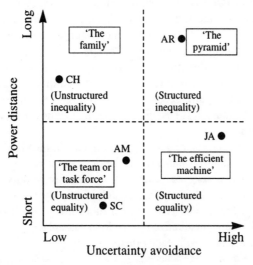

*Figure 9.4 Power distance–uncertainty avoidance*

This is classic Geert Hofstede (except for the fact that my interpretation of Japan is different from his). Figure 9.4 can also be found in his book on culture and work-related values (1980; 1984, p. 265).

The combination of power distance and uncertainty avoidance typical for a culture affects the structure of organizations that will work best in that culture. Where subordinates are more dependent on superiors and superiors on their superiors, greater centralization of power is bound to occur. More structuring of activities (more uncertainty avoidance) implies the need for more rules and regulations and less structuring of activities means fewer such rules and regulations.

Where power distance is short and uncertainty avoidance is low (such as in *America* and *Scandinavia*), organization triangles are generally flat and the number of written rules is low. If rules exist, they are of a more general type. Conflicts in such organizations are not uncommon because autonomy, variety and frankness are asked for, and deviant behaviour is accepted. Vertical communication may also be extensive – in both directions. Organizations are more or less 'implicitly structured' and the ideal model is 'the team or task force'.

Where power distance is short but uncertainty avoidance is high (such as in *Japan*), the organization triangles are much steeper and individuals are emotionally attached to their companies and identify themselves with their place of employment. The ideal organization model is 'the efficient machine'.

Where power distance is long and uncertainty avoidance is low (such as in *China*), organizations are run autocratically and are centralized, that is, organization pyramids are tall and there is a preference for order over freedom. Relations between people are unequal. Change, when it takes place, always starts from the top. The direction of change, however, is generally more in an imitative direction than in an innovative one. Flexibility is highly valued in business, and this is, again, accomplished from the top, in this case by the organization being much less structured there than at the bottom. The implicit model is 'the family'.

Where power distance is long and uncertainty avoidance is high (such as in *Arabia*), there are a large number of political processes going on in the organization, which is very steep. Loyalty and a sense of duty are important in Arab organizations. The implicit model is 'the pyramid'. However, as noted previously, this model is not much more than a shell among Arabs. Inside this shell, many personalized procedures take place, procedures which may even be inconsistent with each other.

Another relation of interest here is *power distance–skills wanted* (Figure 9.5).

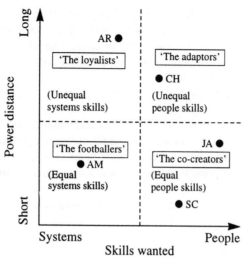

*Figure 9.5    Power distance–skills wanted*

Different cultures ask for different skills in people. The longer the power distance, the more the status is ascribed and the more orders have to be taken from above. The skills asked for could either be given beforehand in terms of content as well as orientation from the firm, then seen as a system, or the required skills could be more or less creative and flexible people skills.

Where power distance is short and systems skills are asked for (such as in *America*), people work in a project-oriented culture, where people are given specific tasks in an arrangement which is targeted upon shared objectives. People are expected to be problem-oriented, professional, practical and cross-disciplinary. The important skills are similar to what 'the footballers' have when they are at their best. American football is a very systems-based game. Trompenaars (1995, pp. 139 ff) refers to this culture as 'the guided missile' (see Figure 2.3).

Where power distance is short and where people skills are asked for instead (such as in *Japan* and in *Scandinavia*), connections between people become diffuse with spontaneous relationships growing out of a shared creative process. People should be process-centred, *ad hoc* and inspirational, participating in the process of creating new reality. These people could be called 'the co-creators'. Trompenaars (1995, pp. 139 ff) refers to such a culture as 'an incubator'.

Where power distance is long, even if people skills are still asked for (such as in *China*), people will relate to an organic whole, but in a diffuse fashion. If people are 'family' members, they are expected to act like them, otherwise they are not expected to contribute much more than following directions and sticking to the rules. However, the direction could be changed at very short notice (they may even be expected to go from manufacturing shoes to assembling computer chips in one year) and people are expected to be very flexible when this takes place. Such people may be called 'the adaptors', being able to live up to the personal whims of 'the father' as well as to follow quick turns in the direction of the firm.

Where power distance is high and systems skills are asked for (such as in *Arabia*), the system is very different from the American one. People are now supposed to become morally involved with and emotionally dependent on their employer; promotion can only take place through a private selection by the person(s) at the top, and 'political' skills become crucial. Loyalty is seen as a virtue and more important than efficiency and management skills. Such people may be called 'the loyalists'.

The next relation of interest is *uncertainty avoidance–attitude to change* (Figure 9.6).

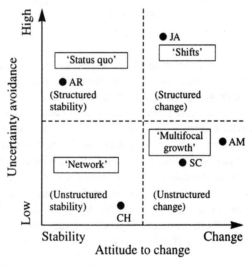

*Figure 9.6   Uncertainty avoidance–attitude to change*

The type of change asked for depends on whether the members of a culture are in need of a structured life or not. In general, the more structured the culture, the more public change, if any at all. In an unstructured culture, change can grow naturally from below and spread in many directions.

Where uncertainty avoidance is low and stability is asked for (such as in *China*), a lot of micro-activities still take place, however, not in a structure or in a hierarchy, but in a 'network'. Change is controlled such that this network is not destroyed and such that change moves in a balanced direction (Yin and Yang).

Where uncertainty avoidance is low combined with where change is asked for (such as in *America* and *Scandinavia*), the belief is that change can be steered and guided by the preferences of human beings. However, change is seen as a process, which is not possible to plan in detail, and which can take many directions at the same time, depending on the interests involved. Change can, therefore, be characterized as 'multifocal growth'.

Where uncertainty avoidance is high, but change is still asked for (such as in *Japan*), change can only take place as carefully prepared and controlled in steps ('shifts') from one position to the next. It is all very structured and the people involved must be committed to change, otherwise the structure itself can stop any attempts to move.

Where uncertainty avoidance is high and stability is asked for (such as in *Arabia*), change has not got much chance. Participants are happy with the *status quo*.

One interesting relation is *uncertainty avoidance–aims* (Figure 9.7).

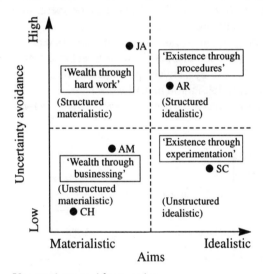

*Figure 9.7   Uncertainty avoidance–aims*

This combination gives people an opportunity to classify what members of different cultures are looking for in life, what is motivating them and what makes them tick. The vertical axis (uncertainty avoidance) opposes motivation by individual effort to motivation by belonging. The horizontal axis (aims) opposes material needs to idealistic needs. Hofstede presents a similar picture (1984, p. 219), but refers to the aims variable as a masculinity scale (motivated by traditional masculine needs, including material ones, versus motivated by traditional feminine needs, including idealistic ones).

Where uncertainty avoidance is low and people are mainly focusing on materialistic aims (such as in *America* and *China*), growth is measured quantitatively, especially in terms of wealth. Americans believe that the most important path to success is through a business career, and the Chinese see business in almost anything. It can be stated, therefore, that people here are motivated by 'wealth through businessing'.

Where uncertainty avoidance is low and people are mainly focusing on idealistic aims (such as in *Scandinavia*), quality of life has a real meaning, and people are searching for it. They are motivated by 'existence through experimentation'. People in this category are motivated by 'quality of human relationships and the living environment' according to Hofstede (1984, p. 256).

Where uncertainty avoidance is high and people are still driven by idealistic aims (such as in *Arabia*), rules govern life and progress in life. People need only think of the ritualistic Muslims and their belief that religion should have an impact on all aspects of life, including business, to understand the label 'existence through procedures'.

Where uncertainty avoidance is high and people are controlled by materialistic aims (such as in *Japan*), people want to achieve wealth, and believe that they can do it best by actively participating in a successful business corporation, that is, 'wealth through hard work'.

The next relation presented here is *social orientation–time orientation* (Figure 9.8).

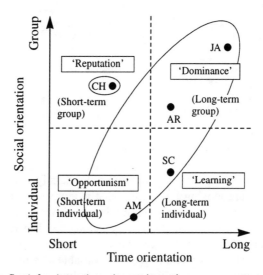

*Figure 9.8   Social orientation–time orientation*

This relation, like the previous one, can be interpreted in terms of what people want, and what they are looking for, if they judge success through themselves or through others and in what time perspective it is all seen.

Where social orientation is the individual and time orientation is short (such as in *America*), freedom and competition are important, and in this race, time is money. The winner may be the one who is best at 'opportunism'.

Where social orientation is the individual but time orientation is long (compared to some others of the five cultures) (such as in *Scandinavia*), people like independence, but also responsibility and do not want to be seen as 'standing out', or trying to be better than others from a materialistic point of view. People want, instead, to develop from within, that is, be constantly 'learning'.

Where social orientation is the group and time orientation is long (such as in *Japan* and *Arabia*), progress is often measured from the whole nation's point of view, and ultimately in terms of superiority and 'dominance' in specific business sectors.

Where social orientation is the group and time orientation is short (such as in *China*), relationships count more than market efficiency and groups and networks more than individuals. However, relations and networks are accessible only as long as a person has a (good) 'reputation'. Continuing business stands and falls with this.

It may be noticed in this picture that four cultures follow a certain pattern, while the Chinese culture breaks it.

Another relation is *attitude to change–skills wanted* (Figure 9.9).

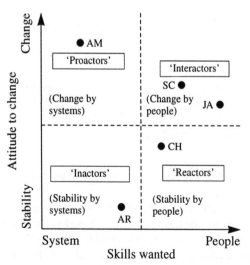

*Figure 9.9   Attitude to change–skills wanted*

This relation will tell us how change (and stability) is expected to be achieved, that is, whether by talented people or by an appropriate system.

Where stability and system skills are asked for (such as in *Arabia*), change does not come naturally. People trust the established way of life and like it as it is, that is, they are 'inactors'.

Where stability and people skills are asked for (such as in *China*), change takes place through people (systems may not even be trusted), but typically only as an answer to new circumstances, that is, as 'reactors'.

Where change and people skills are asked for (such as in *Japan* and *Scandinavia*), change takes place through a process of consensus-building, that is, where people are 'interactors'.

Where change and systems skills are asked for (such as in *America*), people look at it as professional to approach change through advanced planning, decisions and control systems, that is, to be 'proactors'.

One further relation is *aims–problem-solving* (Figure 9.10).

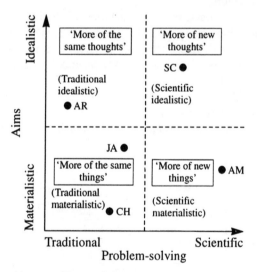

*Figure 9.10    Aims–problem-solving*

This relation tells us how people approach problems and what they expect from solving them.

Where there are materialistic aims and problem-solving is traditional (such as in *China* and *Japan*), the business logic is based on personal commitment and problems are approached intuitively, not logically. Good intuition is based on relevant traditions and adequate experience. People want socially recognized results in terms such that the environment can see what they have done; this in turn will promote their societal status, that is, they want 'more of the same things'.

Where there are materialistic aims and problem-solving is scientific (such as in *America*), people appreciate what is modern, up to date and youthful. With a rational and practical approach also follows rational and practical results, that is, 'more of new things'.

Where there are idealistic aims and problem-solving is scientific (such as in *Scandinavia*), the approach is objective, but the outcome is more subjective. Furthermore, people find it important to learn continuously. They want 'more of new thoughts' and they do not value success so much in terms of things.

Where there are idealistic aims, but problem-solving is traditional (such as in *Arabia*), people still want to feel that they are improving. However, they want to improve on an established frame of reference, not learning new ideas. New ideas may even be seen as heresy. They want to get 'more of the same thoughts', that is, learn more of the established truth.

One interesting relation, which is associated with the last one (as mentioned earlier in this chapter problem-solving and communication are directly related, unbroken across all or five cultures), is *aims–communication* (Figure 9.11).

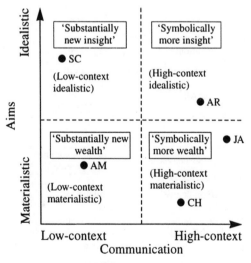

*Figure 9.11   Aims–communication*

In general, it is more important for members in high-contextual cultures to judge their achievements against members of the same culture. Outsiders may not even understand what they are struggling for even as they obviously gain in status and respect among their own. Achievements in low-contextual cultures, on the other hand, are for everyone to see and directly understand, insiders as well as outsiders. To what extent they lead to higher status and respect, however, is secondary. Achievements are less symbolic in low-contextual cultures. Status symbols have a real deep meaning only in high-contextual cultures.

Where there are materialistic aims and problem-solving is scientific (Figure 9.10), the communication environment is low-contextual (such as in *America*), and people want 'substantially new wealth' (Figure 9.11).

Where there are materialistic aims but problem-solving is traditional, that is, the communication environment is high-contextual instead (such as in *Japan* and *China*), people want 'symbolically more wealth'.

Where there are idealistic aims combined with traditional problem-solving, that is, with a high-contextual communication environment (such as in *Arabia*), people want 'symbolically more insight'.

Where there are idealistic aims, but problem-solving is scientific, that is, the communication environment is low-contextual (such as in *Scandinavia*), people want 'substantially new insight'.

The last relation that is discussed here is attitude to *environment–problem-solving* (Figure 9.12).

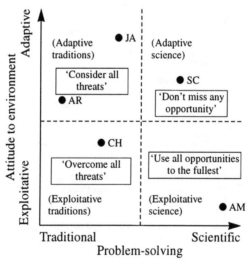

*Figure 9.12    Attitude to environment–problem-solving*

This relation tells us what means various cultures find appropriate and acceptable to use when solving problems they see in the environment. In general, cultures with a scientific approach look at the environment as mainly opportunities; cultures with a traditional approach as mainly threats. Cultures with an exploitative attitude to the environment look at it as a failure not to use their situation to the fullest; cultures with an adaptive attitude look at it as a failure not to recognize relevant aspects of it. The result is four combinations as usual.

Where the attitude to the environment is exploitative and problem-solving is traditional (such as in *China*), the way to go is to 'overcome all threats'. The Overseas Chinese (which are the Chinese looked at in this study) have proved they have been able to do so in business in the past 40–50 years or so.

Where the attitude to the environment is exploitative, but problem-solving is scientific (such as in *America*), the ambition is to 'use all opportunities to the fullest'. With this attitude and with the giant resources available in America, it is small wonder that the Americans are leading in many business fields.

Where the attitude to the environment is adaptive and problem-solving is scientific (such as in *Scandinavia*), people have the creative and open attitude to explore all openings and not neglect any alternatives. Scandinavians have come up with several innovative approaches to business, because they 'do not miss any opportunity', or at least try not to.

Where the attitude to the environment is adaptive, but problem-solving is traditional (such as in *Japan* and *Arabia*), the ambition is to be well prepared for any change that may occur, that is, to 'consider all threats'. If the culture also has other progressive attributes, such as willingness to change and democracy at work (such as in *Japan*), it could be difficult for any opponent to counter business moves from such a culture. If such progressive attributes are not at hand (such as in *Arabia*), change is rare.

## WHAT ABOUT THE FRONTIER, THE BEDOUIN AND SO ON?

Five questions were raised at the end of Chapter 3:

1. How much of a Frontier is there still in an American?
2. How much of a Bedouin is there still in an Arab?
3. How much of a Mandarin is there still in a Chinese?
4. How much of a Samurai is there still in a Japanese?
5. How much of a Viking is there still in a Scandinavian?

A brief answer to these questions is given below:

*Americans* are future-oriented and find it possible, even mandatory, to improve on the present. To change for the better is to control the environment technologically and to steer any changes. Americans see opportunities in the future, embrace what is new and modern and live in a very entrepreneurial society. There is still much of a Frontier among Americans.

*Arabs* are still to a large extent *badawi* (Arabic = 'inhabitants of the desert' = Bedouin) or have this background. However, at least in business, Arabs want to embrace a more 'modern' lifestyle and even if they are careful to keep many old traditions and customs, these are increasingly difficult to derive from the Bedouins. There is less and less of a Bedouin in an Arab.

*Chinese* Mandarin (upper-class) supervision from the north in China itself was the major obstacle to the rise of an indigenous capitalist class and for the merchant class to use its talents and contacts to the fullest. Southerners were eventually forced to leave to exploit their trade elsewhere with unprecedented economic consequences in Southeast Asia. There is little, if anything, of a Mandarin in an Overseas Chinese today.

The *Japanese* want to prepare the battleground carefully by gathering information. Their conquest of world markets is very much like a well-directed military campaign – 'it was almost as though this country had been in training for centuries, toughening itself through self-denial and work-as-duty to be ready for an all-out economic blitz' (Hoover, 1988, p. 130). The Japanese press on in business, neglect obstacles, permit nothing but attack, guided by the warrior code of *Bushido*. There is still much of a Samurai mentality among Japanese.

*Scandinavians* are persistently looking for new markets and applications; they are export-oriented and doing well with their multinational business efforts. They do not spread the same fear as once the Vikings did, but are at least respected in several business fields. Coming from small countries far away from the centre of the interest of the world, 'daring to travel to far-away places' as Scandinavians obviously still do, makes it possible to say that there is still a bit of a Viking in a Scandinavian (and he is very proud of it).

# 10. The cultural business leader

## THE CULTURAL COMPLEX

'Culture' seems to have become a concept that almost all business-oriented people (researchers as practitioners) have found useful and have opinions about. These opinions sometimes differ widely. I have claimed that every concept which has gradually come to contain more and more, sooner or later will become cumbersome and even meaningless. This also goes for the concept of culture. The concept is more manageable and useful for researchers of business if it only contains factors behind our behaviour, not behaviour in itself. In this study culture is defined as consisting of norms, values and assumptions which people carry around as a result of a social life. Behavioural consequences from culture and other expressions such as fine art, institutions and buildings, are called *cultural manifestations*, but not culture in itself. However, even with this 'limited' definition of culture, there are still differences between understanding, managing and influencing norms as compared to doing the same for values or assumptions.

A group must have been together for a while for its members to develop a mutual social understanding. The same goes for an organization of, for instance, a business firm. Yet the culture may become more or less pervasive and more or less strong as was pointed out in Chapter 2. It is still possible for a group of people to develop several slightly different subcultures within itself even though the group has existed for a long time, for the simple reason that members have only associated in smaller units within the whole group. Unless people in a group (for example, a company) associate and develop common social mechanisms of integration, they will tend to develop idiosyncratic explanations for what is going on and come up with their own understanding of their situation (Wilkins and Ouchi, 1983, p. 474).

A common set of shared values (which then probably means that norms and assumptions are shared as well) can be such an integrative link. This normally means less dependence on commands and a more frequent use of consensus.

> Although a value system may be most visible in the few words that make up an advertising slogan, many successful companies have a very rich tradition of values, beliefs, and themes that have developed over the years. Where do these values

come from? They mostly come from experience, from testing what does and doesn't work in the economic environment (Deal and Kennedy, 1988, p. 25).

Basic for the development of values is that people tend to stick to what they see as well known to them, which in turn means an environment which becomes increasingly taken for granted and a more habitual way of life (Daun, 1989, pp. 28–29). People develop a preference for what they have grown accustomed to in a certain social situation; increasingly more of their 'knowledge' disappears into subconsciousness. People are generally not aware of the constant reinforcement of their culture and the fact that what they take to be 'their own thing' or 'natural' is often culturally conditioned. People's eyes are not opened until they meet unusual situations or other cultures. Before people know their own culture, it may needlessly tie them up and hamper them.

One essential cultural manifestation is that *network* which exists in all organizations. This network constitutes the primary means of communication in the organization. Important aspects of this 'cultural net' are (as mentioned previously):

a.  stories and myths;
b.  rituals and symbols;
c.  leadership and management style;
d.  structures and systems.

It is the case, for instance, that stories being told in various organizations are different from one organization to the next one, and these stories reflect those values ruling in the organization in question. And where the culture is stronger, stories are more frequent.

According to Deal and Kennedy (1988, pp. 25–26) most of what goes on of importance to the business takes place in the cultural network, not as formal events in the hierarchy (see Chapter 2). Even in the context of a very controlled meeting, there is a lot of informal communication going on – bonding rituals, glances, innuendoes and so on. The real process of gathering support, of presenting opinions and of making decisions, happens before the meeting – or after. The network is important not only because it ties people together; the meaning and importance of information is also interpreted there. Top managers and business leaders must recognize this fact and use it. To use the cultural network can sometimes be the only way to get something done.

Individual people can be of great importance to create the values and standards of the organization, that is, its culture:

> In a new organization, in a company with a new leader, or in a company determined to modify its culture, the role of the leader is critical in (re)developing the

corporate values. Such leaders shape organizational cultures to the extent that they are able to indoctrinate their subordinates with their own beliefs, or cultivate ideas that their subordinates adopt as their own (Humes, 1993, p. 129).

Business leaders, wherever they are in the hierarchy and in the network, may also be conclusive actors in various stages of a business. However, business leaders can never let go of their cultural responsibility. The most important ability of business leaders may be to clarify 'what we believe'. Those business leaders who realize this could be called 'cultural business leaders' (this will be discussed further later in this chapter).

Looked at from the international perspective of today people are *influenced by other cultures almost no matter what they do*. It is becoming harder for people to isolate themselves, and strictly domestic business is becoming more and more impossible. However, even business managers in organizations directly involved in international business, for example, in multinational corporations, are becoming more proactive by looking at cultures in countries where they operate, as well as their own corporate culture, as very powerful factors and instruments. This may be because they have faced mergers and joint ventures with companies from another cultural background, because they have tried to expand into countries with a different way of life, diversified into product lines requiring diversified strategies, experienced rapid growth or retrenchment, seen serious conflicts between various groups, or simply been inspired by that intensive public discussion and by the variety of writings going on in cultural issues (Humes, 1993, p. 129). Harris and Moran (1987, pp. 23–24) provide several reasons why all managers should improve their cultural learning or why multinational companies should include it in their human resource development strategies. Some of these reasons are:

- Culture gives people a sense of identity, whether in nations or corporations, especially in terms of what human behaviour and which values are encouraged. This can improve loyalty and performance in the organization.
- Cultural knowledge provides insight into other people; managers as well as other employees may benefit from understanding general as well as specific cultural aspects in order to improve intercultural communication, client relations, and productivity.
- Cultural awareness and skills can be useful in influencing the organizational culture. Culture within global corporations, for example, has an impact on job performance and on customer relations; furthermore, such units as subsidiaries, divisions, departments or specializations have subcultures which may foster or undermine organizational goals and communications.

- Cultural insights and tools are useful in studying comparative management, so that people become less bound by culture in their attempts to practise leadership and management. Those who have a position where they are to operate practically among people from other nations can become more effective in local negotiations and organizational relationships.
- Cultural astuteness and acumen enable people to comprehend the diversity of market needs that exists, and to improve strategies with minority and ethnic groups at home, or foreign markets abroad.
- Cultural perspicuity and clear-sightedness are applicable to all relocation experiences, whether domestic or international. This is valid for individual managers or technicians who are facing a geographic transfer, as well as for their families and subordinates involved in such cultural change.

Cultural learning is a means for managers and other leaders to become more global and cosmopolitan in their outlook and behaviour, as well as more effective and profitable in their practices.

Diversity can be a strength and frequently accompanies change. Too much diversity and too large differences may, however, divide the organization. It is a challenge facing every multinational to develop and manage its international network such that it not only accommodates its diverse operations in some kind of common denominator but also allows local differences and needs to function. Such a denominator could be culture seen as 'only' norms, values and assumptions, at the same time as variations in cultural manifestations and expressions are allowed. Every multinational corporation with many operating units spread over the world consists of a panoply of values from home, host country, industry, market, technology and professional dominance, just to mention a few sources of variation.

Taggart and McDermott (1993, p. 43) provide an action list for multinational managers, which can be used to cope with international cultural differences:

1. be culturally prepared: forewarned is forearmed;
2. learn the local language and its nonverbal elements;
3. mix with host nationals, including socially;
4. be creative and experimental, without fear of failure;
5. be culturally sensitive; do not stereotype or criticize;
6. recognize complexities in the host culture;
7. perceive yourself as a culture bearer and ambassador;
8. be patient, understanding and accepting of your hosts;
9. be most realistic in your expectations;

10.   accept the challenge of intercultural experiences.

'Cultural business leadership' is a huge topic, which in itself could form the basis of several book volumes. In this final chapter there is, therefore, room for only a few general aspects of the subject, including who the cultural business leader is and his or her task plus characteristics and ways of functioning in different types of culture.

## SYMBOLS, COMMUNICATION AND LANGUAGE

The number-crunching financial person may feel strongly that the primary role of a business firm is to make money and its success is measured by profits being created. Shared and common values and distinct corporate cultures may possibly seem like a luxury to him or her, a luxury which is affordable only when more money has come into than gone out of the business. According to such a person, the soft side of business should come in second place. Of course, nobody can deny that a business has to be fiscally sound, but this does not happen by itself. Nothing takes place in a company unless somebody acts, and acting is more purposeful if it is directed by 'shared and common values and a distinct corporate culture'. Moreover, there is research showing that companies whose only articulated goals are financial do not do nearly as well financially as companies that have broader sets of values (Peters and Waterman, 1984, p. 103).

Perhaps business leadership has traditionally been pursued by a person who sat at the top of the hierarchy and made decisions as problems arose, and business leaders may 'in the old days' have acted as detached, cold, analytic, centrally placed and strategic planners. The cultural business leader's reality of today could hardly be different. Such a person should rather be a lover of purposefulness, and a preacher of visions and common values. He or she should have the ability to involve others in an intellectually stimulating and emotionally engaging operation and development of business.

A cultural business leader could also be called 'a symbolic business leader'. Organizational life is full of symbols and the cultural business leader understands this – and understands how to use it:

> Organizational life is rich in various forms of ritual activity, tradition, patterns of humour, story-telling, and various kinds of metaphorical imagery which contribute to the development of distinctive kinds of cultural milieux within the organization. Such activities may be consciously contrived to produce certain effects within the organization, or may arise spontaneously to give shape and form to significant patterns of meaning in areas of work life which are otherwise devoid of valued intrinsic content. Thus, organizational traditions and stories may be

consciously developed as a means of achieving improved managerial control. The managerial style of a chief executive may be shaped in many diverse ways to evoke feelings of paternalistic loyalty from employees, or to create a system of attitudes and beliefs which foster a competitive, aggressive organizational atmosphere. On the other hand, the symbolic character of organizational life may take form in opposition to managerial values, providing an escape route from the toil imposed by formal organizational requirements (Morgan *et al.*, 1983, pp. 9–10).

Symbols can be highly individualized but also well spread and anchored in an organization. Furthermore, even though symbolism is important, it is easy to forget. In Chapter 2 it was stated that three aspects in an organization are often studied from a symbolic point of view, that is, *rituals, language and myths*. These three aspects are worth repeating and stressed further here because symbolism is so important to the cultural/symbolic business leader:

1. Many activities carried out in companies take place according to rules or in a predestined fashion. Such activities could be called *rituals*. Managers are also engaged in many such rituals even if they may be reluctant to admit it (Deal and Kennedy, 1988, p. 68). Examples of rituals are:

   - the boss's morning routine walking around talking to the closest staff;
   - a recurrent Monday meeting in the senior group;
   - a monthly speech by the general manager to the personnel, televised internally;
   - a standing agenda at meetings.

   Many subactivities may also be structured or taken so much for granted that they are more to be seen as rituals.
   This does not mean that rituals must be a waste of time or that they have no meaning. They have a *supportive* role (people feel they do their job) as well as a *cohesive* role (observers, including participants, feel at home) to play. What may be surprising is that much more of the operations of a business than is normally understood could be characterized as rituals.
   Insightful managers spend a lot of time fine-tuning the rituals (Deal and Kennedy, 1988, p. 76). By looking at rituals as cultural manifestations, they can consciously make the cultural values of the company coherent and accessible to every employee.

2. A *language* contains much symbolism, as people know. Even if a language is more or less taken for granted, the language being used in a company consciously or unconsciously influences almost everything

going on there (remember that there are both verbal and nonverbal aspects of a language). Additionally, language as communication does not necessarily mean understanding.

Language is, of course, important to the cultural business leader because language is the mirror of culture. It is a common saying that business leaders have visions, for instance. However, if a vision is to be of any importance, it is not only essential that its source is credible; the form and process by which it is communicated can be crucial (Pettigrew, 1979, pp. 577–578). It may be expected, for instance, that the power of the vision is conditional on the degree of complexity and simplicity with which it is expressed, the extent to which it uses the technical language of the business economist or the jargon of 'the grass roots', and whether it is given as a public announcement or is spread through the company's network backed up by relevant action.

3. *Myths* are stories which are based on metaphors, the transferred meaning of which cannot be made literal, at least not directly. Myths require an interpretation which will extract a hidden meaning. This means that myths have a symbolic reality. If a company member 'believes' a myth about his or her own culture, this myth may play a very important role as a prototype. People have all heard of the free and sharp American eagle or the demonic Chinese dragon, but there is also tremendous pride and motivational power behind the employees who call their company 'a gypsy society' (Kanter, 1983, p. 132), 'a shamrock' (Peters, 1992, p. 150), or 'a spider plant' (Morgan, 1993, p. 64).

## THE CULTURAL BUSINESS LEADER – WHO IS IT?

The way in which a business leader looks at culture will influence his or her leading style. If he or she looks at his or her company *as culture*, he or she will see culture in the attitudes and values of the colleagues, in how problems are approached and solved, in how the company acts towards customers, suppliers and competitors and in how the members of the company in practically all matters are operating now and in the future.

I refer to a business leader as a 'cultural business leader' if he or she has this view. I also claim that it is important to have this view in business, because organizations consist of people. To manage people as people means to act through the humble as well as subtle cues and signals of the culture.

As mentioned in Chapter 3, leaders do not have to be appointed as top managers to be of interest to the project presented in this study. A cultural business leader may be a formal as well as an informal leader, functioning in hierarchies as well as in networks, playing transactional as well as transforming roles. Another name for such leaders is leading actors or key players of the culture.

Some say that good strategic planning and an appropriate vision will ensure an institution's future. I am afraid it is not that simple – and not that impersonal. An institution, for example a company, stands and falls with its leaders ('Leadership jazz', June, 1994, p. 28). In strong cultures, leaders take an active part in supporting and creating the culture. This is so at the national level as well as at the corporate level.

## THE CULTURAL BUSINESS LEADER'S TASK

Whichever way culture is understood, values are its core. It is, therefore, important for a cultural leader to know and understand the values ruling his or her organization. What brings values to life, however, is the awareness of everyone in the organization of their existence, but also that people share them and understand that they are important. Cultural business leaders (the leading actors of the culture) participate in this sharing and they take the responsibility for this sharing to take place.

A number of factors other than money affect the motivation of employees to perform for the organization. Some of these factors relate directly to individual needs such as needs for achievement, recognition, responsibility, advancement, personal growth and so on. Other factors relate to group or organizational needs such as peer relations, supervision, status, job security and so on (Boulton, 1984, pp. 168–170). How the specific needs package looks will, of course, very much depend on which national culture a person belongs to, for instance, one of the five cultures discussed in this study.

Rewards that employees receive for their contributions to an organization can be both monetary and nonmonetary in nature. I want to claim, however, that the *conclusive* inducement for an individual to engage him- or herself long term and in depth in the place where the individual is employed is that the person in question has a feeling that what he or she is doing is meaning-ful, both as far as the content of his or her task, as well as in relation to other tasks (other people), is concerned. It could even be said that the cultural business leader's main task is to create and confirm this meaning.

This is no easy task, however. Among other things, it requires a lot of time and not to look at things and events as trivial but to look at them as a challenge and a chance to reinforce and distribute cultural values. Cultural business leaders 'spend a lot of time thinking about the values, heroes, and rituals of the culture, and they see their primary job as managing value conflicts that arise in the ebb and flow of daily events' (Deal and Kennedy, 1988, p. 141). In order to perform this task something much more than knowing about and applying traditional administrative techniques is needed. Again, a cultural leader is a symbolic leader, that is, a person who sees organizations as full of symbols and knows how to use them intelligently.

It could also be said (and it has been mentioned previously) that a leader's job *is* culture. The leadership aspect of culture is related to creating purpose and commitment. One important mechanism for this (as also mentioned previously), is the corporate language. To speak 'their' language is to understand their world view (their system of categories for organizing the world). If nothing else, it generates respect. Generally, to repeat what was said in Chapter 3, the more leaders are able to understand what motivates their subordinates and colleagues and the more they reflect this understanding in carrying out their actions (including language actions), the more effective they are likely to be as leaders.

In organizations with effective leaders people feel generally more empowered. This may express itself in different ways, for example (Bennis, 1989, pp. 38–39):

- people feel significant, that they are counted;
- people feel they really contribute;
- people feel part of a social community and not alienated;
- work becomes more exciting.

How this looks in detail will also very much depend on the national culture in question.

Everybody wants to see a meaning in what he or she is doing, even the leader. It could be said, however, that the difference between the cultural leader and the other organizational members is that the former also wants to see *the meaning with the meaning*, that is, understand the purpose behind creating and maintaining meaning for others (and for him- or herself):

> What we learn from this is that the inherent preferences of organizations is clarity, certainty and completion; the nature of human relations is unclear, uncertain and incomplete. How to satisfy, balance and integrate both these needs – that is the real art of management (Pascale and Athos, 1982, pp. 102–103).

Someone has expressed it such that leadership is like playing jazz ('Leadership jazz', June, 1994, p. 24). It takes place in a group; everybody wants to perform as improvising individuals and as a harmonic group, and the leader depends on the members of the group. The idea is to have a perfect voice and touch!

One important aspect of what is required for a leader to succeed is *consistency*. Followers cannot afford leaders who make casual promises. Leaders put themselves on the line to the people they lead. An enormous chasm separates the private world, where people often smile indulgently at broken promises, from the public one, where unkept promises do great harm, both to the leader and to the culture he or she is supposed to stand for. In order to build a strong culture, a business leader should be convinced of what values he or she can and should promote and then never divert from them.

A unique aspect of leadership, which some people say differs from being a manager, is the ability to influence and change other people more permanently, or as it was stated in Chapter 3, leaders can influence other people's attitudes and opinions, not only their actions and decisions. This may be because cultural leaders understand the power placed in the mentality 'we against the rest of the world', and, therefore, may be able to give extra nourishment to supernatural efforts and, in some cultures, to new initiatives among followers.

Cultural leaders are often brave change agents, who understand other people, who are driven by values, who are lifelong learners, who are able to manage complexity, ambiguity and uncertainty, and who are visionary. These leaders may not be taken back by bureaucracies and hierarchies and may not even follow their own national culture! These leaders' leaders stand out even more from the rest of the crowd. They look at the world in large terms – they work for their own visions and ideas, not for those of others.

Managers and leaders have different power bases (Table 10.1). Some of these differences are (Arvonen, 1989, p. 149):

*Table 10.1   Managers' and leaders' power bases*

| The manager's power base | The leader's power base |
| --- | --- |
| Management is performed in a formal position | Leaders create their own 'informal' legitimacy |
| The power of managers is based on 'authorization' from the employer | Leaders base their power on their own, personal characteristics |
| Managers communicate through formal channels (the official way) | Leaders communicate directly and personally, mainly through networks |
| Managers' communication is objective and neutral | Leaders use signals and symbols |
| Managers develop control and systems to check on behaviour and results | Leaders develop control through identification and social bonds |

Two tasks (and associated behaviour), which are often pointed out as a result of (Western) research on business leadership and which vary among the five cultures, are to what extent cultural business leaders:

1. accept different subcultures in their organization and even use them as a cultivator of change;
2. trust colleagues and subordinates, and delegate in order to increase and spread commitment and engagement.

The successful Western business leader is expected to accept different subcultures as well as being willing to delegate freely.

There are major variations among the five cultures; also to what extent soft factors such as personnel and participation or hard factors such as resources and systems are used, and to what extent control takes place using rules, goals and/or visions.

Of less interest here is to what extent business leadership depends on industry or stage of the cycle of the business ('The four faces ...', May, 1994).

## THE TYPIFIED CULTURAL BUSINESS LEADER

At this stage I will try to come up with some kind of picture of basic characteristics of the cultural business leader, traits and behaviour which I think exist among cultural business leaders in all the five cultures, even if (naturally) the ways in which these aspects and moments are manifested in more detail and their importance vary among the five. I am aware that the consequences of this attempt will lead me on to very thin ice. It is known, for instance, that the five cultures even have different opinions about what a business leader is to start with and, therefore, different conceptions of their function:

- the *American* business leader (the foresighted manager) wants to be a *pathfinder* (a person who finds new roads which other people want to follow);
- the *Arab* business leader (the benevolent autocrat) wants to be a *cultural ideal* (a person who other people seek to emulate);
- the *Chinese* business leader (the well-connected paternalist) wants to be a *central figure* (a person who everybody seeks to have contacts with and asks for advice);
- the *Japanese* business leader (the participative facilitator) wants to be a *catalyst* (a person who triggers an activating process among other

people);

- the *Scandinavian* business leader (the broad-minded negotiator) wants to be an *equilibrist* (a person who is active in coming up with a solution but makes other people feel that the solution is theirs).

As can be seen from the above, it is implicitly understood that *the typified American business leader is to be at the front of a change process*, that *the Scandinavian business leader is to prepare for interested parties* (including him- or herself) *to participate in a change process* and that *the Japanese business leader is to make other people change. The Arab and the Chinese business leaders expect no change to take place unless they change themselves!*

Another factor 'normally' associated with business leaders is, as mentioned earlier, their more 'permanent' influence on their business followers. This is an implicit function for all the business leaders in the five cultures. However, this typically takes place as a consequence of co-action with followers for the Japanese and for the Scandinavian, as a consequence of being a good example to others for the American and the Arab, and as an opportunity offered only to members of the family and other network members for the Chinese. The two themes – 'culture-change relations' and 'leaders' influence on their followers' – will be discussed again later in this chapter.

First, a few possible general and fundamental characteristics of traits and behaviour of cultural business leaders in all the five cultures will be discussed. Typified cultural business leaders (almost everywhere):

- *understand what a culture means and how it is to be used.* They appreciate the manifestations of culture in daily life, look at themselves as players in the cultural drama and have a definite understanding of the importance of culture to the long-term survival of its carriers as well.
- *are extremely symbolically oriented.* They have, for instance, a feeling for language and pay more attention to other people. They are also more convincing in their own language games, which means (Pascale and Athos, 1982, pp. 97–98): (a) being able to use the right words; (b) moving easily between concrete and abstract topics; (c) using metaphors and myths; and (d) using plain language.
- *are constantly not only users, but also supporters and maintainers of the culture* (in words and in actions). They have the ability to travel in the network when needed but also (probably less often) to act from a hierarchical position. Looked at from a network position point of view they are not just leaders but also followers and they probably worry more about the process than the result itself (they know that the result

will go their way anyway if the process is right). One day in their life is full of little things that do not matter, little things that partially matter and big things that matter a lot. The first are called trivia, the second events and the third drama. A cultural business leader knows how to distinguish among the three (Deal and Kennedy, 1988, p. 142). A cultural business leader is also happy to talk about his or her culture.

- *create and maintain meaning for the members of the culture, but also look at meaning in a more holistic perspective* (see 'meaning within the meaning', as mentioned earlier). The ability among cultural business leaders in their language games to be able to shift between concrete and abstract topics (which has just been mentioned) can also be expressed such that they can combine the most mundane details with the broadest visions and ideas (Bjerke, 1989, pp. 704–705). They can also change between being distant and being close to their culture.

- *do not hesitate to defend their own culture but also take care of change if that is necessary and then work actively to accomplish such a change within their own culture* (first as manifestations, but possibly in its more basic value components as well). They are brave and have a conviction when creating and fine-tuning the culture. The trick, of course, is to know their own culture well enough to be able to tailor the problem-solving process in the right direction. Cultural business leaders are probably more visible in critical situations where they point to the organization culture, clarifying 'what we believe' and possibly modifying the culture according to new requirements.

- *can generally interpret people exceptionally well.* They can 'read' their subordinates and colleagues and know to what extent they can be trusted to ensure success. In a special way, all the qualities of a good cultural leader stem from his or her awareness of the human spirit, its possibilities and its limitations.

The above points are not independent of each other, of course.

One good summary of the characteristics of successful leaders (and consistent with the points mentioned above) is provided by Bennis (1989, pp. 37–38). After several years of observation and conversation with such persons (in his case in the Western world), he defined four competencies evident in all leaders:

1. *Management of attention* through a set of intentions or a vision, not in a mystical or religious sense but in the sense of outcome, goal or direction.
2. *Management of meaning* by, often using metaphors or models or their own examples, being able to communicate and make ideas tangible and real to others so that they can support them.

3.   *Management of trust* in the sense of breathing confidence, so that other people feel they know what their leader stands for.
4.   *Management of self* by knowing personal strengths and weaknesses and acting accordingly.


## CULTURE AND CHANGE

If culture has not been considered in a firm before, it will without exception come up for discussion when there is a problem implementing a decided strategy. Generally, in the traditional view, culture may have three alternative ways of preventing strategic change (Lorsch, 1986, pp. 97–100):

1.   Managers do not perceive the necessity to change strategically, because their culture gives them a limited view of their firms and the possibilities and necessities to change.
2.   Managers perceive the necessity to change strategically, but cannot come up with suitable new strategic plans, because their culture makes them think according to the existing culture, that is, traditionally.
3.   Managers perceive the necessity to change strategically, come up with strategic plans for how to accomplish change, but the culture in the rest of the company prevents them from implementing these changes.

This traditional view is missing the point of culture completely. A corporate culture (or any culture) is something that is not turned on or off, or something which arises only under certain circumstances. A corporate culture is not a tool among other tools in a company or one of its systems. A corporate culture is there from the start in a strategic process and *is* the company in the sense that it is an inevitable part of it, the human part of it. A corporate culture is reflected in its structure, in its control systems, in the people who hold power – and in its strategy:

> It is [the] social processes of strategy formulation that have received so much attention in the work of those writers and researchers who have sought to understand how some businesses seem to perform consistently so much better than others – the so-called excellent companies. And the general conclusion that these writers come to is that processes of strategic management need to be understood as an essentially cultural process (Johnson and Scholes, 1988, p. 38).

> The symbolic power of strategy draws attention to how the strategic management process enacts culture and in giving it visible expression, modifies it in much the same way that speech gives meaning to language. Its effectiveness in motivating people and bringing about organization change depends crucially on the extent to which people know about it, understand it and have faith in it. The creation of

such knowledge, understanding and faith through the strategic management process, transforms strategy from a sophisticated economic plan into a potent social symbol signifying change. The symbolic content of strategy highlights the role of senior management and especially the CEO in the strategic management process. Their visibility, the extent to which other organization members interpret their actions, their control over internal resources, and the ritual adulation of leaders, founders, exemplars and heroes in organizational stories, myths and legends, places them at the epicentre of the cultural arena. More than anybody else, therefore, they have to understand their organization's structure of shared meaning in order to manipulate its symbols and create new ones in the furtherance of (their perceptions of) organization purpose (Green, 1988, p. 126).

As mentioned in Chapter 2, it is a pity that those tools which are most often used in order to try to control strategies (and consequently cultures) are of a purely technical nature (such as budgets, formal reports and ROI calculations) rather than formulated in symbolic terms. The challenge is, at least partly, to control a strategy in irrational terms or at least also in terms of networks, to *mix* explicit procedures and formal controls with implicit social control. It is also a pity that external consultants are more likely to be called in when there is disharmony between strategies and culture in a firm. This is exactly the moment when the corporation would need their own (cultural) leaders the most!

To manage change (if change is appropriate), a business leader must, as mentioned previously, at least understand what a culture is in general and what his or her own culture is like and how it functions in particular. As mentioned many times throughout this study, this is in itself no easy task. A person's ambition to understand a culture becomes more difficult, the more he or she gets used to it: a person's initial model of another culture is little more than an amalgam of the observer's own prejudiced presuppositions (Green, 1988, p. 124). To get rid of a person's prejudices against other people is possible, even if it is difficult. It requires both talent and training, however. To get rid of prejudices against oneself (to really understand one's own culture) is granted to only a few!

People may also talk about different degree of change. The most drastic change, of course, is to change the very culture itself:

> When we speak of ... cultural change we mean real changes in the behavior of people throughout the organization. In a technical sense we mean people in the organization identifying with the new role-model heroes. We mean people telling different stories to one another to explain what is occurring around them. We mean people spending their time differently on a day-to-day basis – calling on different accounts, asking different questions, carrying out different work rituals. And we mean for this behavior to be pervasive – to involve virtually all the people in the organization. This kind of deep-seated cultural change is what we mean when we say that change takes a long time to achieve. Most meaningful [in the

real sense of the word] change – for example, developing a 'marketing orientation' or becoming more 'cost effective' – involves just such cultural transformation (Deal and Kennedy, 1988, pp. 158–159).

One source ('The corporate culture ...', 17 October, 1983, p. 70) estimates that the time it takes to realize such a cultural transformation is 6–15 years. A review of the evidence suggests that anybody who tries to unearth a corporation's culture, much less change it, is in for a rough time. The values and beliefs people espouse frequently have little to do with the ones they really hold; these tend to be half-hidden and elusive.

Having grown out of a company's history, values are strengthened daily in a myriad of subtle ways, from observation of how people get ahead in the organization to the words employees choose to describe their companies. Moreover, people cling tightly, even irrationally, to their values and beliefs. It is not uncommon, for instance, to blame the circumstances if something goes wrong or to say that sooner or later a negative trend *must* turn.

It may be easier to change people instead. In the long term, according to many human-resource specialists, the key to culture is who you hire and promote, and people of a certain kind will support other people of the same kind to be hired and promoted (ibid.).

## THE TRANSACTIONAL AND THE TRANSFORMATIONAL LEADER REVISITED

James Burns's (1978) distinction between transactional and transformational leaders was introduced in Chapter 3. The difference between the two is worth a few more words. Transactional leaders were fine for an era of expanding markets and non-existent competition. These managers changed little; they managed what they saw as problematic but left things pretty much as they found them when they came, before they moved on.

Transformational leadership is about change, innovation and entrepreneurship. The transformational leaders are in contrast to those who stress the transactional aspect. Activities among the former go far beyond duty. There is also an emotional tie to the leader among those who follow him or her. Transactional leaders only influence other people's intellectual capacities. Transformational leaders also influence their motivation and self-esteem, maybe even their view of the world.

One source describes transformational leadership as a drama in three acts (Figure 10.1).

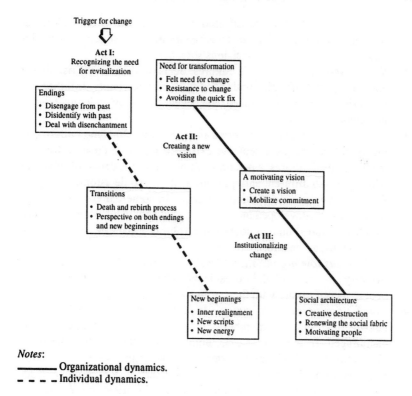

Notes:
———— Organizational dynamics.
– – – – Individual dynamics.

*Source*: Tichy and Devanna (1986, p. 246).

*Figure 10.1    Transformational leadership: a three-act drama*

## BUSINESS LEADERS IN DIFFERENT CULTURES

As previously discussed, there is a qualitative foundation in all cultural business leaders. At the same time as different cultures (for example, the five being discussed in this study) consist of different basic norms, values and beliefs, cultural leadership will express itself differently from one culture to the next. To reiterate, I mention here a few cultural dimensions again and very briefly give some examples of variations in cultural business leadership behaviour (a similar list such as the one below can be found in Hodgetts and Luthans, 1991, pp. 36–37):

- *Centralized versus decentralized decision-making*    In some societies, all important decisions are made by top managers. In other cultures, these decisions are more diffused throughout the organization and members at lower levels participate more actively in decision-making and even make their own decisions sometimes.

- *Safety versus risk* In some cultures, decision-makers are risk-averse and have great difficulty with conditions of uncertainty. In other cultures, risk-taking is encouraged, and decision-making under uncertainty is common.
- *Individuals for themselves versus in a network* In some cultures, an individual is seen as a separate existence and as a creative force in itself. In other cultures, a person's self is seen as the centre of relations, which leads to different entrepreneurial spirit and decision-making.
- *Few social rituals versus many rituals* In some cultures, norms are relatively little developed and correct social behaviour is more unclear. In other cultures, human coexistence follows a pattern which is clear and obvious, at least for an outsider.
- *High versus low organization loyalty* In some cultures, people identify very strongly with their organization or employer. In other cultures, people identify more with their occupational group.
- *Competition versus cooperation* In some cultures, competition is encouraged among its members; in other cultures, cooperation is encouraged. In the former case, human interaction tends to be modelled after the adjudication system and the bargaining of conflicting interests. In the latter case, which is a fiduciary system, political leadership and a strong government are essential (Tu, 1984, pp. 97–98).
- *Rationality versus irrationality* In some cultures, economic systems are built on logical and objective grounds. In other cultures, economic systems are generated from subjective (possibly shared and common) values.
- *Stability versus innovation* In some cultures, stability and resistance to change are encouraged. Other cultures put high value on innovation and change.

Another aspect of business leaders in different cultures is what representatives of one type of culture can expect when working in another culture and how he or she should act. A few examples of this are shown in Tables 10.2–10.5 (Trompenaars, 1995, pp. 45, 61, 106, 136). The cultural dimensions used were presented in Chapter 9.

There are many possibilities to train in and to learn cross-cultural 'abilities and knowledge' (Figure 10.2).

Probably a combination of the above possibilities is to be preferred. Theoretical knowledge becomes empty without experience from the field. Practical knowledge becomes incoherent if it is not placed in a theoretical perspective.

*Table 10.2   Conducting business with 'scientists' and 'traditionalists'*

| Scientists (as traditionalists) | Traditionalists (as scientists) |
|---|---|
| 1. Be prepared for 'rational', 'professional' arguments and presentations that push for your acquiescence. | 1. Be prepared for personal 'meandering' or 'irrelevancies' that do not seem to be going anywhere. |
| 2. Do not take impersonal, 'get down to business' attitudes as rude. | 2. Do not take personal, 'get to know you' attitudes as small talk. |
| 3. Carefully prepare the legal ground with a lawyer if in doubt. | 3. Carefully consider the personal implications of your legal 'safeguards'. |

*Source*:   Trompenaars (1995, p. 45).

*Table 10.3   Conducting business with 'individualists' and 'collectivists'*

| Individualists (as collectivists) | Collectivists (as individualists) |
|---|---|
| 1. Prepare for quick decisions and sudden offers not referred to HQ. | 1. Show patience for time taken to consent and to consult. |
| 2. Negotiator can commit those who sent him or her and is very reluctant to go back on an undertaking. | 2. Negotiator can only agree tentatively and may withdraw an undertaking after consulting with superiors. |
| 3. The toughest negotiations were probably already done within the organization while preparing for the meeting. You have a tough job selling them the solution to this meeting. | 3. The toughest negotiations are with the collectivists you face. You must somehow persuade them to cede to you points which the multiple interests in your company demand. |
| 4. Conducting business alone means that this person is respected by his or her company and has its esteem. | 4. Conducting business when surrounded by helpers means that this person has high status in his or her company. |
| 5. The aim is to make a quick deal. | 5. The aim is to build lasting relationships. |

*Source*:   Trompenaars (1995, p. 61).

*Table 10.4   Conducting business with 'positionists' and 'self-developers'*

| Positionists (as self-developers) | Self-developers (as positionists) |
| --- | --- |
| 1. Make sure your negotiation team has enough data, technical advisers and knowledgeable people to convince the other company that the project, jointly pursued, will work. | 1. Make sure your negotiation team has enough older, senior and formal position-holders to impress the other company that you consider this negotiation important. |
| 2. Respect the knowledge and information of your counterparts even if you suspect they are short of influence back home. | 2. Respect the status and influence of your counterparts, even if you suspect they are short of knowledge. Do not show them up. |
| 3. Use the title that reflects how competent you are as an individual. | 3. Show the title that reflects your degree of influence in your organization. |
| 4. Do not underestimate the need of your counterparts to do better or do more than is expected. To challenge is to motivate. | 4. Do not underestimate the need of your counterparts to make their ascription come true. To challenge is to subvert. |

*Source*:   Trompenaars (1995, p. 106).

*Table 10.5   Conducting business with 'exploiters' and 'adaptors'*

| Exploiters (as adaptors) | Adaptors (as exploiters) |
| --- | --- |
| 1. Playing 'hard ball' is legitimate to test the resilience of an opponent. | 1. Softness, persistence, politeness and long, long patience will get rewards. |
| 2. It is most important to 'win your objective'. | 2. It is most important to 'maintain your relationship'. |
| 3. Win some, lose some. | 3. Win together, lose apart. |

*Source*:   Trompenaars (1955, p. 136).

Is it possible to learn a foreign culture completely? I think not! After all, a person can live a whole life with a marriage partner without fully understanding him or her. However that should not prevent a person from trying:

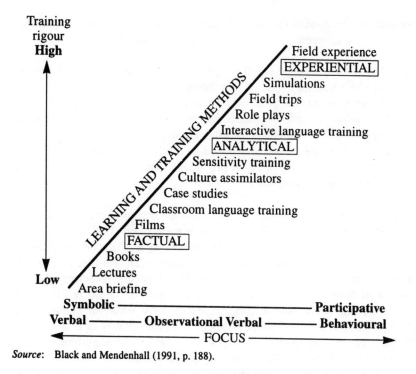

Training
rigour
**High**

Field experience
EXPERIENTIAL
Simulations
Field trips
Role plays
Interactive language training
ANALYTICAL
Sensitivity training
Culture assimilators
Case studies
Classroom language training
Films
FACTUAL
Books
Lectures
**Low** Area briefing

LEARNING AND TRAINING METHODS

**Symbolic** ——————————————— **Participative**
**Verbal** ———— **Observational Verbal** ———— **Behavioural**
◄——————————— FOCUS ———————————►

*Source*: Black and Mendenhall (1991, p. 188).

*Figure 10.2  Cross-cultural learning and training methods*

Other cultures are strange, ambiguous, even shocking to us. It is unavoidable that we will make mistakes in dealing with them and feel muddled and confused. The real issue is how quickly we are prepared to learn from mistakes and how bravely we struggle to understand a game in which 'perfect scores' are an illusion, and where reconciliation only comes after a difficult passage through alien territory.

We need a certain amount of humility and a sense of humour to discover cultures other than our own; a readiness to enter a room in the dark and stumble over unfamiliar furniture until the pain in our shins reminds us where things are. World culture is a myriad of different ways of creating the integrity without which life and business cannot be conducted. There are no universal answers but there are universal questions or dilemmas, and that is where we all need to start (Trompenaars, 1995, p. 177).

## TO FIT A CULTURE

As mentioned previously, smart business leaders are very much dedicated to culture. A conclusion can be drawn from this that successful companies place a great deal of emphasis on values. In general, according to Deal and Kennedy (1988, p. 22), successful companies share three characteristics:

1.	They stand for something, that is, they have a clear and explicit philosophy about how they conduct their business.
2.	Management pays a great deal of attention to shaping and fine-tuning these values to conform to the economic and business environment of the company and to communicating them to the organization.
3.	These values are known and shared by all the people who work for the company – from the lowliest production worker right through to the ranks of senior management.

However, be very careful when interpreting such statements about successful companies. It is important that one thing is understood. This study has presented *typified* pictures, that is, it has looked at logical consequences of following specified values, norms and assumptions. In real life, people will always diverge more or less from these pictures. A person, whether an American, an Arab or whatever, may not recognize him- or herself or his or her friends in this study. And a business leader, from whatever culture, may strongly oppose my description of his or her firm. That is as it should be. People can (at least partly) choose to live their lives according to their national cultural norms, values and assumptions or not.

Similarly, it cannot be said (after completion of this study) that if a company fits its national norm, it is a better or a more successful company. There exists no general model of an outstanding and excellent company, not even in its own national culture. People may speculate and say that successful companies have strong corporate cultures, that they blend the best elements from different kinds of culture (Deal and Kennedy, 1988, pp. 107–108), that they are limited to being driven by a handful of explicit themes (Peters and Waterman, 1982, p. xxii), or that they must not lose their innovativeness even if they have strong corporate cultures (Pascale, 1985, p. 37). However, if it is so (or has been so) somewhere under some cultural circumstances, it can only last for a while. Business leadership must always mean, at least partly, to keep on beating everybody, including oneself!

It is probably the case that business leadership can never be *completely* understood. *Otherwise there would be no followers left.*

# References

'A Japanese buddy system that could benefit U.S. business' (1991, 14 October), *Business Week*, p. 11.

'A survey of business in Asia' (1996b, 9 March), *The Economist*, survey attachment.

'A survey of business in Europe' (1996, 23 November), *The Economist*, survey attachment.

'A survey of government governance' (1994, 29 January), *The Economist*, survey attachment.

'A survey of Japan' (1994, 9 July), *The Economist*, survey attachment.

'A survey of Japanese economy' (1993, 6 March), *The Economist*, survey attachment.

'A survey of Japanese finance' (1990, 8 December), *The Economist*, survey attachment.

'A survey of Japanese technology' (1989, 2 December), *The Economist*, survey attachment.

'A survey of management education' (1991, 2 March), *The Economist*, survey attachment.

'A survey of the Middle East' (1991, 28 September), *The Economist*, survey attachment.

Ahrne, Göran (1994), *Social Organizations*, London: Sage Publications.

Ajiferuke, M. and J. Boddewyn (1970), '"Culture" and other explanatory variables in comparative management studies', *Academy of Management Journal*, **13**, pp. 153–163.

Ali, A.J., A. Ali-Aali and R.C. Camp (1992), 'A cross-national perspective on strategic behavior and business environment', *International Journal of Management*, June, pp. 208–214.

Allport, G.W. (1937), *Personality. A Psychological Interpretation*, New York: Henry Holt.

Al-Mubarak, M.I. (1988), 'Empirical analysis of the effects of environmental interdependence and uncertainty on purchasing activities: a cross-cultural study', *Industrial Marketing and Purchasing*, **3** (1), pp. 19–24.

Alvesson, M. and P-O. Berg (1988), *Företagskultur och organisations-symbolism* (Corporate Culture and Organizational Symbolism), Lund, Sweden: Studentlitteratur.

Andersen, Bent Rold (1984), 'Rationality and irrationality of the Nordic welfare state', *Journal of the American Academy of Arts and Sciences*, Winter, pp. 109–139.

'And never the twain shall meet ... ' (1997, 29 March), *The Economist*, pp. 73–74.

Arbnor, I. and B. Bjerke (1997), *Methodology for Creating Business Knowledge*, 2nd edn, Thousand Oaks, CA: Sage Publications, Inc.

Arvonen, Jouko (1989), *Att leda via idéer* (Leading through Ideas), Lund, Sweden: Studentlitteratur.

'Asia's new giants' (1995, 27 November), *Business Week*, pp. 30–40.

Athos, A.G. and R.E. Coffey (1968), *Behavior in Organizations: A Multidimensional View*, Englewood Cliffs, NJ: Prentice-Hall.

At-Twaijri, M.I. (1989a), 'Saudi approach to business' (unpublished), Saudi Arabia: King Fahd University of Petroleum and Minerals.

At-Twaijri, M.I. (1989b), 'Three practical cultural styles of strategic management perspectives' (unpublished), Saudi Arabia: King Fahd University of Petroleum and Minerals.

Axtell, Roger E. (1990) (ed.), *Do's and Taboos Around the World*, New York: Wiley.

Barnes, L.B. and M.P. Kriger (1986), 'The hidden side of organizational leadership', *Sloan Management Review*, Fall, pp. 15–25.

Bass, B.M. (1981), *Stogdill's Handbook of Leadership: A Survey of Theory and Research*, rev. edn, New York: The Free Press.

Bauman, Z. (1978), *Hermeneutics and Social Sciences: Approaches to Understanding*, London: Hutchinson & Co.

Bedeian, A. (1975), 'A comparison and analysis of German and United States managerial attitudes toward the legitimacy of organizational influence', *Academy of Management Journal*, **18**, pp. 897–904.

Bennis, Warren (1989), *Why Leaders Can't Lead*, San Francisco: Jossey-Bass, Inc.

Bennis, W. and B. Nanus (1985), *Leaders: The Strategies for Taking Charge*, New York: Harper & Row.

Berger, P.L. and T. Luckmann (1966), *The Social Construction of Reality*, Garden City, NY: Doubleday & Company, Inc.

Bhagat, R.S. and S.J. McQuaid (1982), 'Role of subjective culture in organizations: A review and directions for future research', *Journal of Applied Psychology Monograph*, **67**, pp. 653–685.

Bjerke, Björn (1989), *Att skapa nya affärer* (Creating New Business Ventures), Lund, Sweden: Studentlitteratur.

Bjerke, Björn (1996), 'Explaining or understanding entrepreneurship', paper presented at *UIC/AMA Research Symposia on Marketing and Entrepreneurship*, 14–15 June, Stockholm.

Bjerke, Björn (1997), 'Managing entrepreneurship – on whose terms?', paper presented at *UIC/AMA Research Symposia on Marketing and Entrepreneurship*, 31 July–3 August, Chicago.

Bjerke, Björn (1998), 'Some aspects of inadequacies of Western models in understanding Southeast Asia entrepreneurship and SMEs', paper presented at *43rd ICSB World Conference*, 8–10 June, Singapore.

Bjerke, Björn (1999), 'A typified, culture-based, interpretation of management of SMEs in Southeast Asia', *Asia Pacific Journal of Management* (forthcoming).

Bjerke, B. and I.A. Alzamel (1990), 'Saudi Arabia economy and industrial development' (unpublished), Saudi Arabia: King Fahd University of Petroleum and Minerals.

Bjerke, B. and U. Kazi (1990), 'Joint ventures and Saudi economic development' (unpublished), Saudi Arabia: King Fahd University of Petroleum and Minerals.

Bjerke, B. and A.R. Al-Meer (1993), 'Culture's consequences: management in Saudi Arabia', *Leadership and Organization Development Journal*, **14** (2), pp. 30–35.

Bjerke, B. and A.R. Al-Meer (1994), 'A behavioral consciousness view of corporate culture', *The Association of Management 12th Annual International Conference*, Dallas, Texas: Proceedings of the Organizational Studies Group, **12** (1), pp. 174–179.

Black, S. and M. Mendenhall (1991), 'A practical but theory-based framework for selecting cross-cultural training methods', in M. Mendenhall and G. Oddon (eds), *International Human Resource Management*, Boston: PWS-Kent, pp. 184–206.

Blake, R.R. and J.S. Mouton (1964), *The Managerial Grid*, Houston, TX: Gulf Publishing Company.

Boswell, Jonathan (1973), *The Rise and Decline of Small Firms*, London: George Allen & Unwin.

Bottomore, T. and R. Nisbet (1979) (eds), *A History of Sociological Analysis*, London: Heinemann.

Boulton, William R. (1984), *Business Policy: The Art of Strategic Management*, New York: Macmillan Publishing Company.

Bradbaart, Okke (1995), 'A comparison of Chinese and *pribumi*-managed engineering firms in Indonesia', in R.A. Brown (ed.), *Chinese Business Enterprises in Asia*, London: Routledge, pp. 177–196.

Brewster, C., A. Lundmark and L. Holden (1993), *'A Different Tack': An Analysis of British and Swedish Management Styles*, Lund, Sweden: Chartwell Bratt.

Broms, H. and H. Gahmberg (1983), 'Communication to self in organizations and cultures', *Administrative Science Quarterly*, **28**, pp. 482–495.

Brooke, M.Z. and H.L. Remmers (1978), *International Management and Business Policy*, Boston, MA: Houghton-Mifflin.

Bruner, J.S. and C.C. Goodman (1947), 'Value and needs as organizing factors in perception', *Journal of Abnormal and Social Psychology*, **XLII**, pp. 33–44.

Burns, James M. (1978), *Leadership*, New York: Harper & Row.

Byars, Lloyd L. (1987), *Strategic Management*, 2nd edn, New York: Harper & Row.

Cassirer, Ernst (1953), *An Essay on Man*, Garden City, NY: Doubleday, Anchor Press.

Cateora, Philip R. (1991), *International Marketing*, 7th edn, Homewood, IL: Richard D. Irwin, Inc.

Chau, Theodora Ting (1991), 'Approaches to succession in East Asian business organizations', *Family Business Review*, **IV** (2), pp. 161–179.

Chen, Min (1995), *Asian Management Systems*, London: Routledge.

Chu, Chin-Ning (1991), *The Asian Mind Game*, New York: Macmillan Publishing Company.

Conner, P.E. and B.W. Becker (1975), 'Values and the organization: Suggestions for research', *Academy of Management Journal*, **18** (3), pp. 550–561.

Cuff, E. and G. Payne (1979) (eds), *Perspectives in Sociology*, London and Boston, MA: George Allen & Unwin Ltd.

'Culturing change' (1990, 7 July), *The Economist*, p. 65.

Cummings, L.L. and Stuart M. Smidt (1972), 'Managerial attitudes of Greeks: the roles of culture and industrialization', *Administrative Science Quarterly*, **17**, pp. 265–272.

Czinkota, M.R., P. Rivoli and I.A. Ronkainen (1994), *International Business*, 3rd edn, Orlando, FL: Harcourt Brace & Company.

Daun, Åke (1989), *Svensk mentalitet* (Swedish Mentality), Stockholm: Rabèn & Sjögren.

Davis, Stanley (1984), *Managing Corporate Culture*, Cambridge, MA: Ballinger.

Davis, H.J. and S.A. Rasool (1988), 'Values research and managerial behavior: implications for devising culturally consistent managerial styles', *Management International Review*, **28** (3), pp. 11–20.

Deal, T. and A. Kennedy (1988), *Corporate Cultures*, London: Penguin Books.

Dedijer, S. (1991), 'Development and management by intelligence: Japan', *School of Economics and Management Lund University Working Paper Series*, Institute of Economic Research, No. 15.

Delaryd, Bengt (1989), *I Japan är kunden kung* (In Japan the Customer is King), Stockholm: Svenska Dagbladets Förlags AB.

Doi, Tadeo (1971), *The Anatomy of Dependence*, Tokyo: Kodansha International Ltd.

Dore, Ronald P. (1967) (ed.), *Aspects of Social Change in Modern Japan*, Princeton, NJ: Princeton University Press.

Dredge, C. Paul (1985), 'Corporate culture: the challenge to expatriate managers and multinational corporations', in H.V. Wortzel and L.H. Wortzel (1985) (eds), *Strategic Management of Multinational Corporations: The Essentials*, New York: John Wiley & Sons, Inc., pp. 410–424.

Drucker, Peter (1974), *Management: Tasks, Responsibilities, Practices*, New York: Harper & Row.

Drucker, Peter (1985), *Innovation and Entrepreneurship*, London: Heinemann.

Drucker, Peter (1995), *Managing in a Time of Great Change*, Oxford: Butterworth-Heinemann.

Drucker, P. and I. Nakauchi (1997), *Drucker on Asia*, London: Butterworth-Heinemann.

'European business' (1996b, 13 July), *The Economist*, pp. 19–21.

'Europe's new managers. Going global with a U.S. style' (1982, 24 May), *Business Week*, pp. 78–82.

Everett, J.E., B.W. Stening and P.A. Loughton (1982), 'Some evidence for an international managerial culture', *Journal of Management Studies*, **19** (2), pp. 153–162.

'Facing realities' (1981), Brussels: *European Institute for Advanced Studies in Management*, December.

Fallows, J.M. (1989), 'The myth of convergence', *Speaking of Japan*, **10** (108), pp. 14–24.

Faucheux, C. (1977), 'Strategy formulation as a cultural process', *International Studies of Management and Organization*, **7** (2), pp. 127–138.

Ferraro, G.P. (1994), *The Cultural Dimension of International Business*, 2nd edn, Englewood Cliffs, NJ: Prentice-Hall.

'Fissiparous fortunes and family feuds' (1996, 30 November), *The Economist*, pp. 69–70.

Forss, K., D. Hawk and G. Hedlund (1984), 'Cultural differences – Swedishness in legislation, multinational corporations and aid administration', Stockholm School of Economics, Institute of International Business (monograph).

Frost, P.J., L.F. Moore, M.R. Louis, C.C. Lundberg and J. Martin (eds) (1991), *Reframing Organizational Culture*, Newbury Park, CA: Sage Publications.

Frykman, Jonas (1987), 'Bryt upp! Förändring som livsprojekt' (Make a Break! Change as a Life-project), paper presented at a symposium on *The Swedish Model's Cultural Face*, Umeå University, Sweden, 14–16 January.

Gardner, Burleigh (1945), *Human Relations in Industry*, Homewood, IL: Irwin.

Green, Sebastian (1988), 'Strategy, organizational culture and symbolism', *Long Range Planning*, **21** (4), pp. 121–129.

Guth, W. and R. Tagiuri (1965), 'Personal values and corporate strategy', *Harvard Business Review*, September–October, pp. 123–132.

Haire, M., E. Ghiselli and L.W. Porter (1966), *Managerial Thinking: An International Study*, New York: John Wiley.

Hall, E.T. (1977), *Beyond Culture*, Garden City, NY: Doubleday.

Hannertz, U. (1969), *Southside*, New York: Columbia University Press.

Harbison, F. and C.A. Myers (1959), *Management in the Industrial World*, New York: McGraw-Hill Book Company.

Harris, Marvin (1974), *Cows, Pigs, Wars, and Witches: The Riddle of Culture*, New York: Random House.

Harris, P.R. and R.I. Moran (1979), *Managing Cultural Differences*, Houston, TX: Gulf Publishing Company.

Harris, P.R. and R.I. Moran (1987), *Managing Cultural Differences*, 2nd edn, Houston, TX: Gulf Publishing Company.

Hayes, J. and C.W. Allison (1988), 'Cultural differences in the learning styles of managers', *Management International Review*, **28** (3), pp. 75–80.

Herskovits, M.J. (1955), *Cultural Anthropology*, New York: Knopf.

Hickman, C.R. and M.A. Silva (1984), *Creating Excellence, Managing Corporate Culture, Strategy, and Change in the New Age*, London: George Allen & Unwin.

'Hidden Japan' (1991, 26 August), *Business Week*, pp. 14–22.

Hodgetts, R.M. and F. Luthans (1991), *International Management*, Singapore: McGraw-Hill.

Hofstede, Geert (1980), *Culture's Consequences*, Beverly Hills, CA: Sage Publications.

Hofstede, Geert (1984), *Culture's Consequences*, 2nd edn, Beverly Hills, CA: Sage Publications.

Hofstede, Geert (1993), 'Cultural constraints in management theories', *Academy of Management Executive*, **7** (1), pp. 11–32.

Hofstede, G. and M.H. Bond (1988), 'The Confucius connection: from cultural roots to economic growth', *Organization Dynamics*, Spring, pp. 5–21.

'Home sweet home' (1995, 9 September), *The Economist*, pp. 21–22.

Hoon-Halbauer, Sing Keow (1994), *Management of Sino-Foreign Joint Ventures*, Lund, Sweden: Lund University Press.

Hoover, Thomas (1988), *The Samuraj Strategy*, London: Penguin Books.

'How Japan puts the "human" in human capital' (1991, 11 November), *Business Week*, p. 11.

'How to conquer China (and the world) with instant noodles' (1995, 17 June), *The Economist*, pp. 27–28.

Hughes, G., V.R. Rao and H.A. Alker (1976), 'The influence of values information and decision orders on a public decision', *Journal of Applied Social Psychology*, April–June, pp. 145–158.

Humes, S. (1993), *Managing the Multinational*, Hertfordshire, England: Prentice-Hall.

'Information anxiety' (1997, 9 June), *Business Week*, pp. 52–53.

'Inheriting the bamboo network' (1995, 23 December), *The Economist*, pp. 25–26.

Jansson, Hans (1987), *Affärskulturer och relationer i Sydöstasien* (Business Cultures and Relations in Southeast Asia), Stockholm: Marknadstekniskt Centrum, No. 29.

'Japan's economic plight' (1998, 20 June), *The Economist*, pp. 19–22.

'Japan's intellectual revolution' (1994, 30 April), *The Economist*, pp. 19–22.

'Japan's trading companies. Sprightly dinosaurs?' (1995, 11 February), *The Economist*, pp. 61–63.

Jay, Anthony (1987), *Management and Machiavelli*, rev. edn, London: Hutchinson Business.

Johnson, C. (1985), 'The institutional foundations of Japanese industrial policy', *California Management Review*, I (4), pp. 59–69.

Johnson, C. (1988), 'Japanese-style management in America', *California Management Review*, Summer, pp. 34–45.

Johnson, G. and K. Scholes (1988), *Exploring Corporate Strategy*, 2nd edn, London: Prentice-Hall.

Kanter, Rosabeth Moss (1983), *The Change Masters*, London: Unwin Paperbacks.

Kawasaki, Kazuhiko (1984), *Negotiating with the Japanese*, Tokyo: JETRO.

Kedia, B.L. and R.S. Bhagat (1988), 'Cultural constraints on transfer of technology across nations: implications for research in international and comparative management', *Academy of Management Review*, 13 (4), pp. 559–571.

Keesing, Roger M. (1974), 'Theories of culture', *Annual Review of Anthropology*, 3, pp. 73–97.

Kelley, L. and R. Worthley (1981), 'The role of culture in comparative management: a cross-cultural perspective', *Academy of Management Journal*, 24 (1), pp. 164–173.

Kilmann, R.H., M.J. Saxton and R. Serpa (1986), 'Issues in understanding and changing culture', *California Management Review*, XXVIII (2), pp. 87–94.

Klausen, Arne Martin (1984), *Den norske vaeremåten: Antropologisk sökelys på norsk kultur* (The Norwegian Way to be: Anthropological Searchlight on Norwegian Culture), Oslo: Cappelen.

Kluckhohn, C. and W.H. Kelly (1945), 'The concept of culture', in Ralph Linton (ed.), *The Science of Man in the World Crisis*, New York: Columbia University Press, pp. 78–106.

Kluckhohn, C. and F.L. Strodtbeck (1961), *Variation in Value Orientations*, Evanston, IL: Row, Peterson and Company.

Kluckhohn, Clyde *et al.* (1962), 'Values and value-orientations in the theory of action', in T. Parsons and E.A. Shills (1962) (eds), *Toward a General Theory of Action*, New York: Harper & Row, pp. 388–433.

Kobayashi, Y. (1990), 'A message to American managers', *Economic Eye*, Spring, pp. 1–8.

Koontz, H. and H. Weihrich (1988), *Management*, 6th edn, New York: Harper & Row.

Kosai, Y. and Y. Ogino (1984), *The Contemporary Japanese Economy*, Armonk, NY: Sharpe.

Kotter, John P. (1992), *Corporate Culture and Performance*, New York: Free Press.

Kuhn, Thomas S. (1970), *The Structure of Scientific Revolutions*, Chicago: University of Chicago Press.

Lawrence, P. and T. Spybey (1986), *Management and Society in Sweden*, London: Routledge & Kegan Paul.

Lasserre, P. and H. Schütte (1995), *Strategies for Asia Pacific*, London: Macmillan Press Ltd.

'Leadership jazz' (1994, June), *World Executive's Digest*, pp. 24–28.

'Le Défi Américain, again' (1996c, 13 July), *The Economist*, pp. 25–26.

Lewin, Kurt (1935), *A Dynamic Theory of Personality*, New York: McGraw-Hill.

Lewis, J. (1969), *Anthropology Made Simple*, London: W.H. Allen.

Liang, Su-ming (1974), *The Basics of Chinese Culture*, Hong Kong: Zhicheng Books.

Likert, R. and J.G. Likert (1976), *New Ways of Managing Conflict*, New York: McGraw-Hill Book Company.

Limlingan, Victor Simpao (1986), *The Overseas Chinese in ASEAN: Business Strategies and Management Practices*, Manila, Philippines: Vita Development Corporation.

Lindblom, Charles E. (1959), 'The science of muddling through', *Public Administration Review*, **19** (2), pp. 78–88.

Lindkvist, L. (1988), *A Passionate Search for Nordisk Management*, Copenhagen: Institut for Organisation og Arbejdssociologi, August.

Lodge, G.C. and E.F. Vogel (1987), *Ideology and National Competitiveness*, Boston: Harvard Business School Press.

Lorsch, J.W. (1986), 'Managing culture: the invisible barrier to strategic change', *California Management Review*, **XXVIII** (2), pp. 95–109.

Louis, Meryl Reis (1983), 'Organizations as culture-bearing milieux', in L.R. Pondy, G. Morgan and P.J. Frost (1983) (eds), *Organizational Symbolism*, Greenwich, CT: JAI Press Inc., pp. 39–54.

Mackie, James (1992), 'Changing patterns of Chinese big business in Southeast Asia', in Ruth McVey (ed.), *Southeast Asian Capitalists*, Cornell University, Ithaca, New York: Studies in Southeast Asia, pp. 161–190.

'Managing in China: the toughest test' (1994), *World Executive's Digest*, May, pp. 14–25.

March, J.G. and J.P. Olsen (1976), *Ambiguity and Choice in Organizations*, Oslo: Universitetsforlaget.

Matsumoto, Koji (1991), *The Rise of the Japanese Corporate System*, New York and London: Kegan Paul International.

Mayo, Elton (1933), *The Human Problems of an Industrial Civilization*, New York: Macmillan.

McCaffrey, J.A. and C.R. Hafner (1985), 'When two cultures collide: doing business overseas', *Training and Development Journal*, **39** (10), pp. 18–26.

McMillan, C.J. (1985), *The Japanese Industrial System*, 2nd rev. edn, New York: Walter de Gruyter.

McVey, Ruth (1992), 'The materialization of the Southeast Asian entrepreneur', in Ruth McVey (ed.), *Southeast Asian Capitalists*, Cornell University, Ithaca, New York: Studies in Southeast Asia, pp. 7–33.

'Mighty Mitsubishi is on the move' (1990, 24 September), *Business Week*, pp. 38–41.

Miles, R. and C. Snow (1978), *Organizational Strategy, Structure and Process*, New York: McGraw-Hill.

Mintzberg, Henry (1979), *The Structuring of Organizations*, Englewood Cliffs: McGraw-Hill.

Moore, Franklin G. (1982), *Management in Organizations*, New York: John Wiley & Sons, Inc.

Moran, Robert T. (1988), *Venturing abroad in Asia*, Maidenhead, Berkshire, England: McGraw-Hill.

Morgan, Gareth (1993), *Imaginization*, Newbury Park, CA: Sage Publications.

Morgan, G., P.J. Frost and L.R. Pondy (1983), 'Organizational symbolism', in L.R. Pondy *et al.* (1983) (eds), *Organizational Symbolism*, Greenwich, CT: JAI Press Inc., pp. 3–35.

Morita, Akio (1986), *Made in Japan*, New York: Dulton.

Morris, Jan (1984), *Journeys*, New York: Oxford University Press.

Muna, Farid A. (1980), *The Arab Executive*, London: Macmillan.

Nadler, L. (1984), 'What Japan learned from the U.S. – that we forgot to remember', *California Management Review*, **XXVI** (4), pp. 46–61.

Naisbitt, John (1995), *Megatrends Asia*, London: Nicholas Brealey Publishing.

Nakane, Chie (1967), *Kinship and Economic Organization in Rural Japan*, New York: Humanities Press.

Nakane, Chie (1972), *Japanese Society*, Berkeley: University of California Press.

Namiki, N. and S.P. Sethi (1988), 'Japan', in R. Nath (ed.), *Comparative Management: A Regional View*, Cambridge, MA: Ballinger Publishing Company, pp. 55–96.

Negandhi, Amant R. (1975), 'Comparative management and organizational theory: a marriage needed', *Academy of Management Journal*, **18**, pp. 334–344.

Negandhi, A.R., G.S. Eshgi and E.C. Yuen (1985), 'The management practices of Japanese subsidiaries overseas', *California Management Review*, **XXVII** (4), pp. 93–105.

Ng, L. (1984), 'The "interpretive humanistic" approach to social science and accounting research', *Discussion Paper Series*, no. 28, New Zealand: Massey University.

Nonaka, I. and J.K. Johansson (1985), 'Japanese management: what about the "hard" skills?', *Academy of Management Review*, **10** (2), pp. 181–191.

Normann, Richard (1970), *A Personal Quest for Methodology*, SIAR-19, Stockholm: SIAR.

Oberg, Winston (1963), 'Cross-cultural perspective on management principles', *Academy of Management Journal*, **6** (2), pp. 141–143.

Ohmae, K. (1982), *The Mind of the Strategist*, New York: Penguin Books.

Packard, Vance (1964), *The Waste Makers*, Harmondsworth: Pelican Books.

Pan, Lynn (1991), *Sons of the Yellow Emperor*, London: Mandarin Paperbacks.

Pascale, Richard (1985), 'The paradox of "corporate culture": reconciling ourselves to socialization', *California Management Review*, **XXVII** (2), pp. 26–41.

Pascale, R. and A. Athos (1982), *Japansk företagsledning* (The Art of Japanese Management), Malmö, Sweden: LiberFörlag.

Pearce II, J.A. and R.H. Robinson Jr (1985), *Strategic Management*, 3rd edn, Homewood, IL: Richard D. Irwin, Inc.

Peters, Tom (1989), *Thriving on Chaos*, London: Pan Books Ltd.

Peters, Tom (1992), *Liberation Management*, New York: Alfred A. Knopf.

Peters, T. and N. Austin (1985), *A Passion for Excellence, The Leadership Difference*, London: Fontana/Collins.

Peters, T. and R. Waterman Jr (1984), *In Search of Excellence*, Sydney: Harper & Row.

Pettigrew, Andrew M. (1979), 'On studying organizational cultures', *Administrative Science Quarterly*, **24**, December, pp. 570–581.

Pezeshkpur, C. (1975), 'The effects of personal value structure on decision-making: a study of relationship between values and decisions of university business administration students', unpublished Ph.D. dissertation, Lousiana State University.

Phillips-Martinsson, Jean (1992), *Svenskarna som andra ser dem* (Swedes as Other People See Them), rev. edn, Lund, Sweden: Studentlitteratur.

Pollack, Robert A. (1985), 'A transaction cost approach to families and households', *Journal of Economic Literature*, **23**, pp. 590–598.

Popenoe, David (1988), *Disturbing the Nest: Family Change and Decline in Modern Societies*, New York: Aldine de Gruyter.

Quinn, J.B. (1980), *Strategies for Change*, Homewood, IL: Richard D. Irwin, Inc.

Ralston, D.A., D.J. Gustafson, L. Mainiero and D. Umstot (1993), 'Strategies of Upward Influence: a cross-national comparison of Hong Kong and American managers', *Asia Pacific Journal of Management*, **10** (2), pp. 157–175.

Redding, S. Gordon (1993), *The Spirit of Chinese Capitalism*, Berlin: Walter de Gruyter.

Redding, S. and M. Ng (1982), 'The role of "face" in the organizational perceptions of Chinese managers', *Organizational Studies*, **3** (3), pp. 201–219.

Richardson, F. and C. Walker (1948), *Human Relations in an Expanding Company*, New Haven, CT: Yale University Labor Management Center.

Ricks, David A. (1983), *Big Business Blunders*, Homewood, IL: Irwin.

Roberts, Karlene H. (1970), 'On looking at an elephant: an evaluation of cross-cultural research related to organizations', *Psychological Bulletin*, **74**, pp. 327–350.

Roethlisberger, F.J. and W.J. Dickson (1939), *Management and the Worker: An Account of a Research Program Conducted by a Western Electric Company, Hawthorne Works, Chicago*, Cambridge, MA: Harvard University Press.

Rohwer, Jim (1995), *Asia Rising*, Singapore: Butterworth-Heinemann Asia.

Ronen, S. and O. Shenkar (1985), 'Clustering countries on attitudinal dimensions: a review and synthesis', *Academy of Management Review*, September, pp. 436–454.

Sallivan, J. and I. Nonaka (1988), 'Culture and strategic issue categorization theory', *Management International Review*, **28** (3), pp. 6–10.

Samovar, L.A., R.E. Porter and N.C. Jain (1981), *Understanding Intercultural Communication*, Belmont, CA: Wadsworth Publishing Company.

Sapir, Edward (1949), *Culture, Language, and Personality: Selected Essays*, Berkeley: University of California Press.

Sasaki, Naoto (1981), *Management and Industrial Structure in Japan*, New York: Pergamon.

Schein, Edgar H. (1984), 'Coming to a new awareness of organizational culture', *Sloan Management Review*, Winter, pp. 3–16.

Schein, Edgar H. (1985), *Organizational Culture and Leadership*, San Fransisco: Jossey-Bass.

Schneider, S. and J-L. Barsoux (1997), *Managing Across Cultures*, Hemel Hempstead, Hertfordshire: Prentice-Hall Europe.

Schwartz, H. and S.M. Davis (1981), 'Matching corporate culture and business strategy', *Organizational Dynamics*, Summer, pp. 30–48.

Schwind, H.F. and R.B. Peterson (1985), 'Shifting personal values in the Japanese management system', *International Studies of Management and Organization*, Summer, pp. 60–74.

Seagrave, Sterling (1996), *Lords of the Rim*, London: Corgi Books.

'Second time around' (1995, 12 August), *The Economist*, pp. 56–57.

Senger, John (1970), 'The religious manager', *Academy of Management Journal*, June, pp. 179–186.

Sethi, S. Prakash (1975), *Japanese Business and Social Conflict*, Cambridge, MA: Ballinger.

Sethi, S. Prakash (1983), 'Drawbacks of Japanese management', *Business Week*, 24 November, p. 14.

Shinoda, Y. (1973), 'Japanese management: old ways become modern', in B. Taylor and K. MacMillan (eds), *Top Management*, London: Longman, pp. 387–398.

'Showing Europe's firms the way' (1996a, 13 July), *The Economist*, p. 13.

Sica, A. (1981), 'Hermeneutics and social theory: the contemporary conversation', in S. McNall and G. Howe (1981) (eds), *Current Perspectives in Social Theory*, Greenwich, CT: JAI Press Inc., pp. 39–54.

Sikula, A.F. (1971), 'Values and value systems: relationship to personal goals', *Personnel Journal*, April, pp. 310–312.

Sitaram, K.S. and R.T. Cogdell (1976), *Foundations of Intercultural Communication*, Columbus, OH: Charles E. Merrill.

Sjögren, Annick (1985), 'Förhållandet till barnen visar kulturskillnader' (Relations to the children show cultural differences), *Invandrare and Minoriteter*, no. 4–5.

Smircich, Linda (1983), 'Concepts of culture and organizational analysis', *Administrative Science Quarterly*, **28**, pp. 339–358.

Smith, G.D., D.R. Arnold and B.G. Bizzell (1985), *Business Strategy and Policy*, Boston: Houghton Mifflin Company.

*Sociaal Economische Raad, Opvolging in Familjebedrijven* (1990): The Hague, The Netherlands.

Söderman, S. (1983), *Japan och industriell marknadsföring* (Japan and Industrial Marketing), Lund, Sweden: Studentlitteratur.

Steinberg, M. and S. Åkerblom (1992), 'Swedish Leadership in Singapore – a Cross-cultural Feasibility Study' (unpublished), Stockholm: Stockholm School of Economics.

Steiner, G.A. and J.B. Miner (1986), *Management Policy and Strategy*, 3rd edn, New York: Macmillan Publishing Co., Inc.

Stewart, Edward C. (1972), *American Cultural Patterns: A Cross-Cultural Perspective*, Pittsburgh: Intercultural Communications Network.

Taggart, J.H. and M.C. McDermott (1993), *The Essence of International Business*, Hertfordshire, England: Prentice-Hall.

Tanaka, Y., M. Mori and Y. Mori (1992), 'Overseas Chinese business community in Asia: present conditions and future prospects', *Pacific Business and Industries*, **II**, pp. 2–24.

Tannenbaum, R. and W.H. Schmidt (1973), 'How to choose a leadership pattern', *Harvard Business Review*, May–June, pp. 95–101.

Terhune, Kenneth W. (1970), 'From national character to national behavior: a reformulation', *Conflict Resolution*, **XIV** (2), pp. 203–263.

'The compass swings' (1996d, 13 July), *The Economist*, survey attachment.

'The corporate culture vultures' (1983, 17 October), *Fortune*, pp. 66–72.

'The elusive Euro-manager' (1992, 7 November), *The Economist*, p. 81.

'The four faces of leadership' (1994, May), *World Executive's Digest*, pp. 60–62.

'The Global 1000' (1998, 13 July), *Business Week*, pp. 40–84.

'The lesson in Fokker's fall' (1996, 27 January), *The Economist*, pp. 59–60.

'The overseas Chinese' (1992, 18 July), *The Economist*, pp. 21–23.

'The third opening' (1996a, 9 March), *The Economist*, pp. 19–21.

Tichy, N.M. and M.A. Devanna (1986), *The Transformational Leader*, New York: John Wiley & Sons.

'Time for a reality check in Asia' (1996, 2 December), *Business Week*, pp. 40–47.

'Tokyo's power club' (1991, 8 July), *Newsweek*, pp. 10–15.

Tomasson, R.F. (1970), *Sweden: Prototype of Modern Society*, New York: Random House.

Trompenaars, Fons (1995), *Riding the Waves of Culture*, London: Nicholas Brealey Publishing.

Tu, Wei-ming (1984), *Confucian Ethic Today – The Singapore Challenge*, Singapore: Federal Publications.

Upadhya, Carol B. (1988), 'The farmer capitalists and coastal Andhra Pradesh', *Political and Economic Weekly*, **23**, pp. 1376–1442.

Wang, Gungwu (1992), *China and the Chinese Overseas*, Singapore: Times Economic Press.

Waterman, Robert H. (1982), 'The Seven Elements of Strategic Fit', *Journal of Business Strategy*, **2** (3), pp. 69–73.

Waterman, R.H., T.J. Peters and J.R. Phillips (1980), 'Structure is not organization', *Business Horizons*, June, pp. 14–26.

Wee, C.H., K.S. Lee and W.H. Bambang (1991), *Sun Tzu: War and Management*, Singapore: Addison-Wesley Publishing Company.

Weidenbaum, M. and S. Hughes (1996), *The Bamboo Network*, New York: The Free Press.

Westerlund, G. and S-E. Sjöstrand (1979), *Organizational Myths*, London and New York: Harper & Row.

'What sank Asia? Money sloshing around the world' (1998, 27 July), *Business Week*, p. 10.

'What's good for Japan isn't necessarily good for the U.S.' (1991, 23 September), *Business Week*, p. 8.

White, L. (1949), *The Science of Culture*, New York: Grove Press.

Whorf, Benjamin Lee (1956), *Language, Thought and Reality: Selected Writings*, Cambridge, MA: The MIT Press.

'Why can't little Taro think?' (1990, 21 April), *The Economist*, pp. 19–22.

'Why success won't spoil Japan Inc.' (1990, 31 December), *Business Week*, pp. 10–15.

Wilkins, A.L. and W.G. Ouchi (1983), 'Efficient cultures: exploring the relationship between culture and organizational performance', *Administrative Science Quarterly*, **28**, pp. 468–481.

Wong, Sin-lun (1995), 'Business networks, cultural values and the state in Hong Kong and Singapore', in R.A. Brown (ed.), *Chinese Business Enterprise in Asia*, London: Routledge, pp. 136–153.

Wortzel, H.V. and L.H. Wortzel (1985) (eds), *Management of Multinational Corporations: The Essentials*, New York: John Wiley & Sons, Inc.

Yanaga, Chitoshi (1965), *Japanese People and Politics*, New York: Wiley.

Yang, Bo (1991), *The Ugly Chinaman and the Crisis of Chinese Culture*, St Leonards, Australia: Allen & Unwin.

Yoshino, M.Y. and T.B. Lifson (1986), *The Invisible Link: Japan's Sogo Shosha and the Organization of Trade*, Cambridge, MA: The MIT Press.

Zikmund, William G. (1986), *Exploring Marketing Research*, 2nd edn, Tokyo: The Dryden Press, CBS Publishing Japan Ltd.

# Index